Teaching Mathematics through Problem Solving

Grades 6 –12

P9-CMO-185

Harold L. Schoen
Volume Editor

University of Iowa
Iowa City, Iowa

Randall I. Charles
Series Editor

Carmel, California

NATIONAL COUNCIL OF
TEACHERS OF MATHEMATICS

Third Printing 2006

Library of Congress Cataloging-in-Publication Data

Teaching mathematics through problem solving : grades 6-12 / Harold L. Schoen, volume editor.
    p. cm.
  ISBN 0-87353-541-3 (pbk.)
  1. Mathematics--Study and teaching (Secondary)--United States. 2. Problem-based learning. I. Schoen, Harold L.
  QA13.T4313 2003
  510'.71'2--dc22
                                        2003021743

The National Council of Teachers of Mathematics is a public voice of mathematics education, providing vision, leadership, and professional development to support teachers in ensuring mathematics learning of the highest quality for all students.

Printed in the United States of America

CONTENTS

Preface

Recommendation 1: Problem solving must be the focus of school mathematics in the 1980s.

> —*An Agenda for Action: Recommendations for School Mathematics of the 1980s*

Problem solving . . . can serve as a vehicle for learning new mathematical ideas and skills. . . . A problem-centered approach to teaching mathematics uses interesting and well-selected problems to launch mathematical lessons and engage students. In this way, new ideas, techniques, and mathematical relationships emerge and become the focus of discussion. Good problems can inspire the exploration of important mathematical ideas, nurture persistence, and reinforce the need to understand and use various strategies, mathematical properties, and relationships.

> —*Principles and Standards for School Mathematics*

THE TWO statements above, made twenty years apart by the National Council of Teachers of Mathematics (1980, p. 2; 2000, p. 182), serve as evidence of a long-term commitment of the Council to making problem solving a central theme of school mathematics instruction. The first statement was made at a time when the NCTM was just beginning to assert itself as a leader in efforts to change the nature of mathematics teaching in our schools. The second statement demonstrates that after two decades of curriculum development, research, and considerable reflection, the Council has developed a mature position about the role that problem solving should play in mathematics instruction.

The second statement also captures the essence of what this volume and its companion for prekindergarten through grade 6 are about, namely, that the role of problem solving in mathematics instruction should change from being an activity that children engage in after they have studied various concepts and skills to being a means for acquiring new mathematical knowledge. But to suggest, as do the authors of *Principles and Standards,* that problem solving "can serve as a vehicle for learning new mathematical ideas and skills" (NCTM 2000, p. 182) is one thing; to furnish the sort of coherence and clear direction that teachers need is another matter. These volumes represent a serious attempt to provide teachers with that coherence and direction.

In conceptualizing these volumes, the Editorial Panel was guided by what it saw as a central message of all four NCTM *Standards* documents (1989, 1991, 1995, 2000), namely, their emphasis on the importance of viewing classroom mathematics teaching as a system. According to Hiebert and his colleagues (1997), the five dimensions of this system are (1) the nature of classroom tasks, (2) the role of the teacher, (3) the social culture of the classroom, (4) mathematical tools as learning supports, and (5) equity and accessibility. Changing any of the elements of this system requires parallel changes in each of the other dimensions.

The system of mathematics classroom instruction that has dominated U.S. schools for at least the entire past century can be characterized in terms of the foregoing dimensions roughly as follows. Classroom tasks come mainly from the worked examples and homework exercises in the textbook. These tasks are predominantly short, out of context, and symbolic, with emphasis on mastering and maintaining procedural skills. The teacher's role is to work examples for the students using direct teaching, with the expectation that students will listen to and learn to apply the same procedures that the teacher demonstrates. Students then practice those procedures through individual classwork and homework, in which they try many more exercises that are very similar to those the teacher just demonstrated. If any applications of these procedures to real-world problems are included, they are briefly stated, straightforward "word problems" presented immediately after the procedures that students are expected to use to solve the problems.

The social culture of the traditional classroom includes the agreement that the teacher and the answer key in the textbook are the sole mathematical authorities. Students who develop proficiency in using the procedural strategies given in the textbook and demonstrated by the teacher are rewarded with praise and high grades. The nature of the students' thinking and the strategies, both mathematically valid and invalid, that they may have tried for solving problems are generally of much less interest than getting the right answer using the method shown in the textbook.

The most unfortunate consequence of instruction of the sort just described is that too often students leave school with at best a command of a set of facts, procedures, and formulas that they understand in a superficial or disconnected way. Even worse perhaps, they have little or no notion of how they might use what they have learned as they pursue their lives outside of school.

The chapters of this book together describe in some detail the characteristics of a classroom system called "teaching mathematics through problem solving," in which the main goal is for students to develop a deep understanding of mathematical concepts and methods. The key to fostering students' understanding is engaging them in trying to make sense of problematic tasks in which the mathematics to be learned is embedded. In addition to the mathematics that is the residue of work on the tasks, the kind of sense making and problem solving in which students engage involves doing mathematics. As students attempt to solve rich problem tasks, they come to understand the mathematical concepts and methods involved, become more adept at mathematical problem solving, and develop mathematical habits of mind that are useful ways to think about any mathematical situation.

This approach to classroom instruction involves much more than finding and using a collection of "fun" problems. First and foremost, the problematic tasks that are chosen must have embedded in them the mathematics that is to be learned. Second, the tasks must be accessible and engaging to the students, building on what they know and can do. Third, the teacher's role is very important in ensuring that the classroom norms are supportive of students' learning in this way and in pressing students to think deeply both about their solution methods and those of their classmates and, more important, about the mathematics they are learning. Teachers also have a role in ensuring that students have access to appropriate technological and intellectual tools for learning, including facility with important paper-and-pencil procedures. A final challenge for teachers and curriculum developers is to find ways to ensure that the understanding that comes from learning mathematics through problem solving is accessible to all students.

This volume focuses on grades 6 through 12 mathematics, and its companion volume deals with the elementary grades. The organization of, and the issues discussed in, the two volumes are similar, reflecting the overlap of teaching issues across all grade levels.

This volume consists of three main sections—Issues and Perspectives, Tasks and Tools for Teaching and Learning, and In the Classroom—and a final chapter that presents a research perspective on teaching mathematics through problem solving. No single section addresses the entire set of issues concerning teaching mathematics through problem solving, but the volume as a whole presents much of what we in the mathematics education profession know about, and have experienced with, the topic.

Section 1 (chapters 1–4) deals with the conceptual and historical background of teaching mathematics through problem solving. In chapter 1, James Hiebert and Diana Wearne discuss understanding mathematics, why understanding is such an important goal, how engaging in problem solving can lead to understanding, and what some of the signposts are of classrooms designed to promote understanding. The authors close their chapter with a discussion of the fundamental change that is required to move to teaching through problem solving from direct instruction and a traditional curriculum that focuses on procedural skill.

According to Jeremy Kahan and Terrence Wyberg in chapter 2, mathematics helps students solve problems, and in the process of making sense of problems, they come to an understanding of the related mathematics. Following a task that illustrates this sort of sense making, the authors discuss two main benefits of teaching mathematics through problem solving: (1) students take part, at their level of sophistication, in doing mathematics, and (2) they develop understanding of, and interest in, mathematics. The authors also strongly caution that the intended mathematics is the most important focus of planning for, and teaching through, problem solving.

Kenneth Levasseur and Al Cuoco, in chapter 3, argue that through problem solving, students can and should not only understand the underlying mathematics but also learn habits of mind that transcend topic knowledge and that are essential aspects of doing mathematics. The authors discuss eight habits of mind that are especially relevant in grades 6–12 and offer concrete examples and suggestions for developing these habits when teaching mathematics through problem solving.

In the next chapter, Beatriz D'Ambrosio takes us on a trip from ancient to modern times to take a look at how conceptions of problem solving and the role it plays in the mathematics curriculum have changed over time. She notes that problem solving has been an important component of the school mathematics curriculum for at least 150 years and argues that teaching mathematics through problem solving began to emerge rather slowly and has recently begun to appear in some school mathematics textbooks.

Section 2 (chapters 5–8) provides different perspectives on how to select and use appropriate tasks and learning tools so that the intended mathematical understanding will result, an important dimension of the system of teaching through problem solving described above. Robin Marcus and James Fey begin chapter 5 by posing four questions to consider when selecting quality tasks. These questions bring out some ideas discussed briefly in previous chapters, namely, that the important mathematical ideas and methods must be embedded in the tasks; the tasks need to be engaging and problematic, yet accessible to the target students; and work on the tasks needs to help students develop their mathematical thinking and habits of mind. Through several examples, the authors also make the very important point that the collection of tasks in a curriculum must build coherent understanding and connections among important mathematical topics.

In chapter 6, Paul Goldenberg and Marion Walter discuss problem posing as a tool for both teachers and students in problem-based classrooms. For teachers who want to enrich a standard, procedural exercise, the authors suggest using problem-posing techniques for asking useful questions about the exercise (e.g., questions about existence and uniqueness and "What if not?" questions concerning various attributes of the given exercise). Similarly, the authors argue, students should be encouraged to ask these same kinds of questions on their own because doing so is a fundamental part of doing mathematics.

Technological tools for teaching mathematics are Rose Mary Zbiek's focus in chapter 7. She argues that many benefits can be derived from using a variety of technological tools in teaching mathematics. Through examples, she shows how these benefits can be realized, emphasizing, in particular, that the use of technology helps make students' thinking more visible to an observant teacher while also allowing students to reflect on their own thinking more conveniently.

Arthur Bakker and Koeno Gravemeijer discuss another use of technology (statistical minitools available for downloading from the Internet) in chapter 8, although the authors' focus is on planning for and teaching the fundamental statistical idea of "distribution" through problem solving. They use Simon's (1995) idea of a hypothetical learning trajectory that involves considering in advance the learning goal, the learning activities, and the thinking and learning in which students might engage. The authors illustrate their points about planning, learning, and technology with excerpts from students' solutions and conversations.

Section 3 (chapters 9–15) focuses on how teaching mathematics through problem solving might play out in the classroom, assuming appropriate use of the tasks and tools described in the previous section. Together, sections 2 and 3 serve to describe how the five dimensions of the classroom teaching system discussed previously in this preface might be thought of when problem solving becomes the means through which students attain understanding of important mathematics. Nearly every author in this volume refers to the importance of the teacher's role, and many chapters touch on aspects of that role in some depth, but the opening chapter of this section by Douglas Grouws provides the most complete description of that complex role. In fact, he "examine[s] the teacher's role in instruction before, during, and after lessons designed to teach mathematics through a problem-solving approach" (p. 129). As a result, the reader sees a fairly complete picture of what a teacher needs to do to teach mathematics through problem solving well.

In chapter 10, Chris Rasmussen, Erna Yackel, and Karen King describe ways for teachers and students to develop and sustain a classroom environment that fosters and promotes teaching and learning mathematics through problem solving. On the way, they focus on two aspects of the classroom environment, (1) supporting and promoting students' explanations and justifications of their activities, and (2) the distinguishing features of mathematical explanations and justifications that can and should become the classroom norm.

An essential ingredient of teaching mathematics through problem solving is "listening" to students as they do mathematics. For Mark Driscoll, the author of chapter 11, listening carefully to students as they attempt to make sense of rich problems can be a powerful tool for teachers. "The impact of consistent, purposeful listening, especially in a problem-based classroom, can be a powerful way to elicit and understand students' deeper thinking and, perhaps, to propel them toward a more generalized way of thinking" (p. 175).

An important part of a system of instruction based on teaching mathematics through problem solving is classroom assessment, the topic of chapter 12, by Steven Ziebarth. He illustrates some ways to align classroom assessment with teaching through problem solving, mainly focusing on assessing students' understanding. The author also draws on comments about assessment, both from secondary school teachers who teach through problem solving and from their students, in a discussion of several recurring assessment issues, including how to assign grades.

Larry Copes and Kay Shager, the authors of chapter 13, address the important question of how to phase teaching through problem solving into a traditional educational environment. They give practical and gentle advice for the traditional teacher who wants to move, perhaps slowly, toward teaching mathematics through problem solving. The areas that these authors address are articulating the mathematics, structuring class sessions, sources of rich problems, working in groups, and changes in the teacher's role.

In chapter 14, Sarah Lubienski and Jean Stilwell use a researcher-teacher team approach as the basis for their discussion of tough issues and promising strategies for teaching mathematics through problem solving to low-SES students. They describe strategies for structuring problem-based classes and providing extra support outside class that have potential for helping low-SES students learn in a problem-based environment, but they caution that questions remain in this area that teachers and researchers must continue to address.

The final chapter in this section switches the focus completely, to gifted and talented high school students in Russia who were taught through problem solving. Nina Shteingold, who was a student in this system, and Nannette Feurzeig describe an interesting approach that differs somewhat from the U.S. version of teaching mathematics through problem solving. For example, sample problem sets look more traditional than the rich tasks in many of the other chapters of this volume. However, a deeper look suggests that the differences are at least partially superficial. The Russian students were new to the content of the problem sets when they worked on them, and the problems were carefully sequenced to build toward the mathematical learning goals.

In chapter 16, Mary Kay Stein, Jo Boaler, and Edward Silver address the question of what research tells us about the feasibility and efficacy of teaching mathematics through problem solving. They summarize research in two areas—(1) the impact on student outcomes of recently designed curricular programs that support teaching mathematics through problem solving and (2) particular ways that problem-solving approaches are enacted in classrooms. The authors conclude that the evidence from research supports the feasibility and efficacy of teaching in this manner, while acknowledging that implementers face many challenges, including how to support teachers through appropriate curriculum materials and professional development.

A special feature of this volume is the inclusion of a collection of Teacher Stories that amplify the perspectives and suggestions offered by the chapter authors. These stories, written by secondary school teachers who teach mathematics through problem solving, serve to illustrate many of the ideas discussed in the chapters. The teachers were asked to write about their experiences with their students in their own classrooms. These stories, therefore, were not created to illustrate exemplary practice, to explain what works, or to tell other teachers how to carry out a particular activity or implement a teaching technique. Rather, they are attempts to capture stories of mathematical activity in real classrooms, accompanied by the teacher's own thoughts. In a sense, the stories bring to life many of the ideas about teaching mathematics through problem solving presented in the other chapters. The stories represent a wide range of classroom settings—large cities, small urban centers, and suburban towns. We are grateful to these teachers for sharing their practice with us. We hope that this collection of teachers' stories, together with the perspectives offered by chapter authors, will provide both the coherence and the clear direction concerning how to teach mathematics through problem solving that teachers have been seeking.

Finally, the conceptualization and preparation of this volume were undertaken by a small team of mathematics educators who thought long and hard about what it might mean to use problem solving "as a vehicle for learning new mathematical ideas and skills" (NCTM 2000, p. 182). Without their very able assistance, this volume would never have been completed. Not only did several of them write chapters, but each of them reviewed drafts of chapters and gave us invaluable feedback whenever we asked for it. We wish to extend our sincerest thanks to these dedicated individuals, the members of the Editorial Panel:

Frances Jackson, East Chicago City Schools, East Chicago, Indiana

Jeremy Kahan, University of Minnesota, Minneapolis, Minnesota

Kenneth Levasseur, University of Massachusetts Lowell, Lowell, Massachusetts

Mary Jo Messenger, Howard County Public
Schools, Columbia, Maryland

Chris Rasmussen, Purdue University Calumet,
Hammond, Indiana

Harold L. Schoen
Volume Editor

Randall I. Charles
Series Editor

Section 1

Issues and Perspectives

CHAPTER 1

Developing Understanding through Problem Solving

James Hiebert
Diana Wearne

A CENTRAL learning goal for all students is a deep and rich understanding of the mathematics they study in school. It is not enough for students to know how to solve a quadratic equation, how to add expressions containing fractions, how to calculate the surface area of a cylinder, or how to find the mean of a set of data. It is not even enough to memorize procedures for all these things and execute them with blinding speed. It is not enough, because knowing how to execute procedures does not ensure that students understand what they are doing. To understand, students must get inside these topics; become curious about how everything works; figure out how this topic is the same as, and different from, a topic they already studied; and become confident that they could handle problems about the topic, even new problems they have not seen. Understanding requires more of students than has been expected in the past.

Why Is Understanding Mathematics So Important?

Obviously, the goal of really understanding mathematics is extremely ambitious, almost presumptuous, yet is shared unapologetically by all the authors in this book. Why is it important that all students understand mathematics in this way? At least two reasons can be given. First, understanding a topic ensures that everything one knows about the topic will be useful (Hiebert and Carpenter 1992). One will remember things when one needs them and will use them flexibly to handle new situations. That is just the way it is with understanding. Readers can verify this statement by thinking of something they understand deeply, mathematical or not.

Here is an example from elementary algebra. Students learn how to add and subtract fractions in elementary school. If students really understand what it means to find the sum of two fractions, for example,

$$\frac{5}{12} + \frac{1}{3} = \underline{\quad},$$

then solving such problems as

$$\frac{3}{2ab} + \frac{2}{a^2b} - \frac{1}{3ab^2} = \underline{\qquad}$$

or

$$\frac{2}{x^2 - y^2} + \frac{3x}{x^2 + 2xy + y^2} = \underline{\qquad}$$

does not represent something brand-new to be learned but rather another example of adding fractions. How would students use what they understand about fractions to solve these algebraic versions? They would recognize that the fractions are parts of the same unit, that combining fractions is much easier when the fractions have the same denominator, and that the notion of equivalent fractions (e.g., that 1/3 and 4/12 are two ways to represent the same amount) allows them to rewrite the fractions with a common denominator. The numeric and algebraic problems might look different, but students who understand the simpler, numeric problems can use what they know about those problems to help them solve the algebraic ones.

Being able to use what one knows in a flexible way will be the hallmark of successful citizens and professionals in the twenty-first century. This kind of understanding and flexibility is exactly what students must have to use their mathematical knowledge and to take advantage of the best opportunities that our society offers (National Research Council 2001). Unless society chooses to deny these opportunities to some students, deep understanding of mathematics must be the goal for all students.

We have a second reason to set understanding as a central goal. Understanding something really is fun. It is one of the most enjoyable and satisfying intellectual experiences one can have. Understanding something so well that one just knows how it all works confers an unparalleled sense of esteem and control. Readers can verify how motivated they are by achieving new insights into how something works and how comfortable they feel when talking about things that they deeply understand. By the same token, the experience is equally frustrating and defeating to not understand, to be asked to perform but not have any idea what is happening and why the rules one has memorized actually work. For these reasons, mathematics lessons should give all students the chance to understand what they are learning.

What Does Problem Solving Have to Do with Understanding?

If understanding mathematics is such an important goal, why is this book about problem solving? In simplest terms, the reason is that problem solving leads to understanding (Davis 1992). Students develop, extend, and enrich their understandings by solving problems. Some readers might find this approach to be odd and inefficient. Problem solving takes time. And if the problems are real problems, some students might not even solve them. Why not just teach students the concepts you want them to understand? The answer to this question is not simple. It is the theme of this whole book. As it turns out, understanding is supported best through a delicate balance among engaging students in solving challenging problems, examining increasingly better solution methods, and providing information for students at just the right times (Dewey 1933; Brownell and Sims 1946; Hiebert et al. 1997). Because the traditional teaching approach often has tipped the balance toward telling students too quickly how to solve problems, teachers need to correct the balance by thinking again about how to allow students to do more of the mathematical work. Students' understanding depends on it.

How Can Classrooms Be Designed to Promote Understanding?

On the basis of observations of experts and the convergence of research evidence (see Stein, Boaler, and Silver [this volume]), we can identify several signposts that can be used to tell whether classrooms are moving in the direction of giving students opportunities to develop deep mathematical understandings. The signposts point to problem solving as the core activity and stake out a new kind of balance among allowing students to struggle with challenging problems, examining increasingly better solution methods, and providing appropriate information at the right times. (Other chapters in this book point to other signposts, as well.)

Allowing Mathematics to Be Problematic for Students

The idea that mathematics should be problematic for students is the most radical of the signposts. It is radical because it is very different from the way most of us have thought about mathematics and students. Teachers have been encouraged to make mathematics less problematic for students. Parents assume that teachers should make mathematics less of a struggle; a good teacher, says the common wisdom, helps students learn in a smooth and effortless way.

Allowing mathematics to be problematic for students requires a very different mind-set about what mathematics is, how students learn mathematics with understanding, and what role the teacher can play. Allowing mathematics to be problematic for students means posing problems that are just within students' reach, allowing them to struggle to find solutions and then examining the methods they have used. Allowing mathematics to be problematic requires believing that all students need to struggle with challenging problems if they are to learn mathematics deeply. The reader should note that allowing mathematics to be problematic does not mean making mathematics unnecessarily difficult, but it does mean allowing students to wrestle with what is mathematically challenging.

For many mathematics teachers, this way of thinking is new (see Grouws; and Copes and Shager [this volume]). They have learned that they are supposed to step in and remove the struggle —and the challenge—for students. The extent to which this belief is held by U.S. teachers is revealed in the recent study of classroom mathematics teaching as part of the Third International Mathematics and Science Study (TIMSS). Smith (2000) looked at a subsample of the eighth-grade lessons from Germany, Japan, and the United States and examined the kinds of problems that teachers presented to students and the way in which they helped students solve the problems. She found, in her sample, that about one-third of the problems presented in U.S. classrooms offered students the opportunity to explore relationships and to develop deeper understandings. This outcome was not radically different from the percentages found in other countries. However, U.S. teachers almost always stepped in to show students how to solve the problems; the mathematics they left for students to think about and do was rather trivial. Teachers in the other two countries allowed students more opportunities to wrestle with the challenging aspects of the problems.

Allowing mathematics to be problematic for students does not require importing lots of special problems for students. Rather, it requires allowing the problems that are taught every day to be *problems*. For example, suppose students have been solving such relatively simple absolute-value inequalities as $|x| > 3$. When they encounter a problem such as $|2x + 3| > 3$, teachers often treat it as a new type of problem that requires new procedures. Teachers step in and show students how to solve it. But allowing mathematics to be problematic means allowing even these relatively simple extensions to be real problems for students. Students can be asked to use what they know about the simpler case to work out a solution for the more complex case.

Moreover, allowing routine exercises to be problems can help students deepen their understanding of procedures that they might otherwise execute without thinking. For example, suppose the students have been finding the mean of a set of values and are given the following problem: Team A has 12 students, and Team B has 8 students. The mean length of Frisbee throws for Team A was 25 meters. If the mean length of Frisbee throws for Teams A and B combined was 27 meters, what was the mean length of Frisbee throws for Team B? If students have been following a memorized procedure for finding the mean, such a problem can help the students think about the procedure in a new way.

The key to allowing mathematics to be problematic for students is for the teacher to refrain from stepping in and doing too much of the mathematical work too quickly. But students must play their role, as well. They must see something problematic that they want to resolve. This motivation can come, in part, by creating in the classroom a culture that expects students to adopt problems as their own and supports them in doing so (Hiebert et al. 1996). The motivation also can be enhanced by selecting problems that connect with students' lives (see Marcus and Fey [this volume]). Students must engage in the task if it is to become problematic for them.

Clearly this first signpost changes everything. It affects the way in which all mathematics is treated. It points classroom practice in a new direction. It means that solving problems is the heart of doing mathematics, not a supplement to one's ongoing program.

Focusing on Methods

Allowing students to learn by solving problems sets up the next signpost—focusing classroom activity on the methods used to solve problems. John Dewey (1933) pointed out that the best way to gain deeper understanding of a subject is to search for better methods to solve problems. From a student's point of view, this approach requires the opportunity to share one's own method, to hear others present alternative methods, and then to examine the advantages and disadvantages of these different methods. Suppose a class has been working on solving the following problem:

> Emily is very interested in a particular tee shirt. The tee shirt costs $48 at the department store. On Tuesday, the store is having a 25% off sale. How much will the tee shirt cost Emily on Tuesday?

One student might show a method of finding 25 percent of $48 and then subtracting that amount to find the selling price of $36. Another student might explain that 25 percent of $48 is the same as one-fourth of $48, that one-fourth of $48 is $12, and that $12 from $48 is the selling price of $36. A third student might say that if the shirt was reduced 25 percent, Emily would have to pay 75 percent of the original price, and 75 percent of $48 is $36.

Learning opportunities for these students begin as they search for a method to solve the problem. Learning opportunities continue as they formulate a way to explain their methods to their classmates and justify their validity. Learning opportunities intensify further as students listen to the methods of others and examine them, considering their relative advantages and deciding whether the alternatives provide better choices that they can adopt for subsequent problems. For example, students can recognize that the third suggested strategy discussed in the foregoing would be useful in solving such problems as "Emily bought a tee shirt on sale for $36. Find the original price if the price had been reduced by 25%."

Asking students to think about different ways to solve a problem can also help them connect previous methods with current, more efficient methods of solution. Suppose students were given the following problem:

> Kathryn has 24 meters of fencing to use for her garden. She plans to use the garage as one side of her

garden. If the garden will be rectangular in shape, what is the area of the largest garden Kathryn can build?

One solution method would be to construct a table showing the length of the sides and the associated area and to note the length of sides for which the area is maximum. Elementary and middle school students might use this method. Another method would be to graph the associated function, $y = x(24 - 2x)$ or $y = -2x^2 + 24x$, and to note the coordinates of the vertex of the parabola to find the maximum area. A third, more mathematically sophisticated method would be to use the derivative of the function. Encouraging students to compare different methods helps them understand the more sophisticated methods and appreciate their power.

Analyzing the adequacy of methods and searching for better ones drive the intellectual (and social) life of the class. Students should be permitted to choose their own method to solve problems but should commit themselves to searching for better ones. Discussions in class should revolve around sharing, analyzing, and improving methods. The focus always should be on the merits of the method, not the status of the presenter. Whether presented by the teacher or students, methods should win popularity because of their mathematical advantages—they are efficient, or easy to understand, or easy to adjust to solve new problems.

Why place so much emphasis on examining and improving the methods used to solve problems? Because the payoffs are substantial. A first benefit is that examining methods encourages students to construct mathematical relationships, and constructing relationships is at the heart of understanding (Brownell 1947). Returning to the percent problem, examining the different methods that are likely to be presented provides a perfect opportunity to think about the meaning of percent, the relationship among different representations of the same quantity, and the advantages and disadvantages of the various solution strategies. Many relationships can be constructed here, relationships that extend students' understanding well beyond this particular problem.

A second benefit of focusing on methods is that students can learn from analyzing a range of methods, from flawed to primitive to sophisticated methods. By learning why some methods do not work, students can gain special insights that deepen their understanding and prevent them from making similar mistakes in the future. Allowing students to present their own solutions and methods in class gives them a chance to uncover common errors and examine why they are errors. Teachers are familiar with many of the common errors, such as subtracting the percent itself from the quantity in the foregoing percent problem (a common error made by eighth-grade students; see Wearne and Kouba [2000]) or failing to check for extraneous zeros and reporting, for example, $x = 2$ as a solution to the equation

$$\frac{4}{x^2 - 4} - \frac{1}{x - 2} = 1.$$

In short, focusing on methods creates an environment in which mistakes become sites for learning. This atmosphere is important because when mathematics is allowed to be problematic for students, making mistakes becomes a natural part of learning.

The fact that students learn from analyzing a variety of correct and incorrect methods also means that the class benefits from hearing a variety of methods. This outcome might be more likely when the class is made up of a diverse population of students than when it is homogeneously grouped. Students with different backgrounds and different achievement levels are likely to think of the problem in different ways and produce different methods of solution. The interesting implication is that individual differences in a classroom become a resource that can enhance instruction rather than a difficulty that hinders instruction.

A third benefit of focusing on methods is that the spotlight shifts from people to ideas. As Lampert, Rittenhouse, and Crumbaugh (1996) have found, students can become self-conscious and withdrawn when asked to explain their mathematical thinking. By focusing on methods and the ideas they contain, teachers can show students that all methods and ideas are sites for learning. Every student's contribution can help the class think about ways to improve the correct methods and avoid incorrect ones. When students see that the goals are to help the class, as a group, search for better methods and construct new mathematical relationships, the attention shifts from evaluating students in a negative way toward examining what everyone can learn from their response. This focus is important because it provides a way for teachers to build a classroom culture in which all students feel welcome and appreciated.

Telling the Right Things at the Right Times

A final signpost that can guide classrooms toward providing opportunities for students to develop deep understandings is best phrased as a two-pronged question: What mathematical information should teachers present, and when should they present it? For teachers using a traditional approach, this signpost is curious. Does not good teaching mean presenting mathematical information clearly? Why even ask the questions "What should be presented?" or "When should it be presented?" Should not all mathematical information be presented as it comes along in the curriculum?

The fact that this issue even surfaces shows how radical the first signpost is. Allowing the mathematics to be problematic for students changes everything. In this new environment, teachers need to think carefully about what information should be shared and when it should be shared. Presenting too much information too soon removes the problematic nature of problems. Presenting too little information can leave students floundering.

John Dewey faced the same situation in the 1920s. He recommended that students be allowed to problematize their school subjects. Some educators interpreted this recommendation to mean that students should not be told anything. Dewey (1933) then tried to correct this misinterpretation by saying that, although teachers should not present "ready-made intellectual pabulum to be accepted and swallowed" and later regurgitated (p. 257), in many instances teachers can and should provide information for students.

Here are a few rules of thumb for telling students the right things at the right time. First, teachers can and should show students the words and written symbols that are commonly used to represent quantities, operations, and relationships (e.g., such words as *function, complex numbers, permutation,* and symbols for summation, factorial, or congruent). These representations are social conventions, and students cannot be expected to discover them. When should teachers present them? The best time is when students need them—when the ideas have been developed and students need a way to record the ideas and communicate with others about them. These conventions should be presented as beneficial aids, not as burdensome memorization exercises for the students.

A second rule of thumb is that teachers can present alternative methods of solutions that have not been suggested by students. Over time, teachers can develop a good sense for which solution methods for particular problems help students understand the main ideas and relationships that are contained in a problem. If these methods are not presented by students, teachers should feel free to present them.

For example, suppose the students had been finding surface areas of rectangular prisms by finding the sum of the areas of the six faces. The teacher could suggest an alternative procedure, that of finding the perimeter of the designated base, multiplying that quantity by the height, and adding to the resulting quantity the sum of the areas of the two bases. Doing so would present an opportunity to examine why this method works; how it is similar to, and different from, the other method; and whether it can be used to find surface areas of other polyhedra.

Teachers should feel free to present alternative methods during the discussion of problems that students have already solved. The trick is for the teacher to present the method as one that students should examine, just as they examine other methods, rather than a method that is automatically preferred just because the teacher presented it. A good way to ensure this outcome is to make sure that students use a method because they understand why it is correct and find it useful, not because of who presented it.

A third rule of thumb for presenting information is that teachers should highlight ideas that are embedded in students' methods. Students can invent and present methods for solving problems without being aware of all the ideas on which the methods depend. Teachers can help students see these ideas and construct new relationships. Consider again the percent problem discussed previously. A variety of proportional relationships are embedded in the different solution methods, and these can be made explicit by the teacher. By restating and clarifying students' methods and pointing to the important ideas in them, teachers not only show respect for students' thinking but help focus students' attention on the important mathematics, thereby guiding the mathematical direction of the class.

How Different Is This Approach from Traditional Practice?

Classroom practice described in this chapter, and in this entire volume, represents a fundamental change from business as usual. It will not be achieved by making superficial changes. It will be achieved only by rethinking our beliefs about two issues that lie at the core of mathematics teaching: (1) what learning goals we set for students and (2) how students can best achieve these goals.

This chapter is built on the premise that the traditional learning goals for students must be expanded and reshaped to include a deep and rich understanding of mathematics (National Research Council 2001). Understanding mathematics has long been advertised as a goal for students. Many teachers obviously would like their students to understand the mathematics they study, but when asked to specify the goal for a particular lesson, most U.S. teachers in the TIMSS Video Study talked about skill proficiency; few mentioned understanding (Hiebert and Stigler 2000).

Valuing deep understanding of mathematics as an important goal for students is the first step in changing classroom practice. The second step is to help students achieve this goal. One way to support students' efforts to understand is to allow mathematics to be problematic for them. Why has this point been such a major emphasis in this chapter? Because it is based on a theory about how students construct understanding that is very different from the beliefs that many teachers now hold about how students learn. In particular, the theory places great importance on the role of *struggle* in developing understanding. As mentioned previously, many teachers believe that their job is to remove struggles from students' learning experiences. But struggling, in a healthy sense and on the right kinds of problems for an appropriate amount of time, prepares students to make sense of relevant information, to piece together things in new ways, and to see the benefits of better methods of solution. An important part of this theory is that deep understanding develops over time. Although quick insights can occur, sometimes while working on a single problem, significant and lasting understanding of mathematics develops gradually and accumulates over time as students encounter and make sense of coherent sets of connected problems.

The changes called for in this book are fundamental. Teachers who take the recommendations seriously will face many challenges as they revise their instruction to help students develop understanding through solving problems (Ball 1993; Lampert 2001; Schifter and Fosnot 1993; see also Grouws; and Copes and Shager [this volume]). But the changes need not occur overnight and all at once. Change this important often happens in small steps, small steps that build on previous ones. Small successes can yield dramatic improvement if they are saved and shared and accumulate over time. Steady, gradual improvement is often more lasting than overnight reform. And some encouraging signs are emerging. Many teachers are embracing new learning goals for students, creating for themselves new images of practice, and displaying rich models of what is possible in classrooms. If the mathematics education community can create a system in which teachers can record and accumulate these images and models and share them with others, classroom practice around the country can gradually become more aligned with the visions portrayed in this book.

CHAPTER 2

Mathematics as Sense Making

Jeremy A. Kahan
Terrence R. Wyberg

TEACHING mathematics through problem solving begins by identifying the important mathematics that the students are to learn. The teacher then chooses a problem for which the students' thinking about, and work on, that problem are likely to connect with the important mathematics. The teacher poses the problem to the class, making sure the students have sufficient understanding of the task but without telling them how to solve it. Then students explore the problem, trying to make sense of it, and eventually generate one or more solutions. Finally, with the teacher's guidance, students reflect on the problem, their work, and the important mathematical ideas that have emerged. Through this process of sense making, students encounter—or some would say, create or reinvent—mathematics. Mathematics helps solve the problem, and, as Hiebert and Wearne argue in chapter 1 of this volume, in the process students come to understand the related mathematics.

When problems are well chosen and teaching is effective, students' engagement in making sense of the problem is the mechanism by which they come to understand the underlying mathematics. Our purposes in this chapter are to illustrate what we mean by mathematics as sense making, to consider how that idea relates to teaching mathematics through problem solving, to discuss some benefits for students of using this approach, and to share some cautions regarding teaching through problem solving.

15

An Example

We begin with an example of how sense making and teaching through problem solving might play out in a classroom. Mathematics instruction should begin by teachers' articulating to themselves the important mathematical concepts and methods that they want their students to learn. For example, a teacher who wants students to learn to use divisibility arguments might select the Change Problem that follows:

Can you make exactly 5 dollars with exactly 100 U.S. coins and no nickels? If so, how?

We urge readers to attempt this problem before reading on.

We learned about this problem in 1990 while observing the ninth-grade class of Doug McGlathery at the Cambridge Rindge and Latin High School in Cambridge, Massachusetts. The aspect that made the problem interesting for students was that it forced them to rely on experimentation rather than algorithms and to find multiple solutions, both of which they did. The outcome that made the problem memorable for us, though, was that in the process of solving it, students learned important mathematics. We now use this problem with our classes of preservice teachers to help them understand what we mean by teaching mathematics through problem solving. We begin by having the prospective teachers solve the problem. The approaches described subsequently are ones used by preservice teachers but could just as well be approaches used by high school students.

People often start by experimenting with pennies, dimes, and quarters and come close to $5.00 or 100 coins rather quickly but then start to think that the task cannot be done. We ask them how they can be sure it is impossible. Those who take an algebraic approach often proceed by letting p, d, and q represent the respective number of pennies, dimes, and quarters and writing two equations:

(1) $$p + d + q = 100$$

and

(2) $$p + 10d + 25q = 500.$$

They sometimes object, saying, You expect us to solve for three unknowns with two equations? We tell them to press on. Someone will then subtract equation (1) from equation (2) to obtain

(3) $$9d + 24q = 400.$$

If d and q are whole numbers, then the left-hand side of (3) is a multiple of 3 but the right-hand side is not. So the result is algebraic confirmation of people's experience-driven conjecture that no solution is possible with just pennies, dimes, and quarters.

Often students prove the impossibility of the pennies-dimes-and-quarters case, not with formal algebra but through the systematic examination of cases. They know that the number of pennies needs to be a multiple of 5 (why?) and that it needs to be relatively large. With 55 pennies, they must use 45 dimes or quarters, and the value of the dimes and quarters alone will be at least $4.50, which, added to the value of the pennies, exceeds $5.00; so they need at least 60 pennies. Moreover, if the number of pennies goes as high as 85, even if all the rest of the coins are quarters, students cannot reach a value of $5.00. So the cases to consider are 60, 65, 70, 75, and 80 pennies.

These students then proceed to look at the particular cases as follows. If they have 60 pennies and 40 dimes, that collection is worth $4.60; so they need to arrive at greater value. By trading a dime for a quarter, the value rises by $0.15 cents to $4.75. Doing so again produces $4.90. Repeating the trade yields $5.05. So they cannot do the problem with 60 pennies. Students repeat the process for 65 pennies. Sixty-five pennies and 35 dimes are worth $4.15. Trading dimes for quarters increases the value in increments of $0.15, but students are $0.85 short, so they miss $5.00 again (and again they miss the same way, never hitting $5.00, only $4.90 and $5.05). Students repeat the process for 70, 75, and 80 pennies, often parceling out the tasks to different group members and sometimes using spreadsheets; obtain similar results; and conclude that no solution is possible.

We have discussed solutions that use equations and tables. A possible graphical approach is pictured in figure 2.1. This graph was constructed by first fixing the number of pennies at 60, thus leaving 40 dimes and quarters. Each dot on the dotted line segment labeled $p = 60$ represents a different combination of dimes and quarters to make 40 coins and the corresponding value of the collection of coins. For example, when the number of pennies is 60 and the number of dimes is 39, then the number of quarters must be 1 (40 minus 39) and the total value is $4.75; this point is represented by the rightmost dot on the graph. The dotted line segments for other numbers of pennies were generated similarly. (In subsequent discussion we refer to these five dotted segments as lines.)

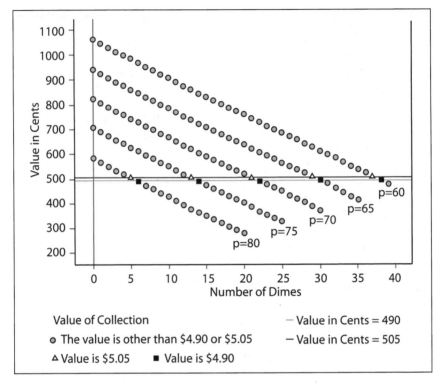

Fig. 2.1. Graphical solution for the Change Problem

Several features emerge from the graphical representation:

- No points are plotted between the horizontal lines for $4.90 and $5.05, demonstrating that no collections have a value of $5.00.

- The five lines are parallel. That property makes sense because each line has slope $0.15, corresponding to the loss of 15 cents when trading a quarter for a dime.

- The intercepts on the vertical axis are evenly spaced at 120-cent intervals, a spacing that makes sense because it corresponds to trading 5 quarters for 5 pennies.

- The bottom-right points on the lines themselves are collinear and evenly spaced, because they are separated by trades of 5 pennies for 5 dimes, with a change of 45 cents in value.

- Proceeding horizontally to the right from line to line, we find that the same value is achieved with 8 more dimes, 5 fewer pennies, and so 3 fewer quarters. This observation is particularly important for the horizontal lines shown at $4.90 and $5.05.

- All the plotted points have values that are one more than a multiple of 3 (cents). This result follows because within a diagonal line all possible transitions are by multiples of 15 cents, and 15 is a multiple of 3. Going from line to line, one can go horizontally for a shift of 0 in value, or vertically for shifts in multiples of 120, or diagonally as for the bottom-right points with shifts in multiples of 45 cents. Regardless, transitions between any two points on the graph add multiples of 3 and stay on numbers of cents that leave remainders of 1 when divided by 3, which 500 does not.

Some Reflections

At this point in the discussion, we encourage the class to compare the solution methods and note the relative merits of each. We also spend time helping the students recognize that each approach is a different manifestation of the same underlying mathematics. Possible observations to elicit include the following:

- Any collection of 100 dimes and pennies has a value that is one more than a multiple of 3 (cents) because the value of a dime and the value of a penny are both one more than a multiple of 3, and so is 100.

- Trading dimes for quarters adds 15 cents, a multiple of 3, so our value remains one more than a multiple of 3.

- Five hundred is two more than a multiple of 3, and 495 is a multiple of 3, so we never hit either of these values, only 490 and 505, which are both one more than a multiple of 3.

These observations show how divisibility by 3 is at the heart of all the arguments, and one could proceed to draw more parallels between them (e.g., all the arguments proceed by eliminating pennies to focus on the divisibility issue in what remains).

Using half dollars and dollar coins, both ninth-grade students and our preservice ones extended the previously discussed methods to find solutions to the Change Problem. Some then found more than one solution and began to see how to use trades that preserved both value and number of coins (e.g., 5 pennies and 3 quarters for 8 dimes) to generate families of solutions. Programming a computer or a calculator was perhaps the most expedient way for students to find all nineteen solutions and to be sure that no other solutions were possible.

Teaching mathematics through problem solving, as illustrated by the Change Problem, challenges traditional instruction in at least two ways. First, teaching through problem solving places the problem first, not after the student knows everything needed to solve it. Second, teaching through problem solving suggests a more dynamic view of learning than the conventional approach does (Huntley et al. 2000; Schroeder and Lester 1989). Students often bounce back and forth between the problem and the mathematics, using the context to amplify their understanding of the related mathematics and using the mathematics to guide their study of the problem. For example, students who write $p + d + q = 5$ (dollars) self-correct when they think about what this equation says in the context of this problem. Mathematics as sense making is the activity in which students engage to resolve the problem and make sense of the results of that effort.

Some Benefits of Teaching Mathematics through Problem Solving

At least three reasons can be cited for teaching mathematics through problem solving: (1) it helps students understand that mathematics develops through a sense-making process, (2) it deepens students' understanding of underlying mathematical ideas and methods, and (3) it engages students' interest. We discuss the first two of these reasons. The third reason is exemplified in several teacher stories in this volume, including those by Bellman and by Messenger and Ames.

Developing Young Mathematicians and Their Sense of Mathematics

In the Change Problem, we see how through solving the problem, students are led to important mathematical ideas. They also experience doing mathematics firsthand, observing that the need for proof emerges from needing to justify a pattern to a skeptic, that some problems do not yield to the first algorithm one tries, that some problems can yield no solutions or multiple solutions, that a messiness precedes the ultimate order, and that connecting multiple representations or methods deepens mathematical understanding. In this problem, the result itself is unimportant and the problem is contrived (do you ever really need to make $5.00 this way?), but the mathematical ideas (e.g., divisibility) and processes (e.g., algebraic thinking) encountered are neither unimportant nor contrived. Like Bruner (1977), we believe that encountering the fundamental ideas of the discipline and the processes that characterize it is essential for students so that they emerge as young mathematicians, not mathematical libraries.

Those who develop mathematics through engaging in problems like the Change Problem can appreciate the following passage (Mathematical Sciences Education Board 1989, p. 31):

> As a practical matter, mathematics is a science of pattern and order. Its domain is not molecules or cells but numbers, chance, form, algorithms, and change. As a science of abstract objects, mathematics relies on logic rather than observation as its standard of truth, yet employs observation, simulation, and even experimentation as means of discovering truth.

As a science of pattern and order, mathematics has its own methods, which we call *processes*. When teaching mathematics through problem solving, one employs those methods to make sense of problems. Mathematics steers the process of our trials in the Change Problem, for example, suggesting we try multiples of five pennies, use variables, or be systematic so we can find patterns in our explorations. Furthermore, as we keep trying various combinations, making sense of our observations is a mathematical activity. After we try to generate solutions with pennies, dimes, and quarters, mathematics helps us come to understand why we keep failing. In solving this problem, students are learning to think mathematically. In Stanic and Kilpatrick's (1989) metaphor that the problem to be solved is a vehicle, student drivers are using the vehicle to learn to drive.

We also encounter mathematics as an object. For example, in the process of making sense of the Change Problem, we encounter underlying patterns and structures, which we call mathematics or the ideas or concepts of mathematics. The trades of dimes for quarters tie in with the mathematics of function and slope. Regardless of which method is used, the fundamental impossibility of doing the problem connects with the issue of divisibility. By engaging in the problem, students learn not only about the problem but also about deeper mathematical ideas underlying it. In Stanic and Kilpatrick's vehicle metaphor, this mathematical learning is the destination.

Having students use problems to develop mathematics also lends authenticity to their mathematical experience, because historically mathematics often developed in the effort to solve problems. Fermat's note of the statement of his Last Theorem that he had discovered a wonderful proof that the margin would not contain was itself a problem (Kahan 1999). The vexation that this problem caused mathematicians led to hundreds of years of mathematical activity, culminating not only in the proof of the theorem but also in the generation of new mathematics along the way. For some, the theorem remains a problem because they wonder about the existence of a simpler but sound proof that Fermat may have had in mind. Other examples of the development of mathematics in response to problems are the emergence of probability from a discussion by Pascal, Fermat, and others of ways to settle a wager in a game halted with one player leading (Kline 1972) and the expansion of the definition of function in response to the problem of describing the motion of a vibrating string (Kleiner 1989). An important goal of teaching through problem solving is to let students be part of that mathematical process.

Developing Understanding

As Hiebert and Wearne (in chapter 1 of this volume) argue, teaching through problem solving can lead to deeper understanding of mathematics. If understanding is seeing general mathematical reasons behind the rules, not just applying a series of unrelated rules, then problem solving can help. For example, Wertheimer (as cited in Bransford, Brown, and Cocking [2000, p. 57]) demonstrated that as compared with students who learned only to apply a formula, those who learned to find the area of a parallelogram by cutting pieces off and pasting them back elsewhere to form a rectangle were better able to find areas of other figures. Similarly, Hiebert and Wearne (see chapter 1 of this volume) argue that those who learn to add fractions like

$$\frac{5}{12} \text{ and } \frac{1}{3}$$

by solving problems understand the need for a common denominator. Those students can then adapt that knowledge when they later add such algebraic fractions as

$$\frac{3}{2ab} \text{ and } \frac{1}{3ab^2}$$

(where a and b are nonzero).

A somewhat different view of understanding involves students' constructing a new framework of knowledge or extending an existing one (Bransford, Brown, and Cocking 2000, pp. 36–42). When students are taught through problem solving, this criterion for understanding is also met. Students are forced by their engagement with the problem to construct or extend a framework of the knowledge of mathematics required to solve the problem.

Some Suggestions and Cautions

Focus on the Intended Mathematics

As Marcus and Fey elaborate in chapter 5 of this volume, the selection of problems is very important when teaching mathematics through problem solving. The Curriculum Principle (NCTM 2000) describes curriculum as more than just a collection of problems or activities. The curriculum must be coherent; students must be able to make connections between the mathematics they are learning and the mathematics they already know. The primary goal is for students to make sense of and learn the mathematical content of the problems that are used. A teacher might be tempted to organize a set of problems around a particularly entertaining context, but that approach would be appropriate only if the problems provided a coherent context for learning the intended mathematics.

The intended mathematical topics need not change when teaching mathematics through problem solving, but the focus needs to shift to understanding those topics in depth. If we want students to multiply and factor polynomials or use the binomial probability distribution with understanding, our challenge is to select and structure problems that lead to that objective (see chapter 5, by Marcus and Fey, in this volume for ideas for teaching both of these topics). Our point is that one begins from a sequence of cohesive curricular objectives, then chooses appropriate problems.

Real-World Context Not Required (But May Sometimes Help)

We make no assumption about the extent to which the substance of the problem is related to the real world. The Change Problem is somewhat intermediate in this respect, using a fantastical real-world context. In this volume, readers will find a continuum of problems, ranging from a realistic setting involving animal population growth (see chapter 10, by Rasmussen, Yackel, and King) to the more abstract one of adding rational expressions (see chapter 1, by Hiebert and Wearne). Even in teaching such traditional content as solving linear equations, one of those occasions when the teacher is tempted to teach by telling, students could instead learn mathematics through solving problems (see chapter 13, by Copes and Shager).

As we stated previously, problems should be accessible and engaging to students, and they should have the potential of leading to the intended mathematical outcomes. On the one hand, not all problems need to be set in a real-world context, although for some students an interesting context may help engage the student's knowledge level and interest. On the other hand, finding a real-world problem to investigate, say, the distributive property of multiplication over addition, is possible, but the context may obscure the underlying mathematics. Many good problems that are not set in a real-world context can be used to investigate this important mathematical idea. We advocate using a blend of problem types. Some mathematical ideas may be better developed through solving authentic real-world problems, whereas other ideas may be better developed through solving problems set in less-than-authentic contexts.

Conclusion

We have focused on mathematics and the process of sense making, but we do not want to leave the impression that the teacher's job is over once a problem is selected and posed to the class. The teacher's role remains complex and is discussed in detail in various chapters in this volume (see chapter 9, by Grouws; chapter 10, by Rasmussen, Yackel, and King; and chapter 13, by Copes and Shager). One challenge that teachers face is that different students may need more and different guidance as they struggle with the problem.

Yet we emphasize that the mathematics-as-sense-making approach described in this chapter is intended for all students. Some people may argue that high-ability students would be better off with a more direct instructional approach. To the contrary, we contend that those students can benefit from learning mathematics through problem solving because they can take the problem and run with it, developing the mathematical ideas and processes with little intervention from the teacher. Some people may also argue that low-achieving students need the structure found in a traditional mathematics classroom and do not have what it takes to draw the mathematics out of a problem situation. We agree that these students, and maybe all students, need structure; this structure can be provided when teaching mathematics through problem solving. Low-achieving students may need additional help from the teacher to understand the problem, but they will not need the teacher to solve or trivialize the problem for them. (See chapter 14, by Lubienski and Stilwell, and its accompanying teacher story by Messenger and Ames.)

Ultimately, we value students' mathematical understanding resulting from teaching through problem solving. By making sense of and solving well-chosen problems with gentle guidance from an effective teacher, students encounter mathematics and mathematical thinking that are useful and important as well as rich and beautiful.

CHAPTER 3

Mathematical Habits of Mind

Kenneth Levasseur
Al Cuoco

THE FIRST two chapters of this volume present a view of doing and learning mathematics as actively making sense of problematic situations. We extend that view by making the point that mathematical thinking involves more than just understanding important mathematical ideas and learning to apply useful methods and procedures. Modes of thought, or habits of mind, exist that transcend content knowledge and are taken for granted by mathematicians as essential facets of their work. These habits of mind are useful for reasoning about the world from a quantitative or spatial perspective and for reasoning about the mathematical content itself, both within and across mathematical fields.

Our teaching experience over the years has convinced us that these habits of mind should not, and probably cannot, be taught by studying the "top-ten habits of mind." Rather, the requirement is an integrated program of immersion in developing concepts and skills with accompanying reflection, solving problems of all types, making and using abstractions, and building and applying mathematical theories. In short, students develop these habits of mind as a by-product of learning mathematics through problem solving using approaches described in the other chapters of this volume. We begin by describing some of the most important mathematical habits of mind using sample problems to illustrate the meaning of each habit. We then discuss how students acquire these habits of mind and offer some suggestions for teachers who want to help students develop these habits.

Habits of Mind

In this section, we identify some of the most significant and useful habits of mind. Space limitations preclude any attempt on our part to present a comprehensive classification of habits of mind. Some habits on this list will overlap to some extent, and surely some habits exist that will be missing. For more exhaustive lists, see Cuoco and others (1996) and Goldenberg (1996). We present each habit with a brief description and an example of its use in a problem situation.

Guessing Is Not Necessarily Bad—We All Do It!

When students are engaged in mathematical problem-solving activities that are challenging to them, they should be encouraged to develop the habit of trying reasoned guessing to help them better understand the problem and move toward a solution. For example, consider the triangle-dissection problem:

> What triangles can be divided into two isosceles triangles?

Please do not read any further if you have not tried the problem!

With enough experience doing geometry problems, students learn that problems that involve triangles often have a solution that is special—maybe an isosceles or right triangle. So guessing that the solution to the triangle-dissection problem is special in some way is reasonable. You as the teacher should encourage this kind of guessing. Isosceles triangles would be a reasonable guess, but they lead to a dead end. They cannot generally be "cloned." In contrast, right triangles do lead to a solution. If we brainstorm what we know about right triangles, the image in figure 3.1 might come to mind. Adding a radial line to the right angle in figure 3.1 makes it clear how right triangles satisfy the conditions of the problem.

The answer to the triangle-dissection problem is all right triangles. Right? We return to this question in our discussion of the next habit of mind.

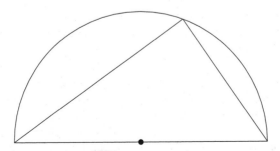

Fig. 3.1. Right triangle inscribed in a semicircle

Challenge Solutions, Even Correct Ones

Once students have found a potential solution to a problem, they need to develop the habit of challenging the solution by looking back over the problem. For example, "all right triangles" seems like a nice solution to the triangle-dissection problem. The solver is tempted to "check off" this problem and move on to the next, but another family of solutions to this problem remains to be found. Reflecting on the way right triangles solve the problem is probably the most natural way to discover the second family. With right triangles, the dissection line is a leg of both isosceles triangles. If we try to fit two isosceles triangles together so that the dissection line is a base of one triangle and a leg of the other triangle, we are forced to draw a picture something like figure 3.2. A new family of solutions, not totally disjoint from the first, emerges. Is that all there is? We leave this question to the reader and go on to the next habit of mind.

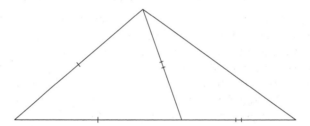

Fig. 3.2. Isosceles triangle dissected into two isosceles triangles

Look for Patterns

Students should be in the habit of looking for patterns. Consider the two-pan-balance problem with powers of 3:

> Given weights of 1, 3, 9, 27, 81, 243, and 729 grams, what weights can you measure? If you want to upgrade your set of weights, what is the next weight you might buy?

You would expect your students to try a few examples, but taking the step to create an organized table of examples is far more useful (see table 3.1). Once the results have been tabulated, students are then in a better position to recognize patterns. What patterns do they see here? Where are the natural dividing lines in the cases, and where will the next one occur?

Table 3.1. Small weight measurements using powers of 3

Weight	Left Pan	Right Pan	Weight	Left Pan	Right Pan
1		1	9		9
2	1	3	10		9, 1
3		3	11	1	9, 3
4		3, 1	12		9, 3
5	3, 1	9	13		9, 3, 1
6	3	9	14	9, 3, 1	27
7	3	9, 1	15	9, 3	27
8	1	9			

Work still remains to be done to describe how the patterns in table 3.1 help answer the question, but the patterns can be a key, and they are unlikely to be obvious as the solver starts working on the problem.

Conserve Memory

One habit of many mathematicians is that they try to memorize as little as possible. Students should be encouraged to develop the same habit. For example, most mathematicians use the identity for the cosine of the sum of angles infrequently. Instead of memorizing the identity, they might just remember the general pattern for the sin (or cosine) of a sum (or difference), which is

$$(\text{SC})(\alpha \pm \beta) = (\text{SC})(\alpha)(\text{SC})(\beta) \pm (\text{SC})(\alpha)(\text{SC})(\beta),$$

where each (SC) is either sin or cos. They should not have difficulty remembering that exactly two of the SCs on the right are cosine and two are sine. Knowing a few of the more basic facts about the trigonometric functions lets us find the right combination if we really need it. For example, if we are looking for $\cos(\alpha + \beta)$ and we consider the specific case where $\alpha = \beta = 0$, we can rule out the case where each term on the right has sine as a factor.

Does this process seem like more work than just memorizing? Before deciding, two considerations should be kept in mind. First, this derivation is done on a personal level—it is internalized and does not have to play out completely in many cases. Second, the correct identity,

$$\cos(\alpha + \beta) = \cos\alpha \cos\beta - \sin\alpha \sin\beta,$$

is now in the short-term memory. It will be memorized for a while, and this temporary retention is sufficient because people tend to use identities and other facts in clusters.

A good understanding of underlying mathematical ideas is required to conserve memory, but the habitual practice of conserving memory in this way helps develop mathematical understanding. In fact, we believe that this sort of mutually supportive relationship with mathematical understanding holds true for each of the habits of mind.

Specialize—Sometimes Everything Is Special

Sometimes insight can be gained about a given problem by analyzing a special case. A classic example of turning a problem into a special case is completing the square. Instead of just learning the mechanics of completing the square, your students should be aware of its significance. In fact every quadratic equation can be reduced to the special case of solving $x^2 = c$.

Special cases also arise when mathematicians begin the solution of a problem with "Without loss of generality...." This statement is a kind of code for saying that we are going to make an assumption that does not restrict the problem in any way. Consider the commuter problem that follows:

> If I drive to work at 60 miles per hour and come back home along the same route at 50 miles per hour, what is my average speed for the two-way commute?

We are not told the distance between home and work; so we reasonably start by making an assumption about the distance: "Without loss of generality, we assume that the commute to work is [fill in almost anything] miles." With that assumption, the solution emerges, and upon reflection we realize that the commuting distance has no bearing on the average speed. In this example, the special case not only adds new insight but actually leads to a solution of the original problem.

Use Alternative Representations

Another mathematical habit of mind that we want to encourage students to develop is to represent a problem in various ways. For example, consider the postage-stamp-arithmetic problem that follows:

> Given an unlimited supply of 7-cent and 10-cent
> stamps, what postage amounts can you make?
> Which ones can you not make?

The postage-stamp-arithmetic problem can be approached using only arithmetic, but new insights can be gained by introducing coordinate geometry to the analysis. See figure 3.3. The problem essentially asks what positive numbers can be expressed in the form $7a + 10b$, where a and b are both nonnegative integers. These nonnegative combinations of 7 and 10 can be represented as lattice points on the first quadrant, including the axes.

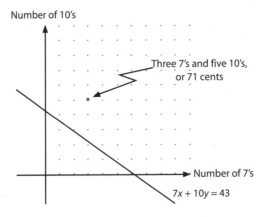

Fig. 3.3. Graph of solution set of the postage-stamp-arithmetic problem

Now the question reduces to asking, Which lines of the form $7a + 10b = k$ pass through these points? This inquiry is not a solution, but it is a different, sometimes useful way to look at the problem. Encourage your students to look for different representations of the same problem. Many more examples of this type appear in a recent yearbook of the National Council of Teachers of Mathematics (2001).

Carefully Classify

Another good mathematical habit is to carefully classify the outcomes in a problem, especially in one that involves complex counting. For example, the dial of a lock pictured in figure 3.4 was made by the Simplex Company. Simplex advertised "thousands of combinations." A combination is an ordered sequence of zero to five pushes. In each push, the user presses from one to five buttons. Once a button is pressed, it stays in, so it cannot be reused in a subsequent step. Does the Simplex Company's advertisement tell the truth?

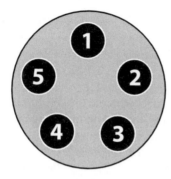

Fig. 3.4. Dial of a lock made by the Simplex Company

One way to solve the combination-lock problem is to classify the possible button sequences according to their "shapes." By shape, we mean the number of buttons that are pressed, such as 3-1-1 or 1-2-1. Counting the number of shapes is a manageable problem, and the number of button sequences with each shape is relatively easy to compute. For example the number of button sequences with the shape 1-2-1 is

$$5 \times C(4,2) \times 2 = 5 \times 6 \times 2 = 60,$$

where $C(4,2)$ is the binomial coefficient "4 choose 2." Counting all 1082 of the button sequences is mostly a matter of organizing this process. For more details, see Velleman and Call (1995).

Think Algebraically

Using the logic of algebra and perhaps, but not necessarily, algebraic symbol manipulation is also a good habit for students to develop. Consider the "arithmagon" problem from Mason (1985).

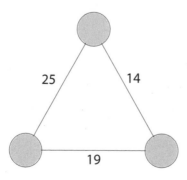

Fig. 3.5. Arithmagon problem with sums of secret numbers on the edges

Each of the vertices of the triangle in figure 3.5 has
been assigned a secret number. Each edge is labeled with the sum of the secret numbers of vertices it
connects. What are the secret numbers?

The "arithmagon" problem is not really challenging for those of
us who teach algebra. Starting from the top and going clockwise,
if we let the unknown numbers at the vertices be x, y, and z, then
the problem reduces to solving the linear system

$$x + y = 14,$$

$$y + z = 19,$$

$$x + z = 25.$$

However, thinking algebraically does not necessarily mean knowing how to create or solve this system. In fact, the observation that
if we add the three numbers 14, 19, and 25, we will get two times
the sum of the secret numbers leads to what some people might
consider a more elegant solution. To make this observation, we
must be able to think abstractly about the numbers, and the logic
is definitely algebraic. It is also a line of reasoning that has been
observed from, and understood by, "prealgebra" students. The
point is that a teacher does not need to start with formal algebra
to expose students to the logic that is used in the subject.

How Can Students Acquire Useful Habits of Mind?

The habits described here should not ordinarily be the explicit objects of our teaching; rather, each student should internalize
them as they do mathematics. Part of the way this outcome can
be achieved is by teachers' modeling the very habits we want students to develop. However, the crucial element is that students be
given the opportunity to develop mathematical understanding
through problem solving. The problems should not all be difficult,
but they should challenge students to think about, and make
sense of, the problems and the mathematics that underlies them.
Reflection on solution methods is also crucial. In short, classrooms in which mathematics is taught through problem solving as
described in this volume are excellent settings for these habits of
mind to develop.

Teachers can facilitate students' development of these
habits by making the habits explicit and by encouraging their stu-

dents to reflect on them when opportunities arise. We have found that student journals are a good tool to foster explication of, and reflection on, habits of mind. We suggest that students record the highlights of their solution methods as they attempt a problem. They should not record everything that pops into their heads, but rather, they should aim for entries that show insights into their thinking as described in the foregoing habits of mind. Here are some items that you might want to suggest for your students' journals. Their connections with the various habits should be clear.

- A rewording of the problem, including an identification of variables, assumptions, and what is to be solved for or proved.

- A question of clarification about the problem. Even if as the teacher you are going to answer the question immediately, encourage students to record the question first.

- A strategy that might help solve the problem. For example, tabulating some data might lead to a solution to some problems. Encourage students to record what they are going to try before actually launching the attempt.

- Conjectures. Some conjectures are based on "gut feelings" that are difficult to explain, but you should encourage students to record them. Conjectures that are based on a plausible reason are even better. For example, suppose that you ask for the dimensions of a rectangle with given perimeter having maximal area. A guess that the solution is a square might be purely a guess, but it also might be based on an understanding that at the extreme (a very long skinny rectangle) the area is nearly zero.

- Guesses. Many nonroutine problems are "inverses" of routine ones. For example, many students can easily solve this problem:

Mary drives from Boston to Washington, D.C., a trip of 500 miles. If she travels at an average of 60 mph on the way to Washington and 50 mph on the way back, how many hours does her trip take?

But they have a difficult time with this one:

Mary drives from Boston to Washington, D.C., and she travels at an average of 60 mph on the way to

Washington and 50 mph on the way back. If the total trip takes 18.5 hours, how far is Boston from Washington?

Both problems involve the same functional relationship, but the second one requires that the relationship be inverted. Repeatedly guessing at an answer to the second problem and then checking each guess allow students to formalize the underlying relationship so that it can be inverted (see Cuoco [1993]).

- A drawing, symbolic notation, or alternative representation of anything that relates to the question. Suppose that a student is working on a problem that involves a line of people who are facing left or right. A representation using left and right arrows reveals something about the student's facility with abstraction.

- Solutions to special cases of the problem. For example, in the triangle-dissection problem, a description of all isosceles triangles that can be divided into two isosceles triangles is, in a sense, an extremely small step. Yet in many problems, such small steps can be scaffolded to a complete solution.

- The statement of another related problem, with or without a solution. What triangles can be divided into two similar triangles or two right triangles? Such a problem may prove to be either challenging or trivial, but in either situation, thinking of related alternative problems should be encouraged.

As students compose, enter, and reexamine journal entries about many different problems, they are likely to witness the emergence of many of the described habits of mind as patterns in their thinking. Their explicit recognition of the habits in their journals has the effect of further strengthening the habits for students.

Conclusion

Mathematical habits of mind develop as a by-product of teaching mathematics through problem solving. As you select problem sequences for teaching any particular content area, you can anticipate that certain habits will be strengthened. One aspect that makes the process fascinating is that students often come up with a surprising, unanticipated approach that fosters a different habit. Periodically, you might want to review a list of habits that you collect from this chapter and other references. If you note that your class has not encountered a particular habit as frequently as you would like, you might try to lead students in the direction of that habit through problem selection or by your own modeling of the habit. You might use the habit of mind as you introduce a concept or as you reflect on a problem that the class has done.

Finally, we want to emphasize a facet of the process that we did not have the space to address in this chapter, namely, the design and selection of orchestrated problem sets. Most of the problems we have used in this chapter can be extended to form such a problem set. For example, an introduction to geometric proof could be built around the triangle-dissection problem. For more details on selecting and creating problem tasks and task sequences, see chapter 5, by Marcus and Fey, in this volume.

Devising and perpetuating a problem-solving environment that fosters good mathematical habits of mind in students is a habit that all mathematics teachers should acquire.

Teaching Mathematics through Problem Solving:
A Historical Perspective

Beatriz S. D'Ambrosio

> In the following work, the object has been to furnish an elementary treatise, commencing with the first principles, and leading the pupil, by gradual and easy steps, to a knowledge of the elements of the science. . . . For this purpose, every rule is demonstrated, and every principle analyzed, in order that the mind of the pupil may be disciplined and strengthened so as to prepare him, either for pursuing the study of Mathematics intelligently, or more successfully attending to any pursuit in life. (Ray 1848, p. 3)

THIS statement, found in the preface of *Ray's Algebra*, was written by one of the nineteenth century's most prolific authors of United States mathematics textbooks, Joseph Ray. It captures a perspective toward mathematics learning and teaching that was prevalent in mathematics education in the United States during the nineteenth century. It also suggests a specific role for problems in the mathematics curriculum.

Educators in the mid- to late 1800s believed that effective teaching involved showing students mathematical procedures, followed by students' application (i.e., use of the procedure to solve word problems) and practice of those procedures. Educators believed that such practice would strengthen the mind, as Ray indicates above. In fact, all the word problems posed throughout Ray's many books give students opportunities to apply the skills and rules presented in the books. Ray emphasizes in the preface to one of his arithmetic books that "the pupil is never required to

39

perform any operation until the principle on which it is founded has first been explained" (Ray 1857, p. 3). Indeed, this view of problem solving, as the application of "principles" that have been taught—that is, explained by the teacher or presented in the textbook—has dominated the mathematics curriculum and many teachers' views of mathematics teaching and learning for at least 150 years.

As might be expected, conceptions of problem solving and the role it plays in the mathematics curriculum have undergone major changes since the time of Joseph Ray. In this chapter, I review some of these conceptions and argue that the position espoused in this volume—using problem solving as the backbone of mathematics instruction—emerged slowly and has recently begun to be reflected in some school mathematics textbooks.

Conceptions of Problem Solving from Ancient to Modern Times

In their seminal article tracing the history of problem solving in the mathematics curriculum, George Stanic and Jeremy Kilpatrick (1988) describe the role of mathematical problem solving from early civilization until the latter part of the twentieth century. They suggest that early Egyptian (e.g., the Ahmes Papyrus), Chinese, and Greek writings laid the foundation for the nineteenth- and early-twentieth-century views of problem solving reflected in mathematics textbooks of the times. Using examples taken from textbooks by Brooks (1871), Milne (1897), Wentworth (1899, 1900), Siefert (1902), and Upton (1939), Stanic and Kilpatrick illustrate the underlying belief of the authors of this period that "studying mathematics would improve one's ability to think, to reason, to solve problems that one will confront in the real world" (p. 9). This view was based on mental discipline theory, which, among other things, posited that learning mathematics was the primary vehicle for developing reasoning.

Late in the nineteenth century, new viewpoints on learning began to develop that ran counter to mental discipline theory. In particular, studies published by Edward L. Thorndike about the turn of the twentieth century discredited the concepts of mental discipline and transfer of training. As the results of Thorndike's studies became more widely accepted, mental discipline theory slowly fell out of favor and was replaced by Thorndike's "connectionism" (for further discussion see Thorndike [1922]). However, vestiges of mental discipline theory remain even today in the enduring belief that abstract subjects, such as mathematics, are valuable because they sharpen the mind.

Also at the turn of the twentieth century, mathematics education was coming to be considered a legitimate field of study at the college and university level throughout the United States, with such mathematics educators as David Eugene Smith and J. W. A. Young arguing that mathematics is an appropriate area of study for all students. They also argued that mathematics is an indispensable tool for developing students' power of reasoning. However, Stanic and Kilpatrick (1988) note, "It is ironic that as the number of professional mathematics educators at colleges and universities around the country began to grow, the place of mathematics in the school curriculum came under attack" (p. 12). The controversy revolved around the role of applications in the school mathematics curriculum. Interestingly, such mathematicians as Felix Klein in Germany, John Perry in England, and E. H. Moore in the United States argued in favor of a greater role for applications, but mathematics educators, led by Smith, insisted that to replace the study of pure mathematics with applied problems would be wrong minded. Obviously, the place of problems and problem solving in the school mathematics curriculum has been a controversial topic for quite a long time.

With this quick glimpse into the history of the role of problem solving in school mathematics as a backdrop, Stanic and Kilpatrick (1988, pp. 13–20) go on to discuss various themes that have characterized this role. Their discussion is included here, with permission, in its entirety because these themes can help to illuminate what is special and different about teaching mathematics through problem solving.

PROBLEM-SOLVING THEMES

Three general themes have characterized the role of problem solving in the school mathematics curriculum: problem solving as context, problem solving as skill, and problem solving as art.

Problem Solving as Context

The context theme has at least five subthemes, all of which are based on the idea that problems and the solving of problems are means to achieve other valuable ends.

Problem solving as justification. Historically, problem solving has been included in the mathematics curriculum in part because the problems provide justification for teaching mathematics at all. Presumably, at least some problems related in

(Continued on page 42)

some way to real-world experiences were included in the curriculum to convince students and teachers of the value of mathematics.

Problem solving as motivation. The subtheme of motivation is related to that of justification in that the problems justify the mathematics being taught. However, in the case of motivation, the connection is much more specific, and the aim of gaining student interest is sought. For example, a specific problem involving addition with regrouping might be used to introduce a series of lessons leading to learning the most efficient algorithm for adding the numbers.

Problem solving as recreation. The subtheme of recreation is related to that of motivation because student interest is involved, but in the case of recreation, problems are provided not so much to motivate students to learn as to allow them to have some fun with the mathematics they have already learned. Presumably, such problems fulfill a natural interest human beings have in exploring unusual situations. The problem shown earlier from the Ahmes papyrus is a good illustration. The recreation subtheme also differs from the first two in that puzzles, or problems without any necessary real-world connections, are perfectly appropriate.

Problem solving as vehicle. Problems are often provided not simply to motivate students to be interested in direct instruction on a topic but as a vehicle through which a new concept or skill might be learned. Discovery techniques in part reflect the idea that problem solving can be a vehicle for learning new concepts and skills. And when the mathematics curriculum consisted exclusively of problems, the problems obviously served as vehicles.

Problem solving as practice. Of the five subthemes, problem solving as practice has had the largest influence on the mathematics curriculum. In this subtheme, problems do not provide justification, motivation, recreation, or vehicles as much as necessary practice to reinforce skills and concepts taught directly. A page from an 1854 text by Nelson M. Holbrook entitled *The Child's First Book in Arithmetic* shows a good example of this subtheme. Notice that the "mental exercises" on division follow work on the division table (see Figure 13).

Problem Solving as Skill

Problem solving is often seen as one of a number of skills to be taught in the school curriculum. According to this view, problem solving is not necessarily a unitary skill, but there is a clear skill orientation.

Although problem solving as context remains a strong and persistent theme, the problem-solving-as-skill theme has become dominant for those who see problem solving as a valuable curriculum end deserving special attention, rather than as simply a means to achieve other ends or an inevitable outcome of the study of mathematics.

The skill theme is clearly related to the changes that took place near the turn of the century, although not all advocates of this point of view would claim an association with, for example, the work of Thorndike. Nonetheless,

Figure 13. Pages from Nelson M. Holbrooks' *The Child's First Book in Arithmetic* (Holbrook, 1854)

(Continued)

(Stanic and Kilpatrick excerpt continued)

largely because of Thorndike's influence (as well as the other changes discussed earlier), most educators no longer assumed that the study of mathematics improved one's thinking and made one a better solver of real-world problems. Especially because many of our professional forebears were reluctant to give up their claims about mathematics and to include more applied problems in the curriculum, they essentially allowed educational psychologists like Thorndike to define the new view of problem solving.

Putting problem solving in a hierarchy of skills to be acquired by students leads to certain consequences for the role of problem solving in the curriculum. One consequence is that within the general skill of problem solving, hierarchical distinctions are made between solving routine and nonroutine problems. That is, nonroutine problem solving is characterized as a higher level skill to be acquired after skill at solving routine problems (which, in turn, is to be acquired after students learn basic mathematical concepts and skills). This view postpones attention to nonroutine problem solving, and, as a result, only certain students, because they have accomplished the prerequisites, are ever exposed to such problems. Nonroutine problem solving becomes, then, an activity for the especially capable students rather than for all students.

Problem Solving as Art

A deeper, more comprehensive view of problem solving in the school mathematics curriculum—a view of problem solving as *art*—emerged from the work of George Polya, who revived in our time the idea of heuristic (the art of discovery). Mathematicians as far back as Euclid and Pappus, and including Descartes, Leibnitz, and Bolzano, had discussed methods and rules for discovery and invention in mathematics, but their ideas never made their way into the school curriculum. It remained for Polya to reformulate, extend, and illustrate various ideas about mathematical discovery in a way that teachers could understand and use.

Polya's experience in learning and teaching mathematics led him to ask how mathematics came to be—how did people make mathematical discoveries? Won't students understand mathematics better if they see how it was created in the first place and if they can get some taste of mathematical discovery themselves? Polya's experience as a mathematician led him to conclude that the finished face of mathematics presented deductively in mathematical journals and in textbooks does not do justice to the subject. Finished mathematics requires demonstrative reasoning, whereas mathematics in the making requires plausible reasoning. If students are to use plausible reasoning, they need to be taught how.

Like our professional forebears Smith and Young, Polya argued that a major aim of education is the development of intelligence—to teach young people to think. In the primary school, children should be taught to do their arithmetic insightfully rather than mechanically because although insightful performance is a more ambitious aim, it actually has a better chance of success. It yields faster, more permanent results. In the secondary school, mathematics should offer something to those who will, and those who will not, use mathematics in their later studies or careers. The same mathematics should be taught to all students because no one can know in advance which students will eventually use mathematics professionally.

> If the teaching of mathematics gives only a one-sided, stunted
> idea of the mathematician's thinking, if it totally suppresses

(Continued on page 44)

those "informal" activities of guessing and extracting mathematical concepts from the visible world around us, it neglects what may be the most interesting part for the general student, the most instructive for the future user of mathematics, and the most inspiring for the future mathematician. (Polya, 1966, pp. 124–125)

In Polya's view, mathematics consists of information and know-how. Regardless of how well schools impart mathematical information, if they do not teach students how to use that information, it will be forgotten. "To know mathematics is to be able to do mathematics" (Polya, 1969/1984, p. 574). "What is know-how in mathematics? The ability to solve problems" (Polya, 1981, p. xi).

To Polya, problem solving was a practical art, "like swimming, or skiing, or playing the piano" (1981, p. ix). One learns such arts by imitation and practice. Polya assumed neither that simply solving problems by itself with no guidance leads to improved performance nor that the study of mathematics by its very nature raises one's general level of intelligence. Instead, he recognized that techniques of problem solving need to be illustrated by the teacher, discussed with the students, and practiced in an insightful, nonmechanical way. Further, he observed that although routine problems can be used to fulfill certain pedagogical functions of teaching students to follow a specific procedure or use a definition correctly, only through the judicious use of nonroutine problems can students develop their problem-solving ability.

In Polya's formulation, the teacher is the key. Only a sensitive teacher can set the right kind of problems for a given class and provide the appropriate amount of guidance. Because teaching, too, is an art, no one can program or otherwise mechanize the teaching of problem solving; it remains a human activity that requires experience, taste, and judgment.

There are those today who on the surface affiliate themselves with the work of Polya, but who reduce the rule-of-thumb heuristics to procedural skills, almost taking an algorithmic view of heuristics (i.e., specific heuristics fit in specific situations). A heuristic becomes a skill, a technique, even, paradoxically, an algorithm. In a sense, problem solving as art gets reduced to problem solving as skill when attempts are made to implement Polya's ideas by focusing on his steps and putting them into textbooks. Although distortion may not be inevitable when educators try to capture within textbooks and teachers' guides what is essentially an artistic endeavor, the task is clearly a difficult one.

Of the three themes, we see problem solving as art as the most defensible, the most fair, and the most promising. But at the same time it is the most problematic theme because it is the most difficult to operationalize in textbooks and classrooms. The problem for mathematics educators who believe that problem solving is an art form is how to develop this artistic ability in students.

Because of the caricature most people hold of John Dewey, we are reluctant to bring his work into the discussion. But we believe that Dewey's ideas about problem solving complement those of Polya. Dewey does not provide all the answers; in fact, he demonstrates that the situation is even more complex than one might think. But he does give valuable direction and another way to think about problem solving.

(Continued)

(Stanic and Kilpatrick excerpt continued)

Although Dewey is clearly the major 20th century American philosopher of education and although he is blamed often and by various people for all that is wrong with American education, his influence on the school curriculum in general, and the mathematics curriculum in particular, has been minimal. A host of educators and psychologists ranging from Moore to Thorndike have praised Dewey's ideas; however, except for the lab school at the University of Chicago at the turn of the century, there is no example of his ideas being implemented as they were intended. What has been called progressive education did have an influence on the school mathematics curriculum, but the critique of progressive education Dewey (1938/1963) provided in *Experience and Education* shows how far from his basic ideas most other reformers were. Nonetheless, Dewey remains a major figure in American education because so many people have claimed a link with his work, including a few people who have actually taken the time to read Dewey's own writing rather than second-hand distortions.

Dewey did not often use the term *problem solving,* but it is clear that problems and problem solving were crucial in Dewey's view of education and schooling. What we refer to as problem solving Dewey usually called *reflective thinking.* Rather than being one way in which human beings deal with the world, problem solving was for Dewey the essence of human thought: Being able to think reflectively makes us human. Dewey distinguished among several types of thinking, but when he wrote *How We Think* in 1910 and revised it in 1933, to think meant to think reflectively.

Better than anyone else, Dewey combined the ideas of problem solving as means and problem solving as an end worthy of special attention. Dewey used much of *How We Think* to discuss how thought can be trained, so developing people's problem-solving ability was an important end for Dewey. But it was not an end separate from the progressive organization of subject matter that is a direct result of reflective thinking. That is, the same experiences that lead to the development of reflective thinking also lead to learning important subject matter. As simple and obvious as this may sound, our history of failures to accomplish the twin goals of helping students to develop problem-solving ability and organize the subject matter of mathematics is convincing evidence of how complex the task is.

Perhaps the greatest single misconception about John Dewey is that he was concerned with the child and not with subject matter. The problem, said Dewey (1902/1964), "is just to get rid of the prejudicial notion that there is some gap in kind (as distinct from degree) between the child's experience and the various forms of subject-matter that make up the course of study" (p. 344). Dewey argued that the child's experience "contains within itself elements—facts and truths—of just the same sort as those entering into the formulated study . . . and [even more important] the attitudes, the motives, and the interests which have operated in developing and organizing the subject matter to the place which it now occupies" (p. 344).

For Dewey, experience was central, problems arise naturally within experience, teaching and learning consist of the reconstruction of experience which leads to the progressive organization of subject matter, and the reconstruction of experience requires reflective thinking (or problem solving).

Like Polya, Dewey placed a great deal of emphasis on the teacher. Dewey did not reject the idea of teachers transmitting information to students. In fact, he said

(Continued on page 46)

that "no educational question is of greater importance than how to get the most logical good out of learning through transmission from others" (Dewey, 1910, p. 197). Dewey said that the problem was how to convert such information into an intellectual asset. "How shall we treat the subject-matter supplied by textbook and teacher so that it shall rank as material for reflective inquiry, not as ready-made intellectual pabulum to be accepted and swallowed just as supplied by the store?" (pp. 197–198). Dewey answered his own question by saying that the transmitted information should not be something student could easily discover through direct inquiry; that the information "should be supplied by way of stimulus, not with dogmatic finality and rigidity"; and that the information "should be relevant to a question that is vital in the student's own experience" (pp. 198–199). According to Dewey,

> Instruction in subject-matter that does not fit into any problem already stirring in the student's own experience, or that is not presented in such a way as to arouse a problem, is worse than useless for intellectual purposes. In that it fails to enter into any process of reflection, it is useless; in that it remains in the mind as so much lumber and debris, it is a barrier, an obstruction in the way of effective thinking when a problem arises. (p. 199).

Teachers, then, can justifiably transmit information, according to Dewey, but only if the information is linked to the child's experience and problems that arise within experience. In a sense, subject matter is even more important for the teacher than for the student. The teacher needs to use her or his knowledge of subject matter in order to help the child reconstruct experience so that subject matter becomes progressively more organized for the child.

In "The Child and the Curriculum," Dewey (1902/1964) compared logically-organized subject matter to a map. The map, said Dewey, is a "formulated statement of experience" (p. 350). As students reconstruct their experience, they make a map of subject matter. They can also use maps constructed by others as guides to future journeys, but no map can "substitute for a personal experience" (p. 350). A map "does not take the place of an actual journey" (p. 350). Like Polya, Dewey was concerned with transforming logically organized subject matter into psychologically meaningful experience for students.

The process of thinking reflectively, of solving problems that arise within experience, was for Dewey, an art form. Dewey (1910) said that "no cast iron rules [for reflective thinking] can be laid down" (p. 78). He believed students should be "skilled in methods of attack and solution" (p. 78), but he expressed concern about an "overconscious formulation of methods of procedure" (p. 112). So, according to Dewey, skill is involved in reflective thinking, or problem solving, but reflective thinking itself is not a skill. In fact, Dewey expressed concern about too great an emphasis on skill acquisition. "Practical skill, modes of effective technique, can be intelligently, nonmechanically *used*," he said, "only when intelligence has played a part in their *acquisition*" (p. 52).

Furthermore, Dewey (1910) believed not only that students should be "skilled in methods of attack and solution" but also that they should be "sensitive to problems" (p. 78). That is, proper *attitudes* were very important to Dewey:

> Because of the importance of attitudes, ability to train thought is not achieved merely by knowledge of the best forms of thought.

(Continued)

(Stanic and Kilpatrick excerpt continued)

> Possession of this information is no guarantee for ability to think well. Moreover, there are no set exercises in correct thinking whose repeated performance will cause one to be a good thinker. The information and the exercises are both of value. But no individual realizes their value except as he is personally animated by certain dominant attitudes in his own character. (Dewey, 1933, p. 29)

What is necessary, said Dewey (1933), is the union of attitude and skilled method. Dewey believed that the three most important attitudes to be cultivated are open-mindedness, whole-heartedness, and responsibility. Developing such attitudes was so important to Dewey that he said if he were forced to make a choice between students having these attitudes and students having knowledge about principles of reasoning and some degree of technical skill in reasoning, he would choose the attitudes. "Fortunately," he said, "no such choice has to be made, because there is no opposition between personal attitudes and logical processes....What is needed is to weave them into unity" (p. 34).

Dewey's connection to Polya seems clear. Polya (1981) suggested that "instead of hurrying through all the details of a much too extended program, the teacher should concentrate on a few really significant problems and treat them leisurely and thoroughly" (Vol 2, p. 123). Dewey (1933) said that "fewer subjects and fewer facts and more responsibility for thinking the material of those subjects and facts through to realize what they involve would give better results" (p. 33)

Polya's and Dewey's belief that mathematics and problem solving are for everyone ties them to our professional forebears in mathematics education and the basic faith they had in human intelligence. Smith and Young could not or would not see in Dewey the opportunity to recast their view of the benefits of the liberal arts in light of a changing society. In a sense, we need to use the work of Dewey and Polya to recapture and revise the tradition embodied in the work of Smith and Young.

CONCLUSION

One consequence of recapturing this tradition is to take seriously the notion that problem solving really is for everyone. We need to look more at what children can actually do and to insist on broad evidence of what counts as ability to solve problems. In other words, we must study more carefully the role of context in problem solving. Some recent research shows that children who have trouble solving mathematical problems in school can solve comparable problems in out-of-school situations that are more meaningful to them. Taking seriously the notion that problem solving is for everyone means studying children in a variety of situations and providing examples to teachers of what children can do when an attempt is made to link subject matter to experience.

Again, neither Dewey nor Polya has all the answers, but they do help us with the basic issues of what problem solving is, why we should teach it, and how it is related to the progressive organization of subject matter. And their work provides for us a vehicle through which we might "critically examine our heritage as a field of study" by carrying on "a dialogue ... with our professional forebears" (Kliebard, 1968, p. 83).

An Emerging Theme: Teaching Mathematics through Problem Solving

Today, as we enter the twenty-first century, we are confronted with yet another shift in focus in the use of problem solving in the curriculum: *teaching mathematics through problem solving,* the theme of this volume. In a chapter appearing in the 1989 Yearbook of the National Council of Teachers of Mathematics, Tom Schroeder and Frank Lester (1989) insisted that, since the role of problem solving is to develop students' understanding of mathematics, teaching via problem solving is the most appropriate approach. They argued that proponents of this approach consider problem solving not as a topic, a standard, or a content strand but rather as a pedagogical stance. This approach has come to be referred to today as *teaching through problem solving.* The influence of Pólya's (1981) and Dewey's (1933) views on problem solving as an art are evident in this view of the role of problem solving in the curriculum.

This new view also closely parallels Stanic and Kilpatrick's theme of problem solving as a vehicle. In fact, problems that serve as vehicles for introducing or developing mathematical concepts began to appear in mathematics curriculum materials in the 1990s. Proponents of teaching mathematics through problem solving base their pedagogy on the notion that students who confront problematic situations use their existing knowledge to solve those problems, and in the process of solving the problems, they construct new knowledge and new understanding. Recent research in psychology and cognitive science has described learning as the individual's process of making sense of ideas on the basis of the individual's existing understandings (Greeno 2003; Sfard 2003). Theories describing how people learn, or construct knowledge, serve as the foundation for teaching mathematics through problem solving. To illustrate how teaching mathematics through problem solving has been put into practice, three examples, one each from the elementary, middle, and secondary school levels are discussed in the following sections.

An Elementary School Example

One elementary school textbook series first published in the late 1990s presents the following situation. A second-grade class has read and discussed the Chinese folktale *Two of Everything* by Lily Toy Hong (1993), in which a poor old farmer finds a magic pot that doubles anything that is put into it. This context is then used to pose the following problem:

Our Class and the Magic Pot

What do you think would happen if our entire class fell into the magic pot? First write about how you would solve the problem. Then write about what would be one good thing and one hard thing about having a double class. (Economopoulos and Russell 1998, p. 46)

Although this problem may not seem very interesting or difficult at first glance, its placement in the curriculum provides an opportunity for children to explore a new mathematical idea before they have received any formal instruction in how to double numbers, especially numbers greater than 10—such as the number of students in the class. The children likely have never seen a teacher solve this problem or any problem like it before. In teaching through problem solving, the teacher trusts that the children will draw on their existing knowledge in a creative way and fosters their thinking about the problem she posed. After the children spend some time, often in small groups, exploring the problem situation, the teacher asks various children to share their solutions and their thinking about the problem. In addition to giving the children practice in problem solving, this activity helps them build their ability to use mathematical language. In this scenario, the entire classroom community holds a mathematical conversation about the solution to the problem.

Children use the mathematics they already know to solve the problem, and from their solutions, a new mathematical concept—the concept of doubling—emerges and may even be formalized. In particular, this problem brings to the children's attention the important mathematical notions of number patterns and relationships, and the teacher may introduce notation that shows the doubling relationship. In this way, the problem-solving experience creates the backdrop against which new ideas begin to take shape in the community of the classroom and in the minds of the children.

A Middle School Example

A middle school textbook contains problems that generate opportunities for students to engage in activities to enhance their emerging mathematical thinking processes, in this example, algebraic thinking (see fig. 4.1). Although this problem might be solved in a straightforward way in a traditional algebra class, it lends itself to investigation at the middle school level before students have had formal instruction in solving systems of equations.

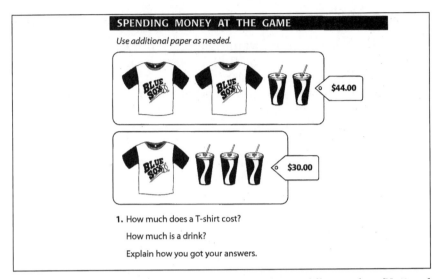

Fig. 4.1. Developing algebraic thinking in the middle grades (National Center for Research in Mathematical Sciences Education and Freudenthal Institute 1998, p.98)

Again, the placement of this problem in the curriculum affords students the opportunity to explore, in this example, the comparison of quantities. Several students' solutions to this problem incorporate the algebraic procedures they will learn more formally in their later study of algebra. For example, as student 1 describes his solution strategy, we can map the solution into formal algebra, identifying each of the student's steps as a formal algebraic manipulation. (The students' discussions of their solution efforts shown below are taken from a research study conducted by the author in collaboration with Jennifer Strabala.)

Student 1:

What I did to figure it out is I took the top picture, and I took 1 t-shirt and 1 drink away. It was $22. So the bottom t-shirt and 1 drink cost $22, but you still had two drinks left that cost $8 total so 1 drink cost $4 and 1 t-shirt cost $18.

Formalized algebraic steps:
$2S + 2D = 44$; so $S + D = 22$.
$S + 3D = 30$, which can be written as $(S + D) + 2D = 30$.
Through substitution, $22 + 2D = 30$.
By solving for D, $2D = 8$; so $D = 4$.
By solving for S, $S + 4 = 22$; so $S = 18$.

Yet another student approached the problem with a very different intuitive sense of what substitutions may be used.

> *Student 2:*
>
> To do this problem, I first crossed out the items common to both pictures. All that was left was a shirt in the $44.00 box and a drink in the $30.00 box. This told me that the shirt cost $14.00 more than the drink (y). I used this info and the original $30 box to make this problem:
>
> $$3y + (y + 14) = 30$$
>
> I modeled the problem like this:
>
> $$yyy \ y \ 14 \wedge 14 \ 16$$
>
> I crossed out the 14 from both sides and got this:
>
> $$yyyy \wedge 16.$$
>
> If $4y = 16$, then $y = 4$. [And] $4 + 14 = 18$. Therefore, a drink costs $4 and a shirt costs $18.

Student 2's use of the fulcrum to represent the equality in the situation is of interest to the teacher, who is using this problem both to draw out what the student knows and to build a more conventional notation to represent the relationship among drinks and shirts and total cost.

A High School Example

The use of problems to introduce new mathematics topics can be found in secondary school mathematics materials as well. For example, in the problem shown in figure 4.2, the students' use of their existing knowledge to approach new problems provides the backdrop for potentially rich mathematical explorations.

Borasi and Fonzi (in press) suggest the following problem as a means of engaging students in exploring concepts related to the area of certain geometric figures. The picture shown in figure 4.2 is given to the class, and the students are asked to propose a formula for the area of all such shapes. The students begin to explore the area of these shapes and draw on their existing knowledge of area. Their solutions reveal their depth of understanding of the area of familiar shapes as well as of the process of finding patterns and drawing generalizations. The problem also requires that students spend a significant amount of time developing and refining the definition for this class of shapes, referred to as "diamonds."

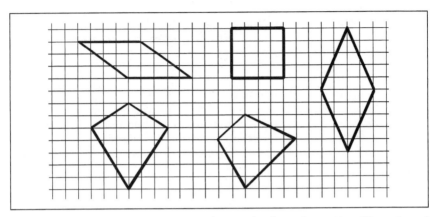

Fig. 4.2. Exploring area in secondary school mathematics (Borasi and Fonzi, in press)

This activity can generate for students several important experiences that simulate the work of mathematicians. First, the classroom community builds definitions and negotiates the limitations of different ways of defining a class of shapes. Second, the community finds the area of the shapes, looking for patterns and generalizing the process of determining area in an attempt to come up with a formula. Third, students propose a formula for the area of the shapes, justifying their thinking and reasoning to defend their proposal. Finally, students evaluate others' proposals, seeking to understand different explanations and challenging ideas that do not make sense to them. This process affords the teacher and students the opportunity to discuss various processes involved in doing mathematics, namely, developing definitions and formulas.

Conclusion

This chapter illustrates that problem solving has been an important component of the school mathematics curriculum for quite a long time—150 years or more—but that its role has changed over time. In some school mathematics textbooks today, problem solving now serves, to borrow from Stanic and Kilpatrick (1988), as a *vehicle* for developing deep understanding of mathematical ideas and processes. Proponents of this approach believe that engaging in productive problem solving leads to increased understanding. This approach, which involves confronting students with truly problematic situations to grapple with, is dramatically different from the approach promoted more than 150 years ago by Joseph Ray (1848) —an approach involving "gradual and easy steps." Whether the future will bring still other ways of thinking about the role of problem solving in mathematics instruction will be interesting to see!

Section 2

Tasks and Tools for Teaching and Learning

CHAPTER 5

Selecting Quality Tasks for Problem-Based Teaching

Robin Marcus

James T. Fey

THE PROPOSITION that important mathematical ideas and methods can be taught most effectively by engaging students in work on interesting problems is one of the most attractive recommendations of recent NCTM *Standards* documents. But it is one thing to set that goal and quite another to select and implement instructional tasks that realize the objective. Designing activities that keep students busy throughout standard class periods is relatively easy, but making sure that such activity leads to learning important mathematics is much more difficult. Finding and adapting problem tasks that engage students and lead them to understanding fundamental mathematical concepts and principles and to acquiring skill in the use of basic mathematical techniques is itself a challenging task for teachers.

Effective use of problem-based materials requires thoughtful selection and use of the available problem tasks. Planning of individual lessons, units, or whole courses requires answers to at least four basic questions:

- Will working on the tasks foster students' understanding of important mathematical ideas and techniques?

- Will the selected tasks be engaging and problematic, yet accessible, for many students in the target classes?

- Will work on the tasks help students develop their mathematical thinking—their ability and disposition to explore, to conjecture, to prove, to represent, and to communicate their understanding?

- Will the collection of tasks in a curriculum build coherent understanding and connections among important mathematical topics?

The importance of these issues is illustrated by analyzing the following tasks.

Roller Derby and Beyond

One of the most important basic ideas of elementary probability is randomness. Most middle-grades students, and many adults, have a naive conception of randomness as something that is totally unpredictable. A more useful understanding is that "phenomena having uncertain individual outcomes but a regular pattern of outcomes in many repetitions are called random" (Moore 1990, p. 98). A teacher can easily design a classroom activity in which students collect results of many tosses of a coin or a die, in some sense revealing the essence of randomness. A more difficult task is to make that activity engaging for students and to connect the empirical notion of probability with useful theoretical methods. A game called Roller Derby (Lappan et al. 2002a, pp. 42–43) shows how clever tasks can lead to significant instructional payoff.

Roller Derby is a game between two teams that is played with a board like that pictured, two six-sided dice, and a set of 12 coins or other markers for each team. To begin play, each team distributes its markers in the boxes of its side on the game board. Then the dice are rolled and the sum of dots on the two top faces is calculated. Each team that has markers in the row corresponding to that sum may remove one of those markers. The dice are rolled again and play continues in this pattern until one team removes its last marker and wins.

Team A		Team B
	1	
	2	
	3	
	4	
	5	
	6	
	7	
	8	
	9	
	10	
	11	
	12	

Once the students have read and understand the rules of the game, the accompanying teacher materials recommend having students play a number of games, perhaps even a class tournament. Then they are asked to think about some follow-up questions, such as those that follow, and to share their ideas in a whole-class summarizing discussion.

1. What strategies in placement of the markers will help your team win?

2. Does a guaranteed-win strategy exist?

3. How could you convince someone else of your ideas for a winning strategy in each version of the Roller Derby game?

4. How would the game board and the winning strategy change if the rules were changed to use the product of the two die results, not the sum?

5. How would the game board and the winning strategy change if the rules were changed to use the difference of the two die results, not the sum?

Questions about the results of rolling two fair dice are a common introduction to basic ideas of probability. The particular attraction is that naive conceptions of probability lead students to mistaken first reactions. For instance, those unfamiliar with dice games often guess that all possible outcomes, 2 through 12, are equally likely. The contrast between naive conceptions and common empirical results makes understanding the game problematic and something to be sorted out by analysis. The adaptation of this activity to the Roller Derby game enhances the problematic nature and the payoff in several important ways.

First, by presenting the mathematics in the context of a contest in which thinking and planning pay off, the activity is immediately engaging to typical middle-grades students. Second, even if some students are savvy about the distribution of probabilities in rolling two dice, they are not guaranteed winners in Roller Derby; this realization is a valuable insight into the empirical meaning of probability. Third, some team will almost certainly place a marker on 1 in the first play of the game, leading in a very powerful way to a revelation of the meaning of impossible outcomes and their probabilities. Fourth, as students are challenged to articulate arguments for winning or at least effective playing strategies, they are led naturally to the basic ideas behind finite sample spaces and theoretical probabilities. Convincing others of their proposed optimal strategies will engage them in communicating and reasoning about mathematics. Finally, the game has some natural extensions that will expand students' conceptions of sample space and make connections with arithmetic skills and elementary number theory ideas.

Problem-based investigations like that developed around the Roller Derby game for introducing randomness are especially attractive and plausible for introducing basic ideas in various mathematical topics. More complex, advanced ideas can also be developed through the same sort of problem-based teaching. For example, fundamental properties of the geometric probability distribution are revealed by work on questions like the following (Coxford et al. 1999a, p. 486):

> To control population growth, China strongly encourages families to have only one child. Many families prefer to have male children. If a family has children until the first male is born, what is the probability of 1, 2, 3, . . . , n child families?

The binomial probability distribution can be developed through student-centered investigation beginning with such questions as the one that follows (Coxford et al. 1999a, p. 490):

> In a supposedly random search of student lockers, administrators at Woodland Hills High School chose ten lockers to be checked for drugs or weapons. It turned out that all ten lockers belonged to male students. The boys complained that they were victims of gender discrimination. *Do you agree?*

Both of these problems are particularly engaging for high school students, and progress toward solving them leads to important mathematics. Starting work on an important mathematical idea by considering a game or rich contextual problem also allows students with a wide range of interests, aptitudes, and knowledge to participate in meaningful ways. The launching scenarios are, however, only the starting points for successful problem-based teaching. Most students will need the assistance of appropriate scaffolding questions and hints and thoughtful classroom summaries that articulate big ideas encountered in work on the problems. Finding the right combination of challenge and support is crucial when using problem-based curriculum materials. When done well, students develop deep personal understanding of mathematical concepts and procedures and important habits of mind for mathematical work. They also learn that persistence pays dividends in problem solving.

A collection of engaging problems that lead to important mathematical ideas is also only the starting point for a full and coherent mathematics curriculum. The three probability problems described previously become most effective when they are used to develop aspects of a probability curriculum that has mathematical coherence and completeness and when they are also tied to topics in other strands of the curriculum. Thus the problems themselves and the classroom discourse surrounding their use should include frequent questions that ask students to identify similarities and differences among the problem structures encountered. The population problem has obvious connections with such algebraic topics as geometric sequences and exponential functions. The locker-search problem has important connections with the binomial theorem in algebra and Pascal's triangle.

Breaking Bridges

Much of secondary school mathematics focuses on fostering students' understanding of, and skill in using, symbolic notation to describe and reason about variables, expressions, equations, inequalities, and functions. For too many students, the experience with algebra is a largely meaningless regimen of arbitrary rules for operations with symbols that do not represent anything real or useful. Problem-based investigations offer attractive alternatives to such experiences.

Consider the mathematical concepts of direct and inverse variation—fundamental tools in the fields of science, engineering, and business. The basic mathematical expressions for these relations are relatively simple: $y = kx$ or $y = kx^n$ for direct variation and $y = \frac{k}{x}$ or $y = \frac{k}{x^n}$ for inverse variation. But most students do not develop good intuition about the relations expressed in these forms, so they do not use the ideas as tools for reasoning about change. Problem-based investigations offer effective preparation for more formal teaching approaches.

For example, an investigation of variation can be launched with such questions as these (Lappan et al. 2000b, p. 5; Coxford et al. 1999b, p. 3):

> Which of the "bridges" pictured is likely to support the greatest weight, and which will support the least?

1. Experiment with bridges made from paper or pasta strips of different length and thickness and pennies for weights to test bridge strength. Organize your data in tables and graphs that display the relationships of interest.

2. If W represents the safe carrying weight; L, the length; and T, the thickness, what sort of equation would best express the relationship between—

   a) carrying weight and length?

   b) carrying weight and thickness?

3. How would each relationship in question 2 appear in tables and graphs of data from your experiment?

4. Which of the following equations would best represent the type of relationship among all three variables, and why?

   (a) $W = L + T$ (b) $W = T \div L$ (c) $W = T \times L$ (d) $W = L - T$

The aim of this sort of exploratory investigation is to develop students' sense about the relationships between symbolic expressions and the types of variation that they represent. The introductory question focuses students' attention on the fundamental issues, and their responses give the teacher information about the understandings that students have at the start of instruction. The bridge setting for thinking about variation provides a tangible metaphor for thinking about other situations with similar mathematical structure. The questions about numeric, graphic, and symbolic patterns in the data help students develop a variety of meaningful images of underlying abstract patterns.

To be sure that students abstract the important mathematical ideas about variation from their experiences with specific problem contexts, the teacher can present other similar contexts for students to examine. For example, the bridge investigation could be followed by several problems similar to this one (Coxford et al. 1999b, p. 5):

The likelihood of a fatal accident in a car, van, or small truck depends on many conditions. Two key variables are speed and mass of the vehicle.

1. What general relationship would you expect among the rate of fatalities in accidents F, the speed of the vehicle S, and the mass of the vehicle M?

2. What sort of equation would model that relation among F, S, and M?

3. If you graphed the relations between *F* and *S* and between *F* and *M* separately, what patterns would you expect in those graphs?

Then to help students articulate their intuitive understanding in notation and ideas that are not limited to specific contexts, the teacher can engage the class in a summarizing discussion around such questions as the following (Coxford et al. 1999b, p. 9):

In relations among variables *x*, *y*, and *z* that can be expressed by equations in the form

$$z = k\frac{x}{y},$$

where *k* is constant:

1. How will *z* change as values of *x* increase or decrease while the value of *y* remains constant?

2. How will *z* change as values of *y* increase or decrease while the value of *x* remains constant?

3. How can the relationship be expressed symbolically in a form that shows how—

   a) *y* is a function of *x* and *z*?

   b) *x* is a function of *y* and *z*?

Be prepared to explain the reasoning that leads you to each answer.

To teachers who have polished explanations of direct and inverse variation that seem to work with many students, a development through student-centered problem-based investigations might seem inefficient and likely to permit formation of incomplete or errant ideas among students. After all, most of us believe that we can give clear explanations of mathematical ideas that students will generally understand and absorb. Unfortunately, a great deal of evidence (see, e.g., Blume and Heckman [1997]; Sfard and Linchesvski [1994]; Clement [2001]; and Stein, Boaler, and Silver [this volume]) suggests that even the clearest teacher explanations leave many students with incomplete understanding and shaky confidence. Ideas that are forged by hard thought and tested in discourse with other students and teachers are much more likely to last and be useful because they have been assimilated into each student's web of understanding.

In addition to helping students learn how to reason and talk about the structure of direct and inverse variation, the problem sequence outlined in the foregoing is part of an extended development of algebra that focuses on the central concept of *change*. Teaching algebraic ideas having connections with real-life contexts is especially helpful in developing that essential understanding, because the variables of science, engineering, computing, and business are most often quantities that change. Important problem-solving tasks often involve describing and predicting the way that change in some variable(s) leads to related changes in some other variable(s). Thus, using problems in context for teaching important mathematical ideas helps the curriculum highlight ideas that integrate specific topics into a coherent development. In fact, classroom investigation through problem solving becomes a unifying curricular theme itself. Students come to see mathematics as a subject that consistently asks them to look for patterns, to solve problems, and to figure out why things work as they do—habits of mind with value that will pay dividends in further study of mathematics and its applications (see Levasseur and Cuoco [this volume]).

Bouncing Balls

To fully understand and be skilled in algebra, students need a variety of experiences in looking for patterns, using various representations to model relations between variables, and analyzing change in various contexts. In the middle grades, students should develop a strong understanding of linear relationships and then expand on this understanding to include families of nonlinear relationships throughout high school. Problem-based investigations can give students algebraic experiences that help them discover the characteristics of function families and the distinctions among them.

In many instances, engaging and mathematically rich investigations can emerge from experiments that involve data collection and analysis. For example, a proven launching point for studying linear and exponential change asks students to investigate the relationship between the height from which a bouncing ball is dropped and the height to which it rebounds. Students measure the height of the first bounce of a ball dropped from varying drop heights and then record their data in a table and a graph. The following questions can guide students in fruitful analysis of the data:

- What variables did you investigate in this experiment? Describe the relationship between the variables.

- Predict the bounce height for a drop height of 2 meters. Explain how you made your prediction. Did you use the table, the graph, or some other method? What clues in the data helped you?

- Predict the drop height needed for a bounce height of 2 meters. Explain how you made your prediction. Did you use the table, the graph, or some other method? What clues in the data helped you?

- What bounce height would you expect for a drop height of 0 meters? Where would this point be on the graph?

- Besides the drop height, what other variables affect the bounce height of the ball?

In almost any reasonably careful experiment, the data plot will reveal a linear pattern. As students describe the relationship between drop and rebound heights and their methods for predicting values based on this relationship, they will develop an informal understanding of the algebraic characteristics of linearity. This investigation can then be followed by activities in which students create and analyze tables and graphs of other linear relations, such as the distance traveled over time at a constant speed or the amount of money earned over time at a constant rate of pay.

Once again, such questions as the following (Lappan et al. 2002c, pp. 7–8) encourage students to summarize what they have learned:

- Look at the table you made for your experiment and the tables you have made for other straight-line relationships. What do you think characterizes the table of a linear relationship?

- What other relationships that you have investigated, in this class or somewhere else, do you now suspect to be linear?

The first question requires students to articulate how a constant rate of change is shown in a table, whereas the second question encourages students to make connections between their new understanding of linearity and previous experiences. Subsequent investigations should connect symbolic representations of linear relationships, both recursive and explicit, with their tables and graphs, guiding students to observe and describe the effect that altering the rate of change or the initial value in various contexts has on the table, graph, and equations. They might later return to the bouncing-ball experiment to write equations for the bounce height of various balls in terms of drop height and to interpret the meaning of the slope in this situation.

The question posed to students about the variables involved in the bouncing-ball experiment is significant. By changing the variables under investigation, new relationships emerge for students to analyze. For example, you can use bouncing-ball experiments to give students experience with situations involving exponential decay. If students measure the height of successive rebounds of a golf ball dropped from a height of at least 8 feet, they will discover exponential decay in the rebound height, with the decay constant equal to the coefficient of x in the linear relationship between drop height and rebound height. An analysis of the variables and relationships involved in the situation will lead to recursive (*NOW-NEXT* notation is helpful at the introductory level) and explicit ($y = \ldots$) formulas for the rebound height as a function of initial drop height and number of bounces.

Students can repeat the experiment and analysis with another ball that will bounce differently. Different groups will collect different data and produce different equations, depending on the types of balls used and the initial height from which the balls were dropped. Sharing results will go a long way toward helping all students in the class develop a deep understanding of both linear and exponential families of functions from numeric, graphic, and symbolic perspectives.

The following questions (Coxford et al. 1999a, p. 442) help students look across the data and equations of the different groups to abstract common features:

- Look back at the data from your two experiments: How do the rebound heights change from one bounce to the next in each case?

- How is the pattern of change in rebound height shown by the shape of the data plots in each case?

- List the equations relating *NOW* and *NEXT* and the rules ($y = \ldots$) you found for predicting the rebound heights of each ball on successive bounces.

- What do the equations relating *NOW* and *NEXT* bounce heights have in common in each case? How, if at all, are those equations different, and what might be causing the differences?

- What do the rules beginning "$y = \ldots$" have in common in each case? How, if at all, are those equations different, and what might be causing the differences?

- What do the tables, graphs, and equations in these examples have in common with those of the exponential growth examples in the beginning of this unit? How, if at all, are they different?

The bouncing-ball experiments and the follow-up questions facilitate strong connections between situations involving constant additive and multiplicative patterns of change and the various representations of such situations—table, graph, *NOW-NEXT* equations, and "$y = ...$" rules. Comparing these representations of the bouncing-ball experiments with those of other situations involving exponential growth allows students to draw out the common characteristic of a constant ratio while articulating the effect of whether that ratio is less than or greater than 1.

Students might then explore other contexts for exponential growth and decay through problem-based investigations, such as pollution cleanup, compounding interest, medicine breakdown, or population change. With sufficient experience in representing and analyzing these kinds of situations, students will be prepared to answer such questions as these (Coxford et al. 1999a, p. 481):

- In deciding whether an exponential model will be useful, what hints do you get from the patterns in data tables? From the patterns in graphs or scatterplots? From the nature of the situation and the variables involved?

- Exponential models, like linear models, can be expressed by an equation relating *x* and *y* values and by an equation relating *NOW* and *NEXT* values.

- Write a general rule for an exponential model, $y = ...$

- Write a general equation relating *NOW* and *NEXT* for an exponential model.

- What do the parts of the equations tell you about the situation being modeled?

- How can the rule for an exponential model be used to predict the pattern in a table or graph of that model?

- How are exponential models different from linear models?

Such situations as the bouncing-ball experiment provide an interesting context for discussing the differences between linear and exponential models. The rebound factor of a ball, for example, 2/3 for a golf ball, provides information about both the relationship between rebound height and drop height and the relationship between rebound height and the number of the bounce. The first relationship is linear, and from this perspective the rebound factor tells us that for every 1-meter increase in drop height, the rebound height will increase 2/3 of a meter. Overall, the values are increasing at a constant rate. The second relationship is exponential, and from this perspective the rebound factor tells us that with each additional bounce, the ball rebounds to 2/3 of the previous rebound height. Overall, the values are decreasing at a decreasing rate.

Organizing lessons and courses so that previously investigated contexts are looked at from a new perspective in later investigations of different mathematical concepts facilitates the building of connections between topics. The consistency in approaching problems by collecting data, looking for patterns, creating models, and making connections among various representations lends coherence that reinforces important mathematical processes. In the example of linear and exponential functions, further connections can be developed as students investigate arithmetic and geometric sequences and series. The rebound heights of successive bounces of a ball form a geometric sequence. Students might investigate the notion of convergence of geometric series by exploring the question of whether the ball ever stops bouncing. The total distance traveled by the ball can be represented by the following expression:

$$h_0 + 2h_0 \sum_{n=1}^{\infty} r^n,$$

where h_0 is the drop height and r is the rebound factor. If the series converges, then the total distance traveled is finite, suggesting that the ball eventually stops bouncing because distance and time are directly related by the familiar quadratic relation in projectile motion

$$h = \frac{1}{2}gt^2.$$

Throughout the various investigations of the bouncing-ball experiment, students are engaged in interesting questions that are based in concrete experience. As students work together to answer those questions, they establish strong intuitive understanding of important mathematical topics on which to build more formal procedures and definitions.

Final Thoughts

The examples described here illustrate ways that middle and high school mathematics instruction can respond to the challenge of teaching important mathematical concepts and skills through problem-based classroom investigations. Each of the tasks we have described engages students by posing questions about a problem in context. The contexts provide concrete accessible settings for students to investigate mathematical concepts and skills before they are formalized. Students are guided to look for patterns within and across contexts to begin the process of generalizing their growing understanding. As students work together to abstract skills and concepts from specific contexts, they are prompted to make and test conjectures, to justify and explain their responses, and to clearly communicate their thinking.

Good tasks focus on significant mathematical ideas and important techniques that connect and extend core strands of the subject. Traditionally, school curricula have too often presented mathematics as isolated bits of information and procedures to be memorized. As a result, students are often limited in their ability to approach new problems for which they cannot recall a previously taught algorithm. In the examples we have described, tasks are structured to draw on students' knowledge and experience and to develop mathematical insights and habits of mind that can be built on in subsequent mathematical investigations to develop coherent understanding.

Selecting tasks is an important step in attempting to make the vision of the NCTM *Principles and Standards* (2000) a reality in mathematics classrooms. However, to realize the full potential for mathematics learning embedded within these tasks, the role of teachers in the mathematics classroom must be reconsidered (see Grouws [this volume]). Furthermore, a classroom environment must be created to support mathematical inquiry, risk taking, and higher order mathematical discourse (see Rasmussen, Yackel and King [this volume]). This work is not easy. Teachers who have attempted to implement problem-based tasks in their own classrooms have encountered many frustrations and difficulties; however, many find that the rewards in student learning and dispositions toward mathematics are well worth the effort, as testified by the teacher stories in this volume.

CHAPTER 6

Problem Posing as a Tool for Teaching Mathematics

E. Paul Goldenberg
Marion I. Walter

W HY SHOULD a book on teaching mathematics through problem solving devote a whole chapter to problem *posing?* One reason is that, in a deep sense, mathematics is about posing problems. It has evolved as much from intellectual curiosity about its own internal objects and structures—problems posed from within—as from the need to solve practical problems posed from without. To experience mathematics as those who love it do, students must develop the habit of asking the what-ifs and whys, and they must spend at least some of their time facing problems for which the solution methods are not already fully mapped out for them. If these problems are their own, all the better. The adventure of setting off on one's own course helps build excitement.

Problem posing is both a tool for teaching mathematics through problem solving and an integral part of learning mathematics in that way. For teachers, posing problems and extending them to enrich students' learning are central to teaching mathematics through problem solving. For students, the process of posing their own problems deepens and widens their ability to solve them and to understand the underlying mathematical ideas. The examples in this chapter deliberately include very traditional

---

The writing of this chapter was supported, in part, by the National Science Foundation, grants ESI-9818735 and ESI-0099093. The opinions expressed are those of the authors and not necessarily those of the Foundation.

The authors gratefully acknowledge the enormous intellectual and editorial contributions of Nannette Feurzeig.

problems made more useful, both mathematically and pedagogi-
cally, through problem posing. Other ways that a teacher can use
problem posing when teaching mathematics through problem
solving are suggested as the chapter unfolds.

What Is Problem Posing, and Why Do It?

This volume focuses on ways students come to understand
mathematics by engaging in problem-solving activities. One part
of that understanding is to be able to derive meaning from the
symbolic language of mathematics and to develop skill at manip-
ulating those symbols to transform and express meaning. Our
first example illustrates the role that problem posing can play in
students' meaningful learning and maintenance of skills in the
area of exponents and logarithms.

Liza, a bright high school junior, wanted to solve for x in

$$\left(8\sqrt{2}\right)^{x} = 16 .$$

Liza could not recall routine procedures for solving this equation. For her, therefore, this expression was a true problem, and
she attacked it as any good problem solver should: she looked for
familiar elements and forms, and she tried to recall relevant problems that she had previously solved. She recognized that 8, 16,
and $\sqrt{2}$ were all powers of 2, and she remembered a problem that
her teacher had shown, in which rewriting everything as a power
of a common base was helpful. Liza rewrote

$$\left(8\sqrt{2}\right)^{x} = 16$$

as

$$\left(2^{3.5}\right)^{x} = 2^4$$

but then did not see what to do next. Her teacher suggested that
she pose a similar problem using simpler numbers. She wrote

$$\left(2^3\right)^{2} = 2^6 ,$$

which led to

$$\left(2^3\right)^{x} = 2^6 .$$

That approach made the method of the computation clear. Sadly,
students seldom realize how very smart they have been. Liza's

approach probably seemed roundabout and groping to her. After all, she was asking for help when she had expected to work this example just by applying a technique semiautomatically. But her approach was perfect, and exactly what mathematicians use when facing genuine problems.

This one small example of problem posing illustrates many important ideas. Liza's steps—rummaging around for relevant knowledge and transformations and seeking similar simpler problems—are two of many principal problem-solving techniques listed by George Pólya, a leading thinker about problem solving. In fact, the technique of using related problems appears in many guises in *How to Solve It* (1945) and in Pólya's other books. Generating these related problems is, of course, problem posing. Pólya writes,

> It is hard to have a good idea if we have little knowledge of the subject, and impossible to have it if we have no knowledge. Good ideas are based on past experience and formerly acquired knowledge ... formerly solved problems, or formerly proved theorems. Thus, it is often appropriate to start the work with the question: *Do you know a related problem?* (1945, p. 9)

Pólya cautions that "mere remembering is not enough for a good idea, but we cannot have any good idea without recollecting some pertinent facts." Still, seeing what is "pertinent" goes beyond mere recall. One does not "know a related problem": one creates a related problem by choosing some attribute of the immediate problem, modifying it in some way, and recognizing a result that is more familiar. Liza recognized the current problem as a type, and she recalled a prototype, or example, that she had encountered before. The transformations, in this instance, were small—rewriting the numbers in a different form and temporarily switching to simpler numbers. For something as closed-ended as this computation, that tactic was enough—all she needed was a numerical value for x.

Liza's intelligent approach is not only an example of good problem solving through problem posing; it also illustrates how Liza used what she knew about exponents, logarithms, and equation solving to try to make sense of the mathematical ideas inherent in the initial problem. Thus, the activity, including her problem posing, helped Liza build on her understanding of exponents and logarithms and also helped solidify her technical skills with equations involving them.

In general, when a student merely changes the numbers or cloaks a routine computation in verbal or numerical camouflage, that alteration is not problem posing. But at some stages of learning, even these small changes can be valuable. When a young child wraps $4 + 3$ in a story problem, such as "Jane had 4 apples and got 3 more...," the child encounters no new mathematical ideas but may learn something about the kinds of camouflage that story problems use. Young students who are still relatively unfamiliar with story problems can benefit from a chance to try their own hand at cloaking something understandable in a "real-world" context. By getting a sense of how to do so, they may learn how to find the kernel of useful information within the morass of irrelevant distractions. Similarly, Liza's modest change in numbers revealed the structure of the problem that had been obscured by the ugly numbers.

Although camouflaging a simple calculation is rarely worthwhile, unlikely to lend insight into the anatomy of problems, students do sometimes learn a lot just by "cloaking" an answer. For example, Liza might start with such statements as the three below—essentially, just a definition of the symbols "$\sqrt[c]{}$" and "log"—and create from them a problem of the type she is typically asked to solve. Starting with

$$\left| \begin{aligned} &\text{If } a = b^c \\ &\text{then } b = \sqrt[c]{a} \quad, \\ &\text{and } c = \log_b a \end{aligned} \right.$$

one substitution yields such statements as $a = b^{\log_b a}$ and $c = \log_b b^c$.

Substituting numbers into the first of these expressions gives such "problems" as $7^{\log_7 4} = \underline{}$ and $10^{\log 7} = \underline{}$. Two substitutions let Liza create exactly the sort of problem she had found hard. Where "simplification" helps solve a problem, "complication" helps give insight into the ways problems are built up!

Although changes that affect nothing but the arithmetic or the cosmetic features of the problem are not, in general, what we mean by problem posing, Liza's small changes were good examples of posing a new problem to help her solve an old one. "Nice" numbers are not merely a kindness to the person who must calculate with them. Elegance is a key principle in evaluating problems, solutions, and presentations in mathematics, and experience is required to develop a sense of elegance. If we want to transmit this important part of mathematical culture, we must use it in the problems we pose. Although we have good sport in making fun of all the problems that "come out even," something is to be said for them, or at least for having students figure out how to create them! In Liza's situation, the use of simpler numbers—affecting only the arithmetic!—led to real insight. Definitions are not reliable here: one person's "problem" is another person's routine calculation. Problem posing is just that—problem posing. One knows it when one encounters it.

Examples of problem posing by computational camouflage

The first two of these problems fall short of real problem posing, as they are posed by us, not by you.

1. Using the same kinds of methods, invent a problem of the form $b^{\log a} = x$ in which b is a "nice" decimal, and a and x are "nice" numbers.

2. Create a quadratic function with roots 2 and –3 but with y-intercept not –6.

3. Pick from a topic that you have taught this term or are about to teach, and invent your own problem by starting with a "nice" answer and applying "algebraic complication," as opposed to simplification.

Problem posing is an essential ingredient in investigative activities of all kinds. It is related to building and testing hypotheses, a valuable skill in its own right and one that is increasingly in demand in curricula that depend on students' investigations. We want students to acquire the habit of asking questions, such as "What if...? What if not...? Could it be that...? Suppose... What are the consequences of...?" and the skills and inclination to pursue a hypothesis to a logical and reliable end. Teachers, too, can use these techniques in various ways when they teach through problem solving. For example, some problem-posing techniques, including computational camouflage, are useful for transforming curriculum and assessment tasks that involve only symbolic skill so that they require more understanding or problem solving. (See also the chapters by Hiebert and Wearne; Ziebarth; and Copes and Shager [this volume].) Problem-posing techniques can also provide a basis for good questioning by teachers who are teaching through problem solving. (See also the chapters by Grouws and by Driscoll [this volume].)

Some Useful Methods for Problem Posing

The examples we gave previously of problem posing by computational camouflage were problems posed by us. They were designed to help students acquire the underlying mathematical understanding and skill and also a strategy that in the future would allow them to pose problems. Most students need some initial ideas, almost a kind of permission, before we can expect them to ask "questions that come to mind" about a mathematical situation that is placed before them. At first, for many, the only question that comes to mind is "Why are we doing this?"

New questions do not arise in a vacuum—some fact, technique, or problem already exists that sets the context for the new question. To illustrate the kinds of questions that are often productive in teaching new content, we give two mathematical contexts in which these questions might arise. The first, problem A, has an investigative quality, and it can serve as the basis for learning some important results and methods in number theory. (A problem-posing approach to problem A for teacher professional development can be found in the module "What Is Mathematical Investigation?" in *Connecting with Mathematics* [Education Development Center 2002].) Problem B is a routine computation, but through problem posing it can be used to generate a rich activity that will enhance students' understanding of the mean of a data set.

A. Which numbers can be expressed as the sum of two or more consecutive counting numbers?

B. Find the mean of 7, 4, 7, 6, 3, 8, and 7.

Next comes the fun! The left column of table 6.1 suggests ideas and questions that can help in creating new problems, often better ones, from contexts A and B above. The right column shows only a tiny fraction of the possible problems that arise. Before reading further, try your hand at posing problems based on these contexts.

Brute-force questioning, like intuition, improves with experience. One begins to stockpile useful questions: "Is a solution possible?" or "Must we use integers?" or "What assumptions are we making?" or "Is redundant information given?" (For further examples, elaboration of some of these questions, and other starting points, see Brown and Walter [1990].) Some may depend on the topic; some may be personal to your own mathematical taste. You and your class may want to keep an evolving list of the questions you find most productive, perhaps on a poster as a resource for all.

In addition to the types of questions illustrated in table 6.1, another technique for problem posing is to examine each word or phrase of a sentence, theorem, or situation to see what its role is.

Table 6.1. Useful Questions and Resulting Problems

Ideas and Useful Questions		Problems Derived from Contexts A and B
Existence: • Does it have a solution?	A_1	Clearly some numbers, such as 2, cannot be expressed this way. Is the solution set completely empty for any of the variants of the problem suggested below?
Uniqueness: • Is the solution unique? • Is the method unique? • In how many ways can this problem be done?	A_2	The number 15 can be expressed as $7 + 8$ or $4 + 5 + 6$ or as $1 + 2 + 3 + 4 + 5$. Which numbers, if any, can be expressed as this kind of sum, but in only one way?
	B_1	Does any set of numbers exist that does not have a mean or that has more than one mean?
Extreme or degenerate cases: • Does a max or min exist?	A_3	Which numbers can be expressed as the sum of two or more consecutive integers? As two or more rational numbers that differ by 1? (These problems are both examples, also, of extending the domain.)
	B_2	Can the mean ever be greater than, or equal to, the largest number in the set?
Specialization: • Does a special case exist? • Can we add a constraint? • Can we restrict the domain?	A_4	Which numbers can be expressed as the sum of consecutive counting numbers starting at 1?
	A_5	Which numbers can be expressed as the sum of an odd number of consecutive counting numbers? What can we say about a solution with two addends? With three addends?
	A_6	Which numbers can be expressed as the sum of two or more consecutive odd numbers?

Table 6.1. Useful Questions and Resulting Problems—Continued

Ideas and Useful Questions		Problems Derived from Contexts A and B
Generalization: • Is it a special case? Can we reduce a constraint? • Can we extend the domain?	B_3	What can be said about the mean of any seven points on a number line?
	B_4	How could we invent a meaningful "mean" of points on the plane? What is the meaning of such a "mean" of two such points (the endpoints of a segment) or three such points (the vertices of a triangle)? (This question also suggests a geometrical interpretation of mean.)
Analogy: • What does the problem remind you of?	A_7	These sums remind me of the triangular numbers (which appear in Pascal's triangle and numerous other contexts involving combinatoric ideas). They also suggest factorials—products of consecutive numbers.
Interpretation and representation: • How can this problem be viewed geometrically? Algebraically? Analytically?	A_8	$1 + 2 + 3 + 4 + 5 + 6 -$ $(1 + 2 + 3)$ $4 + 5 + 6$ $\sum_{i=k}^{n} i = \sum_{i=1}^{n} i - \sum_{i=n+1-k}^{n} i = \frac{n(n+1)}{2} - \frac{k(k-1)}{2} = \frac{n^2 - k^2}{2} + \frac{n+k}{2}.$
	A_9	Old friends have just appeared—the arithmetic mean and the difference of squares. $7 + 9 + 11 =$ $(1 + 3 + 5 + 7 + 9 + 11)$ $-(1 + 3 + 5) =$ $6^2 - 3^2 =$ $(6 - 3)(6 + 3)$ Wow! Again, the difference of squares.

Table 6.1. Useful Questions and Resulting Problems—Continued

Ideas and Useful Questions		Problems Derived from Contexts A and B
Examining the given and the result: • Can we relax the givens and get the same result? (A playful examination of what happens when you relax the initial conditions for the case of the Euler line—for example, using an intersection point of *nonperpendicular* bisectors—can be found in Goldenberg [2001].) Can we get by with less information? • Can we use different given information or data for the same result? For example, can we start with the result and work backward?	**B₅**	Find a set of seven numbers with a median and mode of 7, a mean of 6, and a range of 5. How many such sets are possible? What if we use only natural numbers?
	B₆	If the given numbers were not integers, could the solution still be an integer? What conditions on the given numbers will force the result to be an integer? Can the result be irrational, and if so, how?

Since the important mathematical ideas do not change, the questions that follow are much the same as the ones listed previously, but looking at the words helps one find the places to vary the original situation.

1. Does the wording describe part of the essence of the problem, or is it window-dressing? If it is window-dressing, throw it out altogether.

2. If the wording is essential, can it be made more restrictive or less restrictive?

3. If the wording is essential, how can we alter any of the details (e.g., by changing the domain or creating a variable)?

4. Which implicit questions are left unstated (existence, uniqueness, lack of other restrictions, tacitly implied domain, lack of extreme cases, etc.)?

Applied to problem A, this strategy yields a host of other problems, many of which, although they seem to depart from A, actually help move one from a conjecture about A, which is relatively easy to make, to a proof of A, which seems, at first, daunting in the extreme. Such apparent sidetracks as problems A2 and A5 shed important insights into A itself.

This notion of finding the places to vary the original problem (e.g., by concentrating on each word or symbol of a problem statement) leads to a particularly productive problem-posing strategy: asking "What if not?" (See especially chapter 4 of *The Art of Problem Posing* [Brown and Walter 1990] and also numerous places throughout *Problem Posing: Reflections and Applications* [Brown and Walter 1993].)

Even prosaic starts—often central to the curriculum, and most in need of fresh approaches—can be made interesting in this way. Recall the problem-posing opportunities for Liza and her logs and the routine computation of the mean.

Given the set of productive ideas and useful questions suggested in table 6.1, we were able to generate a few potentially interesting problems based on context B, but how could we use this strategy of analyzing the "attributes" of the problem? Often, "prosaic" starters like context B do not seem to have attributes to change. Before you read what we found, review context B—computing a mean—and take a bit of time to list some of its attributes and assumptions. The ideas you list need not be independent of one another; they can even restate a previous idea in a new way. Also, try not to censor ideas that seem silly or trivial. Even these may trigger valuable new ideas. In table 6.2 we list some of the attributes that we found. (The letter identifiers are used to map these attributes to variations listed subsequently.)

Table 6.2. Attributes or Assumptions in Problem B ("Find the Mean of 7, 4, 7, 6, 3, 8, and 7.")

a.	Seven pieces of data are given
b.	We do not (yet) know the mean
c.	The numbers are not all different
d.	The lowest number is 3
e.	The highest number is 8
f.	The numbers are not given in order of size
g.	The numbers are all whole
h.	One set of data is given
i.	We are given numbers

One can easily skim a list and not notice much. But before reading on, notice at least that some of the nine items that we listed in table 6.2 are, in current youth-vernacular, "pretty lame." That is fine. Even item (i), which looks anything but insightful, can become the jumping off point for truly good problems if it is taken seriously. Table 6.3 lists some "what-if-nots" on some of the attributes that we found for some of the problems.

Often, such new problems take "nonstandard" approaches to the topic that is being studied, giving students opportunities to look at that topic from new angles and in greater depth. For example, computing the mean of seven numbers can be routine and formulaic. When one tries to figure out what sets of numbers have a given mean or how the mean is affected when a set of (unspecified) numbers is transformed in certain ways (e.g., by adding 1 to each number), one goes well beyond mechanically using a formula and may see new meaning in it.

Others of these problems reveal the natural interconnections among different topics in the curriculum. For example, problems i_1 and i_2 raise ideas that students face as they begin to study arithmetic sequences. That connection is explicitly mentioned in problem i_3.

Table 6.3. Variations on Problem B: Find the Mean of 7, 4, 7, 6, 3, 8, and 7.

a_1	What if only five of the seven values are given? Can one determine the missing data if one knows the mean of the original seven?
a_2	What if one computes the mean of each possible combination of only five of the given seven numbers? (How many such combinations exist?) What could one learn from, say, a histogram of those means?
a_3	What if the original seven numbers are sampled from a population consisting of eight numbers? What might one reasonably infer about the eighth number? Do ideas from problem a_2 help answer that question?
b_1	What if one knows the mean but none of the data? What, if anything, could one say about the data? What possible sets of data would fit?
c_1	What if the numbers are all different? Is it possible to find seven different integers whose mean is 6? What if one also had to make the median 7 or the range 5?
e_1	What if the highest number is 18, not 8? Which of mean, mode, median, or range changes?
g_1	What if the numbers are not all whole? What if each number is 1/2 more than listed? How does the mean change?
h_1	What if two sets of data are given instead of one? Suppose the second set is 2, 6, 7, 9. Can the mean of the combined sets (all eleven numbers) be calculated by combining the means of the two sets in some way? Would averaging the means do that job?
h_2	What if one knows only that the means of two sets of numbers are 7 and 10? What, if anything, can be said about the mean of the combined set?
i_1	What if one is given no numbers? Here is one possibility. Suppose that the set has seven members and that the mean is 6. What can be said about the numbers? Next suppose that the lowest number is 1; what can be said about the highest possible number?
i_2	More generally, suppose that the set has n members and that the mean is m. What can be said about the numbers?
i_3	Suppose that a set of n numbers that form an arithmetic sequence has a mean of m. What can be said about the numbers?

In the foregoing tables we illustrated how one might take two starting points and generate new problems. We started by listing some attributes of the original problem or situation. Then, by asking "What if not?" for each of the attributes, we created new situations. Finally, we asked questions about these new situations. Sometimes, the original questions applied to the altered situation, and sometimes the altered situation triggered new questions. The procedure may seem very linear, almost formulaic, but acquiring new skills often involves a somewhat self-conscious rule-following stage. As we teach through problem solving and our students engage in problem posing, problem posing comes much more naturally and with less conscious attention to procedure. Ideas come spontaneously, without first ritually listing attributes or what-if-nots. Most important, a collection of "useful questions" begins to develop.

Another Example

Students are often confused about the concept of area, in part because they rarely encounter problems that require more than substitution into formulas, whose derivation the students may not understand. Problem posing is one way to help students better understand the area formula for a trapezoid. Here we use a routine problem to illustrate this approach.

> $ABCD$ is a trapezoid with the two parallel sides $\overline{AB}$ and $\overline{CD}$. $AB = 6$ cm, $CD = 13$ cm, and $AD = 10$ cm. The altitude is 8 cm. Find the area.

In a way, this problem is already a bit unusual, in that most problems do not provide unnecessary information. Before continuing, take a few minutes to think about and jot down some problems based on this situation.

Here are some that we came up with, using techniques that we outlined previously.

1. Is such a trapezoid even possible? If so, is it unique? (In this case, no!) If not, why not?

2. Can I find the area with less information than given? What information can be left out? Is the answer to this question unique?

3. Does a trapezoid exist with the same area but all different measurements?

4. Does a trapezoid exist with the same area, the same length of parallel sides, and the same altitude but with a different

shape? Does the answer depend on the particular numbers used in this example?

5. Does a trapezoid exist with the same area, the same height, and different lengths of parallel sides?

6. Does a trapezoid exist that has the same altitude but twice the area of the given one?

7. If we try to cover one of these trapezoids with squares, we see eight rows consisting of 6 + 7 + 8 + 9 + 10 + 11 + 12 + 13 squares.

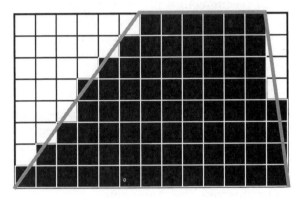

This sum of consecutive counting numbers (context A comes back to haunt us!) is a special case of an arithmetic series, which students learn to compute using such formulas as

$$S = \frac{n}{2}(a_1 + a_n),$$

where n is the number of terms and where a_1 and a_n refer to the first and nth terms of the sequence. (Feinberg-McBrian [1996] elaborates on this connection between trapezoids and consecutive sums in "The Case of Trapezoidal Numbers.") The formula looks very much like the formula for finding the area of a trapezoid, which is sometimes written as

$$A = \frac{b_1 + b_2}{2}h$$

and often described in terms of the mean of the two bases (context B returns). How far can we push this analogy? Is more to be learned from it?

8. What does the computation look like if the trapezoid's bases are equal? And what does the "trapezoid" look like in that sit-

uation? What if one of the two bases is 0? Again, what does the figure look like then?

Even with this simple example, we can see that problem posing—and then solving—can lead to deeper insight into a situation. In this example, students may begin to understand both how the area of a trapezoid depends on its various features and how its computation relates to the formulas for the areas of parallelograms and triangles, the sum of arithmetic series, and the computation of the arithmetic mean.

What Else Can Be Learned about Problem Posing?

Although much more remains to be learned about problem posing, this chapter has focused on the role of problem posing in classrooms in which mathematics is taught through problem solving. (See English [2003] on the same topic from an elementary school perspective.) As the teacher, you choose an initial problem or task with the intent that when your students engage in the process of understanding and solving the problem, they will, at least potentially, learn the important mathematics that is your goal. (See Marcus and Fey [this volume] for more on selecting tasks.) The examples in this chapter show how problem-posing techniques have an important role at several points in the process of teaching through problem solving. You can use problem-posing techniques to create sense-making opportunities within traditional skill-reinforcing tasks. Once your students become engaged in a problem task, practice and experience with problem posing deepen their insight into the problem and their understanding of the mathematics that underlies it. Additionally, both you and your students can use problem posing to transform old problems into particularly interesting new ones by asking questions about uniqueness, interchanging known and unknown quantities, changing the domain, and the like.

You will also begin to sense when the extra time spent on a rich problem "pays for itself" in some way. This payback may come in various forms. It may simply be useful drill and practice but in an investigative context that holds students' interest. It may help students examine the meaning and significance of what might otherwise be rote and meaningless application of rules and formulas. It may establish connections between a new mathematical concept and one already encountered but seemingly unrelated.

Problem posing offers benefits beyond helping students solve problems and understand the underlying mathematics. Some students who feel they are "not good at math" are quite good at problem posing. Getting a chance to exercise that strength often allows these students to gain a more comfortable relationship with the topic at hand and also experience an increase in self-esteem and confidence that carries over to the rest of their mathematical activities. Perhaps most important, as we said at the outset, problem posing helps these students—all students—experience mathematics as insiders do, because, at its core, problem posing is what mathematics is about.

Marion Walter and Paul Goldenberg met more than thirty years ago, when Marion was coteaching a problem-posing course with Stephen I. Brown at the Harvard Graduate School of Education, and Paul entered as a doctoral student. They have remained friends and colleagues and are delighted to be writing this chapter together as their first joint publication.

Snapshots of a Precalculus Course Focused on Problem Solving

Gloria B. Barrett
Helen L. Compton

B Y THE time students reach eleventh grade, we would hope that they are experienced problem solvers. We have found, however, that students entering the North Carolina School of Science and Mathematics (NCSSM) as high school juniors typically have very little experience in this area. Our goal is to provide students with problems and activities that guide them in building meaningful mathematical knowledge. These experiences also serve to enhance our students' ability to solve problems, often in unfamiliar situations. The students almost always use technology and interact with one another. Throughout this process, the role of the teacher varies. In some situations we guide an entire class through a problem-solving activity; at other times we simply walk around the room, listening to students and assessing their progress and understanding as they interact.

Solving an Introductory Problem

The NCSSM precalculus-level course is the first mathematics course taken by most of our entering students. We begin the course attempting to communicate our goals and to build on the

---

The examples in this article were adapted from *Contemporary Precalculus through Applications,* by North Carolina School of Science and Mathematics, Department of Mathematics and Computer Science (New York: Glencoe/McGraw-Hill, 2001).

mathematical knowledge that students bring with them in areas of linear functions and data analysis. The following problem is one that we solve together in class during the first few days of school. Several weeks later we revisit the problem and provide an opportunity for students to reflect on their problem-solving process by sharing the problem and its solution with a parent or other adult. The problem that we pose follows:

> The senior class at the local high school wants to raise money to support the athletic program by selling tickets that will allow a family to attend all athletic events at the school. The class officers are trying to decide the price for a single ticket. When they are unable to agree on a price, they ask parents what they would be willing to pay for an all-sports ticket. The survey results in table TS1.1 reflect answers to the question "What is the most you would be willing to pay for an all-sports ticket good for this school year?"

Table TS1.1

Results of All-Sport-Ticket Survey Responses

Maximum price ($)	50.00	75.00	90.00	95.00	115.00	135.00	150.00	175.00
Expected ticket sales	145	80	45	85	120	80	60	150

The setting for this problem is one that is familiar to students, yet the problem is one that students have not experienced before. After some initial discussion as a class, we encourage students to talk with others in their small groups. Our students sit in pods of four, so they have ongoing access to one another during class. As the teacher strolls about the room listening to students, we hear such comments as "I can't remember how to do this kind of problem" or "I don't think we did problems like this last year." Most students appear to expect to begin the year reviewing something they previously learned, and we quickly assure them that we are not doing review. Rather, we want students to figure out how to use skills they bring into the course to solve a problem unlike any they have ever solved before.

Solving this problem fills several days of class time. On the first day, students need time to brainstorm and to make sure they understand the problem. All students need to realize that they have both an opportunity and a responsibility for sharing ideas and asking questions, and early in the year many students feel more comfortable speaking in a small-group setting. Some students will quickly suggest that they should look at the data graphically. Students use their calculators to create a scatterplot of ticket sales versus maximum price, with those who are more proficient calculator users helping their less experienced classmates. The graph reveals no relationship between these variables, a result that is surprising to most students. After more thinking and sharing of ideas, students should realize, or the teacher may need to suggest, that a parent who is willing to pay $175.00 will certainly buy a ticket at any lower price; thus, a new table (see table TS 1.2) and new graph are needed with cumulative ticket sales as the response variable.

Table TS1.2

Table Revised to Reflect Cumulative Ticket Sales

Price ($)	50.00	75.00	90.00	95.00	115.00	135.00	150.00	175.00
Cumulative ticket sales	765	620	540	495	410	290	210	150

At this point, some students may suggest multiplying price and cumulative ticket sales to see which of the prices included in the survey produces greatest revenue. Doing so will lead to an answer, but is it the best answer? Might we do better with a price not listed in the original survey? How can we predict the revenue associated with other prices?

The teacher encourages students to think about how they can produce a function that relates price and revenue. This process begins with looking at a scatterplot of cumulative ticket sales versus price and observing a decreasing linear relationship between these variables. All precalculus students should be able to write a linear function relating ticket price and the total number of tickets sold; then they can build a revenue function by multiplying ticket price and the function for number of tickets sold. Our students' prior experiences in data analysis vary greatly; some have studied linear regression in second-year algebra, whereas others have not. For this problem we usually encourage students to eyeball a line and use their knowledge of linear equations to write an equation. Often this task is assigned for homework or for group work in class. This assignment results in many different equations, causing students to realize the need for a standard method of fitting a linear equation to the data, thereby laying the groundwork for the data-analysis unit that is next in our syllabus.

The final steps in the solution process involve writing a revenue function and using it to determine the optimal ticket price.

The revenue function is quadratic, and we assume that precalculus students are proficient with graphs of quadratic functions. Students need to make connections among the real-world context of this problem, the function they have created, and its graph to determine that maximum revenue is associated with the vertex of the parabola.

As we conclude work on this problem, we ask students to reflect on the considerations that were involved in the solution process. We want students to think about how they needed to stay focused on the question they were trying to answer as they applied mathematical procedures and concepts that they already knew to an unfamiliar situation. We emphasize to students that they were not expected to accomplish this task alone; rather, they collaborated with their classmates and shared their insight and ideas to produce the solution. Finally, we ask students to think about the solution they produced. Can they be sure that they have determined the exact ticket price to maximize revenue?

Later in the year, the culminating task for a problem like this one typically requires that students write a report explaining their solution. As the final assignment for this problem, we sometimes ask students to assume the role of teacher in sharing the problem with a parent or another adult at home. Before students take this assignment home, we allow class time for them to discuss how they will talk about it with a parent. Then each student writes a lesson plan that outlines the planned discussion and includes notes on how and where calculator work will be incorporated into the discussion. Working through the problem and the solution with someone outside of class requires that students reflect carefully about what they have done; at the same time we are able to share some of our course content and methodology with parents.

To complete the assignment, students and parents fill out an evaluation sheet and comment on the other party's work. The comments give evidence that the sharing activity is worthwhile. Parents are clearly impressed with what the students have been doing. Several parents complimented their son or daughter's patience in responding to their questions. Another commented on how the student struggled to explain the problem at a sufficiently basic level. Working with an adult helped students realize that explaining the problem to someone else increases their understanding. One student commented that "teaching someone with a different background in math broadened my comprehension and interpretations of the problem." Several commented on how difficult it was to help their parents understand what they needed to do without doing the work for them. One student's comment may have been the most revealing: "She [her mother] was a little hesitant to actually think about what she was doing; at first she wanted to let me just tell her what to push on the calculator. After it was clear she had to think, she grasped the concepts quicker than I expected."

The ticket problem sets the stage for our precalculus course. It quickly prompts students' awareness that this course is more than just a collection of new skills; throughout the year they will be expected to connect the mathematics they learn with the real world. Solving the problem in class gives the teacher an opportunity to assess some of what students already know, students' comfort levels with their calculators, and their skill at communicating with their peers.

Investigations for Concept Development

Additional opportunities for using problem-solving strategies within the precalculus curriculum occur in several investigations that ask students to develop their own theories and build new mathematical knowledge. Each investigation of this type is a study of behavior of functions and uses calculator graphs as the tool for gathering information. The first investigation focuses on basic transformations. The second one deals with function composition, and the third one deals with sums and products of functions. Using a carefully navigated set of instructions in each investigation, we ask students to look at two graphs at a time—one very familiar (usually one of our toolkit functions, such as $y = x^2$, $y = \sqrt{x}$, and $y = \sin x$) and the other, similar but with a little twist.

Students should work in groups on these investigations. As they sit huddled over calculator screens, they make conjectures about the graphs of the modified functions by comparing them with the original toolkit functions, then test their conjectures with more examples. A rule that we have adopted in our teaching is that we ask questions rather than give answers during the student investigations. To be sure that all students arrive at the correct theory, we ensure that a whole-class summarizing activity concludes the investigation. This activity might be a general class discussion, group presentations, a written report from each student or group, or a written assignment employing the use of the concepts. In this concluding activity, we focus on the methods and reasoning that different groups used during the investigation. Our main goal at this point is to be sure that students link the mathematical result of the investigation with the reason it is happening.

In the first investigation, the ideas are associated with transformations of functions including $g(x) = f(x) \pm c$, $g(x) = f(x \pm c)$, $g(x) = c \cdot f(x)$, and $g(x) = f(c \cdot x)$. Students are given groups of functions g that are transformations of a familiar toolkit function f. The students first write g as a transformation of the toolkit function f. Then they graph both functions on the same viewing window of the graphing calculator and make observations on relationships. Since this investigation is of a somewhat familiar topic, students are able to begin to build intuition about how functions behave and to learn the power of generalization.

A similar but markedly more challenging investigation soon follows in the study of composition of functions. Prior to the investigation, students have studied the algebra of compositions. They can find an expression for $f \circ g$ given f and g and can determine functions f and g that will produce a given $f \circ g$. The investigation includes compositions of the types $g(x) = |f(x)|$, $g(x) = \sqrt{f(x)}$,

$$g(x) = \frac{1}{f(x)},$$

and $g(x) = f(|x|)$ where the graph of f is familiar. A portion of the investigation appears in figure TS1.1.

Near the end of the course, a third function investigation is included in the unit on combinations of functions. In this investigation, students work to understand how the graphs of f and g influence the graph of $h(x) = f(x) + g(x)$ and that of $k(x) = f(x) \cdot g(x)$. The combination graphs, such as $h(x) = x + \cos x$ and $k(x) = 2^x \sin x$, look strange but exhibit some familiar behavior. Students must consider how to take familiar pieces and develop the new graph. Since this investigation occurs at the end of the course, students bring many skills and a wealth of experience and self-confidence to the task. The experiences and theories from this investigation provide powerful tools for thinking about such concepts as limits in calculus and for such applications as dampened oscillation.

A Final Note

The primary goals of the mathematics courses for our junior-level students focus on their developing understanding of mathematics through problem solving while acquiring techniques to be good problem solvers. At the end of each school year, teachers

Investigating Graphs of Compositions of Functions

a. $f(x) = x^2 - 9; g(x) = |x^2 - 9|$

b. $f(x) = 2\sin x - 1; g(x) = |2\sin x - 1|$

c. $f(x) = 1 + \dfrac{1}{x}; g(x) = \left|1 + \dfrac{1}{x}\right|$

Answer questions 1–3 for each pair of functions.

1. Use function notation to show how g is a composition involving function f. For example, if $g(x) = |2^x - 4|$ and $f(x) = 2^x - 4$, you would write $g(x) = |f(x)|$.

2. Choose an appropriate viewing window, and use a graphing calculator to graph the functions f and g together. Sketch the graphs, and label key points carefully.

3. Compare the graph of g with the graph of f. Note any changes in the domain. Write a few sentences about your observations.

   Write a general statement explaining how the graph of $g(x) = |f(x)|$ compares with the graph of f.

   Explain why the result is reasonable.

Fig. TS1.1. Portion of an investigation of graphs of compositions of functions

write a one-paragraph assessment of each junior. This write-up is always a wonderful occasion to reflect on the growth of that student over the year. Our comments are often focused on the self-confidence that students have acquired to solve unfamiliar problems. Since problem solving is a major goal for our students, we build time into our syllabus for activities to develop problem-solving skills. Group work is emphasized; the classroom furniture stays in pods, and students are encouraged to collaborate outside of class. Our teachers meet weekly to plan and share strategies for implementing new problems and approaches.

Good problem-solving experience helps our students expand their thinking, encourages persistence through difficulties, and empowers them to navigate their own learning. We believe that all these skills are necessary for their success in the new century.

CHAPTER 7

Using Technology to Foster Mathematical Meaning through Problem Solving

Rose Mary Zbiek

THE EXAMPLES in this chapter illustrate some ways to use mathematics technology to facilitate the emergence of mathematical ideas through sense making and problem solving. Whether technology use is a mandate from others or a personal goal, we remain in control of how we use it in our classrooms. Good uses of many different types of technological tools can be a powerful part of students' learning experiences.

Why Use Technology?

Using technology can reap clear learning, teaching, and curricular benefits for students and teachers in problem-solving circumstances. It promotes general mathematical benefits, such as rapidity of generating examples, decreased likelihood of computational errors, and unique opportunities for students to pose their own problems. Using technology also brings instructional benefits, such as the capability of storing, retrieving, sharing, and altering problems and attempted solutions. Technology used effectively helps students stay focused on mathematics and stay engaged in solving problems that intrigue them. Each of the examples in this chapter illustrates in greater detail how we can capitalize on these benefits in a classroom where fundamental mathematical ideas emerge through problem solving.

Available Technology

Technological possibilities for the mathematics classroom abound. Calculators come in several types, from fraction and graphing calculators to those with symbolic manipulation capability. Geometry tools include LOGO microworlds, as well as such interactive environments as The Geometer's Sketchpad (Jackiw 1997) and Cabri Geometry (Laborde and Bellemain 1994). Data-analysis tools range from spreadsheets and databases to more mathematics-specific products, such as Fathom (Finzer, Erickson, and Binker 2001), a dynamic statistics environment. Students may gather data through Internet resources, from video clips using such products as VideoPoint, or through calculator-based products. Mathematics classrooms may also have such communication tools as word processors or such presentation tools as PowerPoint. In addition, special purpose programs and games are available; however, most of these resources were designed initially in past decades, during a time when problem solving was viewed as the object of instruction rather than as a vehicle for learning important mathematical ideas.

We can also employ technology, for instance in World Wide Web–based activities, to connect mathematics with its many applications. For example, students may go to the Virtual Earthquake site at http://www.sciencecourseware.com/VirtualEarthquake/ to determine the epicenter and Richter value for an earthquake. A problem-solving-activity sequence using this site not only can introduce such ideas as intersecting circles but also may serve as the motivation to study logarithms (see CAS-IM [2000] for a sample lesson).

Technology resources vary greatly in the extent to which their developers intended them to be used for mathematical purposes and in students' problem-solving endeavors. However, each of these forms may have a place in our classrooms as students develop mathematical understanding through problem solving. For example, communication and presentation tools obviously provide opportunities for presentation of possible solutions (National Council of Teachers of Mathematics 2000, p. 257). In this chapter, we investigate and reflect on two examples using mathematics-specific technology.

Two Examples

Each example consists of a sequence of two or more related problems that can be adapted for students across grades 6 through 12. The essential part of each description is the mathematical learning focus. If at all possible, the reader is urged to take advantage of the opportunities for interactive work noted in the boxes throughout this chapter to see how students encounter and develop mathematical ideas in these problem-solving experiences. Minimally, students need a graphing calculator and a geometry construction environment, or at least a graphing calculator and by-hand compass and straightedge, for these examples.

Example 1: Combining Transformations

Students encounter Euclidean transformations (e.g., rotations, translations, reflections, dilations) and apply these to simple figures in middle school. These students are ready in subsequent years for a problem-solving experience through which important mathematical ideas about composition of functions and equivalence emerge. Some students use such interactive geometry software as The Geometer's Sketchpad or Cabri Geometry. Adaptations of this example have been used with eighth-grade students and in classes including a mixture of students in tenth through twelfth grades. This example also shows how sharing students' thinking in solving one problem can lead to a subsequent problem from which important mathematics emerges, illustrating the value of focusing on students' solutions, as suggested by Hiebert and Wearne (this volume).

> In figure 7.1, which numbered triangle, if any, is the image of ΔABC under a reflection? Notice what you think about as you tackle the problem.

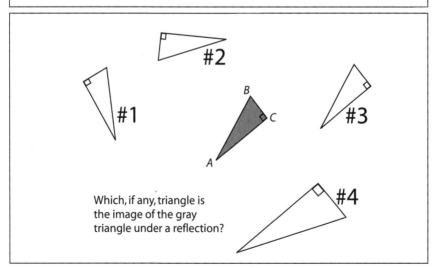

Fig. 7.1. The first transformation problem with gray triangle, ABC

In solving this problem, students learn about relationships among the transformation's preimage, image, and parameters. Students typically identify shape 1 as the image under reflection, then locate a line of reflection as the line that is "halfway between" a point and its image. Asked to discuss the other triangles, students explain that shape 4 cannot be a reflection image because it is "bigger than" $\triangle ABC$ as they learn that reflections preserve size but not orientation. They describe shapes 2 and 3 as a rotation and a translation, respectively. However, mathematical learning does not stop here when students share their solutions. One average-ability tenth-grade student saw shape 2 in a different way:

> If you took number 2 and flipped it down and then if you flipped it over to the right, then that would match into there [$\triangle ABC$], but you'd have to do it at an angle too. I'm thinking of, like, complex things right now.

This student described one triangle as the image of the other not under one reflection but under a composition of two reflections. The thinking she presented in solving the original problem was an ideal source of a new problem! This scenario illustrates how "[i]n addition to using carefully chosen problems with particular curricular purposes in mind, [we] can take advantage of events that occur in the classroom" (National Council of Teachers of Mathematics 2000, p. 338). The challenge in this example is to locate two lines such that reflecting shape 2 over one line and then reflecting that image over another line produces a final triangle that coincides with $\triangle ABC$. Middle school students using a geometry construction program can undertake her challenge.

> Find her two lines. What might she have meant by "you'd have to do it at an angle"? Is the solution to this problem unique? Justify your conclusion.

Students may conclude that the rotation that maps $\triangle ABC$ to shape 2 in figure 7.1 is equivalent to a composition of two reflections. Students solving this problem develop a richer understanding of equivalence. They can use the software to alter $\triangle ABC$—and consequently shape 2—to see that the two lines worked with any other triangle they tried. With the flexibility of the technology, students can find many ways to place the two lines. Most secondary school students will rarely have seen a problem that has infinitely many solutions. Further class discussion may uncover the facts that every pair of lines intersects at the same point and that the point seems to be the center of the rotation equivalent to composition of the two reflections. We as teachers may need to highlight, as Hiebert and Wearne (this volume) note, this embedded idea in the students' solutions.

As Goldenberg and Walter (this volume) suggest, we can play with this student's problem to pose a new one. We were given the image of a rotation and found two reflections whose composition is equivalent to the rotation. But what if we ask students to reverse things and start with any two reflections? Is the composition of any two reflections equivalent to a rotation?

> Experiment! Start with any two lines and a figure. Locate the image of that figure under the composition of two reflections. Does a rotation exist that maps the figure to its image? If so, where is the center of rotation and what is the angle of rotation? Explain how you know whether the rotation you developed really is equivalent to the composition of the two reflections. Try other pairs of lines, and see if you reach the same conclusions.

Access to a geometry construction program makes this experiment far less tedious than conducting it with only by-hand constructions. The technology also allows students to focus more directly on their reasoning. In thinking mathematically, students need to be aware of the possibility of attaining different results for their different cases. The teacher whose students tackle this problem of whether the composition of two reflections is the same as a rotation may need to encourage students to think about the lines they are choosing. The sketches in figure 7.2 (adapted from Glass [2001]) imply that solving this third problem requires considering at least two cases: parallel lines and intersecting lines.

Other mathematical ideas can emerge from problems based on the opening task in figure 7.1. For example, middle school students may pursue similar questions about compositions of pairs or triples of other types of transformations. High school students may use coordinates and then do some complicated curve-fitting work to express the transformations as equations and as matrices. In all these extensions, each task not only launches the next problem but also provides information about how the students understood ideas of transformation.

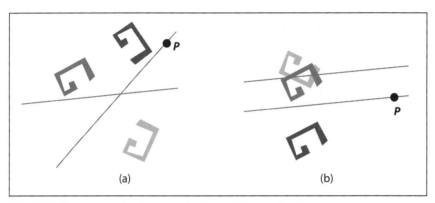

Fig. 7.2. Two cases in the composition of two reflections

Technology is the means of introducing the initial problem in this example. Presenting the task in a dynamic environment allows students to test various lines quickly and accurately as they conduct experiments, as well as to test their solutions. In their work with two given lines of reflection, students may, perhaps unintentionally, move lines in such a way that the figure changes from one with intersecting lines to one with parallel lines, as in dragging point *P* to move from the case in figure 7.2a to that in figure 7.2b. Solving the final problem about compositions of reflections illustrates the importance of cases and conditions in reasoning formally about abstract claims.

Example 2: Investigating Parameters

An important indication that students understand function is their ability to relate symbolic and graphical representations. One way for students to develop this ability is to investigate the effects on a function graph of changing the parameters in a symbolic form of the function. These "parameter explorations" can be done at different levels of complexity, and technological tools are often helpful.

As a very basic example, we could challenge middle school students to use a graphing calculator in as many ways as possible to indicate the vertical intercept of the graph given by $f(x) = 3x - 6$. Students have several solution options. They may use a Trace command to note that the second coordinate where the graph crosses the vertical axis is –6 (as in fig. 7.3a). They could use a computational approach by storing 0 in *x* before computing $3x - 6$ (see fig. 7.3b). Students then could draw on these experiences to solve the problem of determining the effects of parameter *b* for linear functions of the form $f(x) = ax + b$.

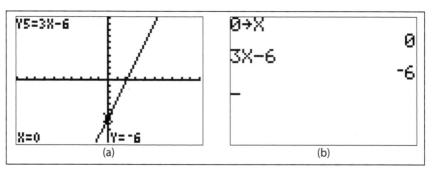

Fig. 7.3. Two graphing-calculator ways of seeing the vertical intercept for $f(x) = 3x - 6$

Similarly, with or without electronic technology, students see that increasing the value of c for functions of the form $f(x) = ax^2 + bx + c$ causes "the graph to move up." With probing from the teacher, students can use their understanding of real-number addition and multiplication to explain why increasing the value of c by, say, k, increases the value of $ax^2 + bx + c$ by exactly k regardless of the value of x. They can also discuss the similarity between this result and the effects of changing the constant in the linear functions and can extend this property to polynomial functions in general.

Access to graphing calculators affords students opportunities to study parameter effects for more complex function families, including exponential functions of the form $f(x) = Ca^{bx}$ and rational functions of the form

$$f(x) = \frac{a}{x + b}.$$

On the one hand, using increasingly "thicker" line styles as in figure 7.4, students observe that output values are positive for functions of the form $f(x) = Ca^{bx}$ for C values of 2, 5, and 9, given $a = 7$ and $b = 1$. On the other hand, output values are negative for the same values of a and b and negative values of C. This and similar technology-generated examples with other values of C, a, and b lead students to formulate and defend a conjecture that if a and b are positive, then Ca^{bx} is positive if the multiplier C is positive but negative if C is negative.

The following discussion presents a more complex example of a parameter investigation that builds on students' understanding of these exponential and rational functions. Students investigate

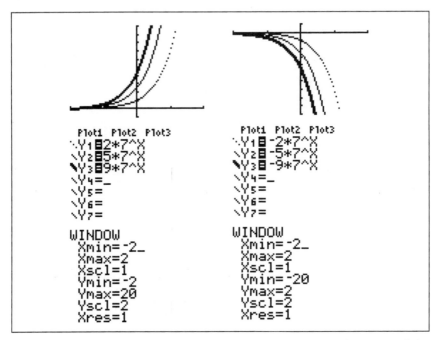

Fig. 7.4. Using increasingly "thicker line" styles to explore functions of the form $f(x) = Ca^{bx}$

a new function family and learn more about zero denominators, vertical and horizontal asymptotes, and limits. The central problem in this example (from CAS-IM [2000]) began as a task through which tenth- through twelfth-grade students also could hone their symbolic reasoning skills.

We asked students to determine the effects of parameters a, b, c, and d on graphs for the family given by

$$y = \frac{a}{1 + b \cdot e^{cx}} + d.$$

Students obviously could use graphing calculators for this task. However, we knew that our students' explorations would be richer if they could generate their examples more quickly and capitalize on the greater visual impact afforded by dynamic graphs. We developed a dynamic graphing setting using The Geometer's Sketchpad, as illustrated in figure 7.5. The generic equation for the family appears in the upper-left corner. As the student slides points a, b, c, or d at the bottom of the screen, the value of the corresponding parameter changes. These changes are shown in the equation in the upper-right corner, as well as in the graph. (A linear dynamic graph appears in E-example 7.5 in the Problem Solving Standard for grades 9–12 in

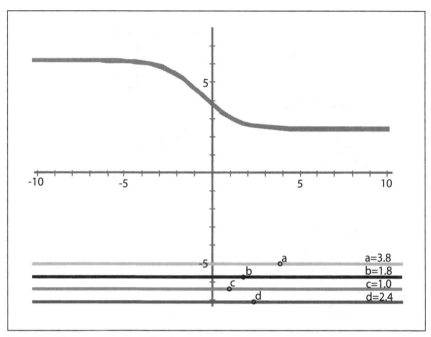

Fig. 7.5. Opening screen for the parameter exploration using

$$y = \frac{a}{1 + b \cdot e^{cx}} + d$$

the electronic version of *Principles and Standards* [available at http://standards.nctm.org/document/chapter7/prob.htm].)

This example involves a large problem that breaks into sub-problems at various levels of difficulty, including subproblems that are accessible to all learners. To illustrate, we consider the following subproblem.

Experiment with graphs as needed to determine the effects of changing the values of parameters *d* and *b* for this family of functions.

All students quickly identify the effects of changing *d*, often without considering examples. They note that increasing or decreasing the value of *d* causes the graph to move up or down, and they relate this outcome to the effects of changing the value of the constant in the general forms of a polynomial expression. However, changing the value of *b* puzzles them. They typically try a few positive values for *b*, then try to think with the symbols. They wrestle with interesting, although perhaps flawed, connections, such as, "*b* is a coefficient of something with *x* in it, so maybe it has to do with the slope, like m in $mx + b$." They test this conjecture with a few examples and see that in places on the graph, the "slope" does not change, and they attribute this phenomenon to the fact that b is in the denominator. At some time during their work, they drag point b so that the value of b suddenly changes from only positive values to a negative value, and the shape of the graph turns suddenly from that in figure 7.5 to that in figure 7.6—an experience that is difficult if not impossible to emulate with a graphing calculator. Immediately students have a new subproblem to solve.

> Explain why the graph appears to "break apart" suddenly at a negative b value.

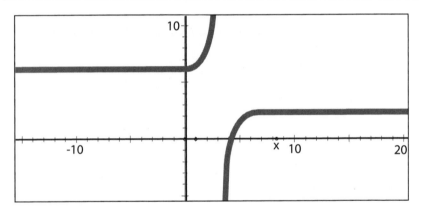

Fig. 7.6. Graph after it "breaks apart"

This example reveals how rich mathematical understanding can emerge as students engage in solving a sequence of subproblems. Students focused on the subproblem of why the graph breaks draw on their understanding of rational functions. They soon observe that a zero denominator indicates where graphs of

$$y = \frac{a}{1 + b \cdot e^{cx}} + d$$

will break apart. This observation prompts students to focus on the equations, $1 + b \cdot e^{2x} = 0$ and then $b \cdot e^{2x} = -1$. They know that $e^{cx} \geq 0$ for any value of c on the basis of their understanding of exponential functions. The students conclude that $b \cdot e^{2x} = -1$ is possible only for some negative value of b. In this way, they solve the subproblem and explain why the break happens for a negative value but not for positive values of b.

In solving this subproblem, learners encounter mathematical ideas about asymptotes, division by zero, and the sign of terms involving exponential expressions. They take those ideas back to the larger problem of finding the effects of b. Students use ideas about the effects of the magnitude as well as the sign of b in the original problem when considering how the effects of one parameter are related to the effects of another. Overall, students not only develop insights into the connection between symbolic and graphical representations, they also learn important ideas about what a limit is and how to reason symbolically about limits.

The graphing assistance from technology is essential in keeping students' focus on the important questions. For example, using geometry construction software rather than static forms of graphing calculators allowed students to see the "break" occur as values of b changed. The break occurred at a value of b to which the students later gave meaning: it is the value of b satisfying $1 + b \cdot e^{cx} = 0$ for a given value of c.

Reflecting on Examples

Using technology in these examples produced many benefits. It allowed students access to new problems and to new approaches. The geometry environments in the parameter investigations and in the composition of reflections fostered new ways to encounter interesting mathematics and to experiment in the process of refining solutions.

Pedagogical benefits also accrued, in that the choice of the technology and its use helped make student thinking more visible to the teacher. For example, students' tendencies to consider only positive parameter values were readily seen by watching them use the dynamic graph. This inclination would be harder to notice if one had to shuffle through several sheets of paper or to follow a sequence of several calculator-generated graphs. Technological tools provide a means for students to reflect on their own solutions and on the completeness of their thinking. Students who saw the sudden "break" in the graph in the last example left with a new understanding of the importance of considering pertinent cases. Having students actively analyze these experiences helps them "take responsibility for reflecting on their work and make the adjustments necessary when solving problems" (National Council of Teachers of Mathematics 2000, p. 55).

The classes described here used technology in ways that helped connect different strands of mathematics. Algebra and geometry issues arose simultaneously in extensions of the transformation problems of the first example. In the second example, the geometry environment generated the dynamic graphs that students studied algebraically. Using such technology as calculators, geometry construction tools, and computer algebra systems, students learn to combine number and operation, as well as geometric figures and properties, with algebraic concepts and symbols. Learning, teaching, and curriculum benefits like those on which we reflected in this chapter should be primary considerations when incorporating technology in a problem-solving approach to teaching and learning mathematics.

Conclusion

Many different kinds of technology can be used in the mathematics classroom in a variety of appropriate ways. Technology can help students and teachers present, pose, interpret, compare, and reflect on problems and solutions. To have an impact on mathematical understanding, however, the use of technology must be consistent with mathematical goals. It must spur rather than suppress or supplant students' thinking as they learn mathematics through problem solving.

CHAPTER 8

Planning for Teaching Statistics through Problem Solving

Arthur Bakker

Koeno Gravemeijer

W HEN presenting rich problems to students, we as teachers offer them the freedom to develop their own strategies and insights. But how do we make sure that students eventually reach the intended mathematical learning goals through problem solving? The point we want to make in this chapter is that freedom for students requires careful planning by teachers and instructional designers. We use the notion of a hypothetical learning trajectory to argue that a well-designed *series* of problems is necessary to give students the opportunity for mathematical growth (also see Marcus and Fey [this volume]).

We elucidate our point with classroom episodes taken from a teaching experiment on statistical data analysis carried out in a seventh-grade classroom in the Netherlands. This teaching experiment is one of a series that builds on earlier teaching experiments carried out in Nashville, Tennessee (see Cobb [1999]; McClain, Cobb, and Gravemeijer [2000]). We used a number of similar tasks and data sets and revised versions of the same software, the so-called minitools (available for download at www.fi.uu.nl/wisweb/en and as the CD of the NCTM publication *Navigating through Data Analysis in Grades 6–8* [2003]).

After explaining what we mean by a hypothetical learning trajectory, we focus on one aspect, namely, its end goal in the instance of statistics: distribution. Classroom episodes demonstrate how students learned to reason with distribution and how their learning was guided by the designed learning trajectory and supported by using the computer tools and discussing students' own graphs.

Hypothetical Learning Trajectory

Many current reform recommendations, and chapters in this volume, suggest that the starting points for mathematics instruction should consist of settings in which students can immediately engage in informal, personally meaningful mathematical problem solving. This activity of problem solving should then bring about the transition to more sophisticated, conventional forms of mathematical activity. Teachers are advised to minimize "teaching by telling" and to help students learn the mathematics for themselves. Note that this goal implies that teachers need to focus the learning processes of students in a more indirect manner. The problem of how to do so gives rise to the following question: How can you as the teacher be sure that your students will learn what you want them to learn? In answer to this question, we put forward this seemingly contradictory thesis:

> The more autonomy you want to allow students,
> the more you must invest in planning.

Just giving students interesting problems to solve will not do the trick. The problems should give rise to solution strategies that the teacher can build on with students. If not, the teacher will be forced to use more and more eliciting or nudging to push the students in the right direction. To avoid too much of this intervention, teachers and instructional designers must plan ahead. This planning concerns the teacher's tasks of selecting instructional activities, choosing topics for discussion, and orchestrating discussions. Details of the actual planning can be elucidated with Simon's (1995) notion of a hypothetical learning trajectory.

According to Simon, the teacher should carry out thought experiments, envisioning what might happen when students work at certain problems. Or as Simon (1995, p. 133) puts it,

> The consideration of the learning goal, the learning activities, and the thinking and learning in which the students might engage make up the hypothetical learning trajectory....

Such a learning trajectory is hypothetical in that the actual thinking and learning of students may differ from what was anticipated. The teacher looks for clues that reveal this discrepancy and then makes adjustments to the hypothetical learning trajectory for subsequent instructional activities.

Central in this notion of a hypothetical learning trajectory, which leads from possible starting points to end goals, are *(a)* the instructional activities and *(b)* the mental activities of students. The choice of instructional activities is a means of influencing the mental activities of students. This choice also encompasses the choice of tools and topics for discussion.

We cannot address every aspect of a hypothetical learning trajectory, but we elucidate the trajectory framework with episodes from the teaching experiment on data analysis mentioned in our introduction. We start our sketch by discussing the end goal of the statistical sequence—the big idea of distribution—and then discuss some instructional activities, some topics of discussion, and the computer tools used.

Distribution

Students tend to have difficulties with viewing data as a plurality of values of one variable. In other words, they are inclined to see data as attributes of individuals (Hancock et al. 1992; Konold and Higgins 2002). In general, students regard "five feet" not as a value of the variable "height" but as a personal characteristic of, say, Chantal. In terms of variables, however, the measurement value is disconnected from the object or person measured and is considered against a background of possible measurement values.

The initial subjective view taken by students clouds their ability to see data as being distributed within a space of possible outcomes. Teachers must therefore try to foster a shift in students' attention from individual attributes to the notion of values of a variable. We contend that having a notion of a data set as an entity, with data distributed within a space of possible values, is a necessary condition for understanding what one might be able to deduce from conventional ways of displaying the data.

To help students come to view data sets as entities, we pose problems that can be solved by reasoning about the characteristics of data sets, not by looking at individual data points. We expect that by doing so, students will construe such statistical measures as mean, mode, median, spread, quartiles, and relative frequency as ways to characterize distributions.

This approach contrasts with statistics courses in which mean, mode, median, spread, quartiles, and frequency are taught as almost independent definitions. By aiming at distribution as the overarching statistical idea and end goal of the hypothetical learning trajectory, we can help students connect these seemingly unrelated statistical measures as characteristics of distributions and data sets, as in figure 8.1. This figure shows two simultaneous perspectives. Reading upward, we can see the mean, for example, as the result of operating on individual data and as a measure for the center of the data set. Reading downward, we can see the mean as a characteristic of a distribution. Likewise, such conventional representations as histogram and box plot come to the fore as ways to display both data and distributions. Hence, apart from addressing a big idea of statistics, this approach of focusing on distribution may also bring more coherence to a statistics curriculum unit.

Distribution (Entity)			
Position and Shape (Global Informal Aspects)			
Center	Spread	Density	Skewness
mean, median, mode, midrange, ...	range, standard deviation, interquartile range, ...	(relative) frequency, majority, outliers, ...	position majority of data, ...
Data (plurality, individual data points)			

Fig. 8.1. Different layers and aspects of distribution

How can "distribution" become an entity for middle school students? The answer lies in the observation that distribution is intimately connected with "shape." For instance, many people colloquially speak of the "bell shape" of a normal distribution (fig. 8.2), although the bell-shaped distribution entails much more than just the image.

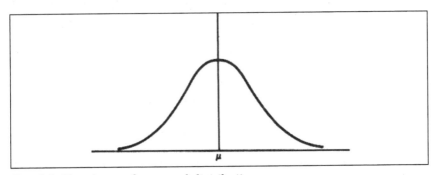

Fig. 8.2. The shape of a normal distribution

What does the graph in figure 8.2 actually mean? Let us assume that it models the distribution of the heights of a very large group of seventh-grade students. We invite the reader to consider the following questions:

- Does a point on the graph tell us a relative frequency?

- What would happen to the shape and position of the graph if we measured the same students one year later?

- What would the graph look like if we took a sample that is twice as big?

At first sight, the height of a point on the graph may seem to signify the relative frequency of a certain measurement value. This interpretation, however, is incorrect, since it would imply the existence of frequencies for infinitesimally precise values—for instance, a height of 74.53728 inch. It is very unlikely that one of the students has exactly this height, let alone that a number of them do. Alternatively, the graph can be seen as an idealization, or as the limit, of a series of histograms having interval widths that approach zero. Another way to think about this graph is as representing a density function. In that interpretation, the height of a point on the graph does not signify a relative frequency but, rather, the (probability) density at the corresponding value.

What happens if we take a sample that is twice as big? On the one hand, we might expect the bell shape to be twice as high (the upward perspective in fig. 8.1). On the other hand, we would expect the shape of the distribution to be the same, because certain phenomena tend to be distributed the same way (the downward perspective in fig. 8.1). These two perspectives can be reconciled by graphing density.

Additionally, we may conclude from this example that both shape and density are important topics for discussion within the envisioned instructional sequence for statistics. Those discussions clearly will not be about just the visual images but about what they stand for. This outcome brings us to the issue of the mental activities we aim for, or how students reason with certain statistical images. We illustrate the relationship between image and meaning with the following classroom episodes.

Classroom Episodes

In the third lesson of a sequence of fifteen, the students dealt with the following problem:

> In a certain hot-air balloon, normally eight adults are allowed. Assume you are going to take a balloon ride with a group of seventh graders. How many seventh graders could safely go into that balloon?

This instructional activity was meant to let students think about sampling, average, variation of weight, and representativeness. A common solution was that students estimated an average or typical weight both for adults and for children. Some used the ratio of those numbers to estimate the number of children that could be allowed, but most students calculated the total weight allowed and divided that value by the average student weight. The students' answers varied from 10 to 16.

This activity formed the basis for a subsequent whole-class discussion on the reliability of the estimated weights. The outcome of the discussion was that the students decided to collect the values of the height and weight for each student in the class. For the eleventh lesson, the students were asked to make a graph for the balloon driver, with which she could decide how many students she could safely take on board. We emphasized that she was not interested in just the mean but that she really needed to know more information. In this way, we expected to focus the students' attention on the whole distribution. The students drew various graphs, but the teacher focused the discussion on two of them, Michael's graph (fig. 8.3) and Elleke's graph (fig. 8.4).

The lighter, smaller case-value bars represent students' weights. (Although all students used the same data set, the values in Michael's graph do not exactly match those in Elleke's graph; Michael's graph is more like a rough sketch.) Michael's graph is espe-

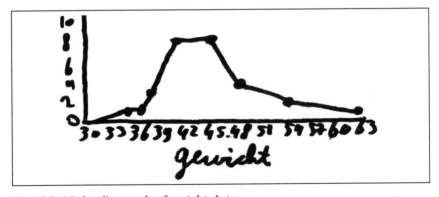

Fig. 8.3. Michael's graph of weight data

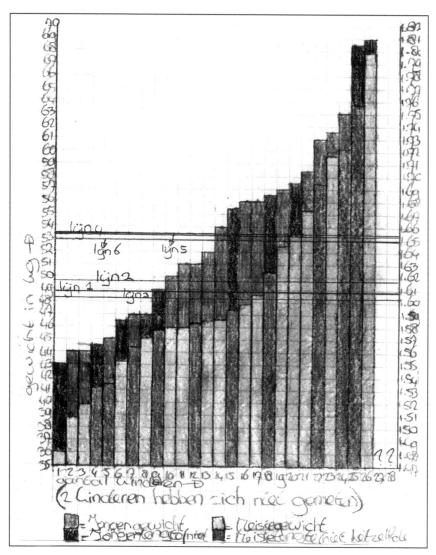

Fig. 8.4. Elleke's graph

cially interesting, since it offered the opportunity to talk about shape. In the class discussion, Michael explained how he got the dots:

Michael: Look, you have roughly, averagely speaking, how many students had that weight, and there I have put a dot. And then I have left [*y*-axis] the number of students. There is one student who weighs about 35 [kg], and there is one who weighs 36, and two who weigh 38 roughly. And then I have put, yeah ...

Teacher: Have just put dots.

The dot at 48 signifies about four students whose weights are around 48 kilograms. After some other graphs, including Elleke's (fig. 8.4), had been discussed, the teacher engaged the class in the following discussion:

Teacher: What can you easily see in this graph [pointing to Michael's graph]?

Laila: Well, that the average, that most students in the class, uhm, well, are between 39 and, well, 48.

Teacher: Yes, here you can see at once which weight most students in this class roughly have, what is about the biggest group. Just because you see this bump here. We lost the bump in Elleke's graph.

Apparently, Michael's graph helped the class see the majority of the data—between 39 and 48 kg. The teacher first used the word *bump* to draw students' attention to the shape of the data. By saying that "we lost the bump in Elleke's graph," she invited the students to think about an explanation. Nadia indeed explained what had happened to the bump in Elleke's graph.

Nadia: The difference between ... they stand from small to tall, so the bump, that is where the things, where the bars are closest to one another.

Teacher: What do you mean, where the bars are closest?

Nadia: The difference, the ends [of the bars], do not differ so much with the next one. In comparing these two graphs, students had to explain this apparent conflict. Eva added to Nadia's remarks as the following discussion ensued:

Eva: If you look well, then you see that almost in the middle, there it is straight almost, and, uh, yeah, that [teacher points at the horizontal part in Elleke's graph].

Teacher: And that is what you [Nadia] also said, uh, they are close together and here they are bunched up, as far as height or weight is concerned.

Eva: And that is also that bump.

These episodes demonstrate that for the students, the bump was not merely a visual characteristic of a certain graph but an indication of a relatively large number of data points having approximately the same value—both in a hill-type graph and in a value-bar graph. For the students, the bump signified a range in which a relatively high density of data points occurred. This perception does not mean that Michael's graph is a conventional density graph, but his representation might be seen as an informal precursor to it. The students often referred to the bump as "the majority." Without actually using the word *density*, the students appeared to be thinking and reasoning about density and shape in the way intended. This outcome is based on students' prior experiences (see next section), and it is substantiated by further observations, later in the teaching experiment, in the thirteenth lesson.

In that lesson we learned that asking students to predict and reason without available data was helpful in fostering a global view of data, for instance, when the teacher asked about the weights of eighth graders as opposed to those of seventh graders.

Teacher: What would a graph of the weights of eighth graders look like?

Luuk: I think about the same, but another size, other numbers.

Guyonne: The bump would be more to the right.

Teacher: What would it mean for the box plots?

Michael: Also moves to the right. That bump in the middle is in fact just the box plot, which moves more to the right.

Luuk reasons with individual numbers, but he still thinks that the shape will be about the same. Instead of moving individual data points to the right, Guyonne sees the bump as a singular entity being shifted to the right. Shifting hills, or box plots, is indeed one of the mental activities we wanted to foster.

Another prediction question also led to reasoning about bumps, this time in relation to another statistical notion: sample size.

Researcher: If you were to measure all seventh graders in the city instead of just your class, how would the graph change, or wouldn't it change?

Elleke: Then there would come a little more to the left and a little more to the right. Then the bump would become a little wider, I think. [She explained this using an informal notion of outliers.]

Researcher: Is there anybody who does not agree?

Michael: Yes, if there are more children, then the average, so the most, that also becomes more. So the bump stays just the same.

Albertine: I think that the number of children becomes more and that the bump stays the same.

In this episode, Elleke refers shape to outliers; she thinks that the bump will grow wider if the sample grows. Michael argues that the majority will also grow higher, implying for him that the bump will keep the same shape. Albertine's answer is interesting in that she seems to think of relative frequency. For her, too, the shape of the distribution seems to be independent of the sample size. Apparently, the notion of a bump helps these students reason about the predicted shape of the distribution and overcome the problem of seeing only individual data points.

Representational Backbone of the Learning Trajectory

The described classroom episodes are part of a series of lessons and, as such, fit in a preplanned learning trajectory in which the already mentioned statistical minitools have been used. To sketch this learning trajectory, we start by investigating what knowledge is necessary to understand the two shown graphs. Elleke's graph (fig. 8.4) is the more straightforward, namely, a value-bar graph: each bar signifies one value, and the length of the bar corresponds with the magnitude of that value. Each dot in Michael's graph (fig. 8.3) signifies the number of cases with similar values. In line with this analysis, the learning trajectory starts with the introduction of a simple computer minitool that displays individual data as value bars (fig. 8.5). Elleke's graph was clearly inspired by that first minitool.

In the first instructional activities with this first minitool (see McClain et al. [2000]), the students started reasoning on the basis

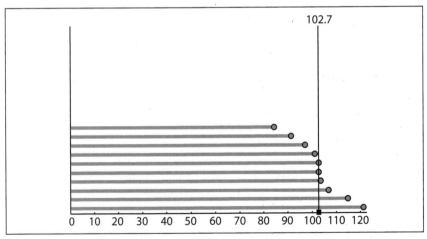

Fig. 8.5. Minitool 1: value bars, ordered by size, with a reference line at 102.7

of the end points of the bars. This occasion justified the introduction of the second minitool, which uses only endpoints and which displays data sets as dot plots (fig. 8.6).

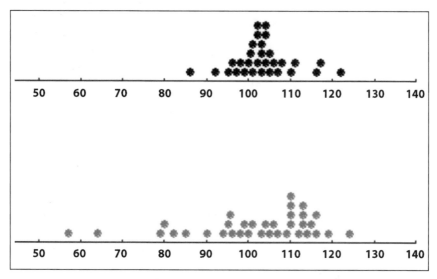

Fig. 8.6. Minitool 2: dot plot, separated by shade to show two subsets

With the dot plot we are getting closer to conventional graphs in which distributions are depicted as curves. The data points in the dot plot of minitool 2 can be structured in different ways. One option is to create equal intervals (fig. 8.7); this activity is meant as a precursor to introduction of the histogram.

When students compare data sets displayed by dot plots to answer a question or to make a decision, they get the opportuni-

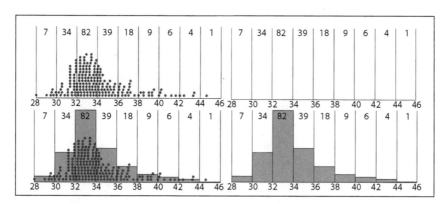

Fig. 8.7. Minitool 2 with equal intervals, histogram option, and hide-data options

ty to reason about the shape of the data set in a more conventional way than with value bars. As a means of support, students can also use another minitool option, one that partitions the data into four equal groups (fig. 8.8), a representation that serves as a precursor to the box plot. In this representation, the interval width emerges as a crude measure for density. The smaller the interval, the more packed up the data points are. Finally, students can use the four-equal-groups inscription to see or describe the hill-shaped curve of a unimodal distribution.

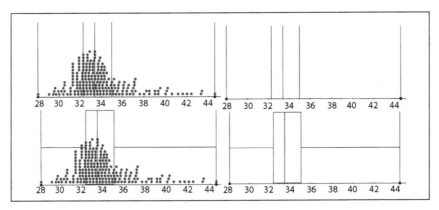

Fig. 8.8. Minitool 2: four equal groups, box plot, and hide data options

These simple minitools are very different from data-analysis software packages complete with many conventional ways of representing data (see, e.g., fig. 8.9). Such packages are powerful tools for those already familiar with expert ways of understanding the statistical ideas related to these conventional representations. However, for students who are just beginning to learn about these statistical ideas, conventional software is not a good starting point, because students do not yet conceptualize data in ways that enable them to make good choices from the array of conventional representations. The ability to use such software is more a possible end point of our hypothetical learning trajectory than a tool for learning conventional graphs. We mention this point to emphasize the importance of choosing the right educational tools in a hypothetical learning trajectory.

Conclusion

At the beginning of this chapter, we posed the question of how to make sure that the problem-solving activity of students eventually results in their reaching certain pregiven statistical learn-

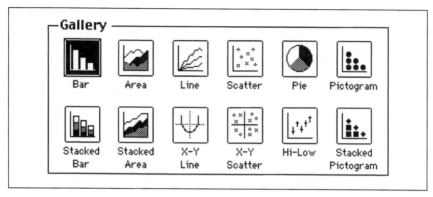

Fig. 8.9. A menu of ways to display data in ClarisWorks

ing goals. We argued that freedom for students requires careful planning by teachers and instructional designers. The notion of a hypothetical learning trajectory can function as a paradigm for such careful planning. This planning must involve the instructional activities, the mental activities of the students, and the end goals of the learning experience. We elaborated the notion of distribution-as-an-entity as the end goal of our learning trajectory in statistical data analysis. Such issues as shape and density turned out to be important topics of discussion, and we showed how these issues came to the fore in students' thinking and reasoning in some classroom episodes taken from a teaching experiment of fifteen class periods. These episodes showed that the students used the word *bump,* which was introduced as a visual characteristic of a graph, for the majority of the data points, and that it became a conceptual reasoning tool.

The whole-class discussions about students' graphs revealed both the power of using students' own contributions and also the importance of planning. The teacher chose specific graphs to make the meaning of the bump in Michael's graph a topic of discussion. The students then made the connection with the straight part in Elleke's graph. We want to emphasize that the students were able to reason about the characteristics of graphs only because of their participation in the preceding activities in the instructional sequence. This foundation allowed the students to interpret Michael's graph in the way they did. We also want to emphasize the important role of the choice of appropriate tools—in this sequence, the statistical minitools—when planning for teaching through problem solving.

Who Is in Charge Here?

Allan Bellman

JULIAN asks, "How long is the skid mark?" Tanya tells you her group needs to know how to determine a coefficient of friction. After Margaret asks about rain, Tu whispers to her group, huddled around a computer screen, "Do we need to know if it's raining?" Three boys and a girl toss a hat toward a trash can, one shouting, "Harder, harder!" A group drags a block of wood attached to a probe across the classroom floor.

This is your class; are you a teacher or a referee?

Modeling and Active Learning

In my mathematics classes, I am both, and I am also a learner, since I do not necessarily know the answer to the problems either. The class is using real data to solve real-life problems—in the same way as the police do or as any company's management does—and here, in the classroom, the process is as important as the answer; the methods the students devise, as crucial as the mathematics used.

Students use mathematical modeling in the problem-solving process to determine from the length of skid marks whether the driver contributed to an accident being investigated by police. When they try to find how far a hat flew when it was caught by the wind, they are being introduced to parametric equations. They drag wood across carpets to see how police find the coefficient of friction at accident sites. Yes, they are investigating real situations.

Allan Bellman spent thirty-one years as a high school mathematics teacher in the Montgomery County, Maryland, School System.

Thirty years ago, we mixed a lot of candy, sent a lot of trains to their destinations, and calculated how Mary's age related to that of every other woman on earth. Now, though, we try to make mathematics more relevant. In a given classroom, three groups of students working on the same problem, but with three different sets of assumptions, may find three different and equally correct solutions. Problems no longer sit lifelessly on the pages of a textbook. Now these problems come from the local police files, the FBI, athletic shoe sales, perceived TV interference, in other words, from everyday life. And that is where we, as teachers, get the data for activities and where we, as today's mathematics teachers, actually teach.

The confluence of a number of factors in the 1980s worked to change the applications that I used and, thus, the way I taught:

- The NCTM *Curriculum and Evaluation Standards for School Mathematics* (1989) gave a call for using applications and problem solving and also provided valuable examples to use as starting points.

- The mathematical-modeling role models that we did not have when we ourselves were students started to appear as more and more workshop sessions were devoted to modeling, applications, and problem solving.

- Technology advanced to the point that it was affordable, available, and useable. Various technological tools allowed us to collect and investigate real data in ways not possible before. We could now engage our students in more authentic problem-solving activities.

In my mind, the advance in handheld technology was probably the most important of the three factors cited above. Once data-collection devices that interfaced with calculators became available, students could design and implement simulations that showed the relationships between the mathematics they were studying and the world in which they lived. Students could not only design and perform these simulations but also take the data home to study. In addition, the graphing and statistical capabilities of calculators often made the use of real data practical.

If you were to visit my second-year-algebra class over any two-day period, on at least one of the days the class would be heavily involved in a problem-solving activity. What would one of these activities involve? To get an idea, let me describe one of my favorites.

A Sample Activity

Mathematically, this activity is used to study the quadratic function, the addition of functions, and the concept of modeling. The students enjoy it because it is studied during the year they are looking forward to getting that all-important driver's license. I have also received strong positive parental feedback that this problem encourages their teenagers to really understand what is happening when they are driving and need to stop.

You work for the accident-investigation unit of your local police department. You have been called to the scene of an accident. A car coming around a blind corner has hit another car, which had broken down and was stopped in the street. Luckily, no one was injured. You will be asked to help determine whether the driver of the car was in some way at fault. Was he speeding? Since he was coming around the corner, did he have sufficiently early warning to stop? Once you have written your report, answer the following questions:

- On what assumptions did you base your model?

- Compare your answer with those of other groups. Do you agree? If not, why not? Did the discrepancy arise because of the use of different information, a different method, or different assumptions?

- If you are driving down the street and a ball rolls in front of you, what factors would determine how long, and thus how far you would travel, before you could come to a complete stop?

- Besides the information that was given to you when you asked, what other details do you think the police would need to know about the situation? Why?

In small groups, students define the problem and determine the information they will need to begin work toward a solution. Next they determine where to find that information. Some information comes from their experiential backgrounds. Some can be found by researching the World Wide Web or a library's resources. Some can be provided by calculator-based-laboratory simulations. If asked, I provide the information that is typically culled from, in this example, the accident site. The groups start to develop a model, revise assumptions, and rework approaches. Sometimes a group scraps all it has done and starts again. The process is dynamic.

My role is to provide the slimmest amount of information possible while monitoring students' progress. I get involved only if necessary to allow a group to maintain its momentum.

For this problem, when asked, I provide the length of the skid mark (89 feet), the distance from the accident to the corner (225 feet), and the speed limit along that stretch of roadway (45 mph). But the students must determine on their own which information is pertinent to the problem.

As students develop their models, different groups typically work with different information. In this example, most of the information was found through a search of the World Wide Web (the Web). One group may have found on the Web the formula $s = \sqrt{30Dfn}$, where s = speed, D = skid, f = coefficient of friction, and n = braking efficiency. Another group may have found the data in table TS2.1 on the Web. A third group may use information from a driver's handbook.

Table TS2.1

World Wide Web Data for the Accident-Scene Problem

Speed	Braking Distance	Perception/Reaction Distance	Total Stopping Distance
10	5	22	27
20	19	44	63
30	43	66	109
40	76	88	164
50	119	110	229
60	172	132	304
70	234	154	388

The students develop the search parameters and perform the search themselves. My function is to determine the type of information that I cannot expect them to find on their own within a realistic time frame. I also continue to monitor their progress, although I function differently in this role as compared with several years ago.

Once each group determines which information it will use, technology again plays a major role. With "real" data, either collected with scientific equipment or found at a Web site, the models and answers rarely involve integers or simple fractions. The ease with which students can analyze the data encourages them to invest the time needed to complete the activities. Without technology, all analysis would be performed by hand, a task that would "turn most students off."

With handheld graphing calculators, students have numerous methods to determine a quadratic model that fits the data in table TS2.1. They could use three points, matrices, and systems of equations. They could use the built-in regression capability of the calculator. They could use the vertex-and-one-point method. Or they could use some of the interactive, dynamic modeling features that have recently appeared on calculators. The screen shots in figure TS2.1 illustrate a linear model being developed by interactive, dynamic "eyeball fit" modeling.

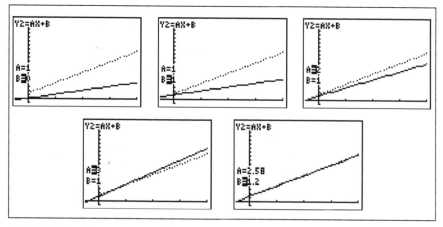

Fig. TS2.1. Changing a and b to eyeball fit a linear model

During the activity, students work on their own, talking within their groups, using the computers in the room, devising and performing simulations, and approaching me for information. I make certain that the individual members of each group are involved in the process and making progress individually as well as with the group. I intercede as necessary to ask probing questions as I move from group to group.

As groups find solutions, they discuss their findings and begin to write their reports. Once the reports are completed, the students confer with other groups. My job remains that of monitoring their progress and activity. I try to allow as much freedom as possible while keeping the classroom as close to "under control" as I think necessary. The classroom can become like a three-ring circus in which I am the ringleader. An observer can see the excitement that is generated as the pieces start to fit together for each group. The process is exciting to watch, almost breathtaking.

Once all group reports are in final (for the time being) form, a class discussion ensues. The members of each group present their solution, the method that they used to reach that solution, the assumptions they made, and where they found the required information. For this problem, the groups used three different solution methods.

During the wrap-up, students can learn new mathematical methods and concepts from one another as they discuss their differing methods and findings. This format allows me an opportunity to direct the learning of mathematics. After this problem-solving activity, I usually schedule a visit from the local police, who discuss how they determine speed at an accident site. The police have always done a nice job with this visit, frequently leaving skid marks in the school parking lot and then discussing their formulas and the many possible variations from the norm.

Reflections on the Activity

Are all the groups usually successful? Yes. Can the same be said about each individual? With this particular problem, I have always thought that everyone was successful by the end of the activity. But what is success? Every student is usually able to answer the two main questions. No matter which method is used, each group is able to determine that the driver was not speeding and that he had more than enough time to stop. The students conclude that the driver contributed to the accident.

For me, getting those answers is not the primary purpose of the activity. Arriving at those answers means that the students developed, or found, a mathematical model and used it correctly. It also means that they were able to interpret the issue of total stopping distance and how it relates to a driver's ability to stop in time. More important to me, they were able to pursue an open-ended question by—

- understanding the underlying mathematical concepts, such as function, and how they relate to this real-world problem;

- developing a reasonable mathematical model for the problem situation;

- determining what information was needed to solve the problem and where to find this information;

- recognizing that their answer was based on a large number of assumptions and that their answer would be different if they had used different assumptions;

- justifying why different groups got slightly different answers;

- recognizing and being comfortable with the fact that the different answers were equally "correct," since those differences arose because of different assumptions;

- recognizing what changes in their assumptions or approach would produce the same answer that another group got using a different method;

- finding estimates either by research or by simulation of the coefficient of friction, reaction time, and braking efficiency as required in the formula; and

- working together with classmates in an undirected but supervised environment.

My second-year-algebra class deals mainly with function families and their properties and applications. Some activities use the functions as they are being studied. Others use functions from previous chapters and serve as a review of previously acquired skills. Others serve as an opportunity to introduce representations that differ from those previously taught in second-year algebra. For example, we have studied logistic growth and used parametric equations to study motion in an average second-year-algebra class. Still other activities, in effect, look into the future. These investigations usually preview functions that are to be studied later. For functions they have not studied before, students devise models as best they can. They realize that these models might not be optimal but are adequate for an estimate of the required answer as long as a number of conditions are met. These, they call the "best-for-now models." This approach allows students to learn about new functions and models as the course progresses.

A Final Note

When I moved entirely to teaching through problem solving, mainly with modeling problems, in my second-year-algebra courses, I was apprehensive. This approach was something for which I had no role models and very few materials and in which I would have to relinquish control in the classroom. But I discovered that a dynamic kind of learning takes place. Students say that they enjoy the course, can see a purpose for mathematics, and have ownership of their work; and they do well in subsequent courses. Ownership might be the pivotal element, since from start to finish, students invest a great deal of time and effort in the problem-solving tasks. They make sense of the problems and the underlying mathematics, and they design and implement their solution strategies. At different times, I might direct, support, and monitor their work, but it remains their work. Imagine my excitement when a student says, "Hey, this function fits the data we had last month. Let's go back to that problem, and see if it changes our conclusion."

Section 3

In the Classroom

CHAPTER 9

The Teacher's Role in Teaching Mathematics through Problem Solving

Douglas A. Grouws

A FEW secondary school students can learn mathematics and become expert problem solvers through independent study and by solving many mathematical problems. Very few. For the vast majority of students, becoming mathematically proficient and developing problem-solving expertise involve studying mathematics under the guidance of a well-qualified teacher who selects problems that embody important mathematical ideas and then ensures that the mathematics involved in these problems is brought to the surface and made explicit. This chapter identifies and discusses teaching strategies that have the potential to help students learn important mathematical ideas as they work on significant mathematical tasks and move toward becoming mathematically literate. Following the organizational framework used by Charles and Lester (1982), I examine the teacher's role in instruction before, during, and after lessons designed to teach mathematics through a problem-solving approach.

The Teacher's Role

The teacher's role in fostering students' mathematical learning is central and deserves greater attention than it has received in recent years. Does effective mathematics teaching involve more than forming small groups and assigning good problems for students to solve? Of course it does, and the purpose of this chapter is to delve into the many decisions that teachers make that influence the quality of the mathematics their students learn. The teacher's role in directing the development of students' mathematical knowledge is indeed complex. The responsibility is difficult to fulfill because it involves simultaneously fostering students' knowledge accumulation and developing their mathematical abilities. The mathematical proficiency we seek requires depth of knowledge and includes the strands of conceptual understanding, procedural fluency, strategic competence, adaptive reasoning, and productive disposition (National Research Council 2001). A teacher must bring all these components together in lessons while simultaneously taking into account students' abilities and backgrounds. No wonder knowledgeable people proclaim that teaching mathematics is one of the most demanding professions.

Before the Lesson

When one watches a great mathematics lesson, the "behind the scenes" time and effort that have been devoted to planning and perfecting the lesson are not often evident. The impact of a lesson on students' learning is greatly influenced by more than what one can observe in watching a lesson. For example, careful attention to the mathematical ideas to be taught is essential in preparing the lesson, and such attention to detail has been shown to be associated with high achievement on the part of students (Stigler and Hiebert 1999). We begin by examining how attention can be given to mathematics content as we consider some of the important decisions that teachers make prior to teaching a lesson that promotes mathematical proficiency. Of necessity, I discuss these teaching decisions one at a time, understanding that all aspects of teaching are deeply interconnected. Teaching decisions in one area must take into account the entire teaching context because changing one instructional component always affects, directly or indirectly, other components.

Using Tasks to Structure Lessons

Teaching mathematics through problem solving has been described carefully in preceding chapters. In reading this chapter, an important point to remember is that successfully implementing such an approach involves many teacher decisions and actions, which include, to name a few, choosing appropriate tasks, conveying tasks to students in ways that stimulate interest, maintaining students' engagement in tasks, and leading discussions in which the important mathematical ideas embedded in the tasks are brought to the surface. As we consider these teaching decisions and roles, we arrive at the clear conclusion that teaching through problem solving is quite different from other activities that sometimes masquerade as such, including discussing problems-of-the-week, playing strategy games, working on logic puzzles, and focusing on application-type problems at the end of textbook chapters. One of the most important distinctions between teaching through problem solving and teaching that simply involves using problems is how tasks are chosen.

Choosing Appropriate Tasks

Mathematics educators usually agree that the mathematical tasks teachers choose to use in their teaching affect not only the mathematics that students learn but also the depth and quality of that learning. In fact, some research evidence shows that using mathematically rich tasks in the classroom, even though used poorly, can have positive effects on students' learning (Stein and Lane 1996).

Teachers can select tasks that develop important aspects of mathemetical proficiency. These components include the learning of mathematical concepts (e.g., prime numbers), skills (e.g., computational estimation), problem-solving techniques (e.g., "guess and check"), methods of reasoning (e.g., pigeonhole principle), and proof techniques (e.g., exhaustion), to name a few. Elaborated examples of how carefully chosen tasks can lead to the preceding learning outcomes can be found in other chapters of this volume. A reasoning example is presented here.

Reasoning example

The importance of developing mathematical reasoning is touted in most, if not all, recent recommendations for school mathematics (e.g., NCTM [2000]; National Research Council [2001]). As we shall see later, mathematical reasoning can be promoted through appropriate teacher questioning when discussing a wide variety of rich mathematical tasks. Many useful reasoning strategies exist that students should acquire, and teachers can make progress toward this goal by carefully selecting tasks in which to engage students. Consider the pigeonhole reasoning strategy, for example. Simply stated, it says that if we have a finite number of holes, say, n, and we place $n + 1$ pigeons in these holes, then we will have a hole with at least two pigeons in it. The strategy has applicability to a wide variety of mathematical problems and situations ranging from the simple to the complex, and from arithmetic to probability to abstract algebra. By carefully choosing an appropriate task, a teacher can help students learn to use the strategy and develop other mathematical ideas at the same time. Consider the following examples chosen from different areas of mathematics:

Probability task

What is the minimum number of times you have to roll a fair die before you can be certain that you will get an outcome that is a repeat of a previous roll?

One solution. Think of each of the six outcomes possible on a single roll of the die as your pigeonholes ($n = 6$); then from the pigeonhole principle, by the seventh roll you will always have a repeated outcome (i.e., two pigeons in the same pigeonhole). Note that one can easily show by example that any number of rolls less than seven will not satisfy the problem conditions.

Number theory task

Given any nine integers, show that you can choose two of them whose difference is a multiple of 8.

One solution. The reader is encouraged to try to find the solution before reading on. Notice that any number divided by 8 has one of eight remainders, 0 through 7. These remainders are our eight pigeonholes. The nine given numbers are our pigeons. By the pigeonhole principle, two of the numbers are in the same hole and thus have the same remainder when divided by 8, say, r. Thus, through some symbolic representation and algebraic manipulation, we can show that the two numbers can be expressed as $8m + r$ and $8n + r$, with m and n being integers. Their difference is $8 (m - n)$, which is divisible by 8.

In choosing tasks that are appropriate and productive, some general learning principles are helpful to keep in mind:

- The tasks presented to students affect the mathematical concepts and skills that students are likely to acquire as they complete the task.

On the one hand, one cannot predict with precision the exact learning path a student will follow during the course of a lesson or in working with a task; yet one can be quite confident that students will interact with a specific mathematical idea if the task is carefully selected to embody that idea, as shown in the preceding examples. On the other hand, if one chooses a task without regard to a given mathematical objective, then the likelihood of a student's learning something about that objective is remote.

- The tasks presented to students affect the problem-solving techniques and habits of mind that students learn.

Students should acquire many problem-solving techniques as part of the secondary school mathematics curriculum. Giving explicit attention to these techniques in lesson planning is appropriate. Familiar techniques that quickly come to mind include making an organized list, guessing and checking, using the method of exhaustion, applying the pigeonhole principle, and making a diagram. A careful choice of tasks allows students to explore and learn a particular problem-solving technique as part of a lesson. The same can be said for habits of mind (see Levasseur and Cuoco [this volume]).

- The tasks presented to students should require a high level of cognitive demand to promote the development of a deep knowledge of mathematics.

What do I mean by high cognitive demand in tasks? One way to think about this idea is simply to consider the amount of thinking and sense making needed to complete the task. If the task focuses primarily on recall or on simple application of a learned procedure, then it is at the lower end of a continuum of cognitive demand. But if the task requires using connections between ideas, or making new connections, or working in a new context, or putting several procedures and concepts together in a new way, or some combination of these approaches, then the task is at the upper end of the continuum. Clearly, a task with a high cognitive demand will not be completed quickly nor have an immediately obvious solution path.

Teachers have numerous good reasons to strive to include tasks that embody a high cognitive demand in their lessons. First, using these tasks allows students to engage in "doing" mathematics and thus gives them opportunities to develop the capacity to think and reason mathematically. Second, research evidence shows that even when teachers begin with high-demand tasks, the tasks have a tendency to decline in cognitive demand as they are implemented in the classroom (Smith 2000; Stein, Grover, and Henningsen 1996). Thus, starting with high-level tasks becomes even more important. Finally, when students engage in tasks that go beyond memorizing facts and applying known formulas and procedures, they develop a better sense of what mathematics is, that is, a discipline in which the ideas make sense, are logically related to one another, and can be used to solve nontrivial problems.

Another way of thinking about choosing tasks is to focus on selection criteria. The following criteria, some of which are discussed in more detail by Marcus and Fey in this volume, are important in choosing good tasks. A good task generally has the following characteristics:

- It is centered on an important mathematical idea, concept, or skill that is part of a course of study.

- It is clearly stated, that is, it is not unintentionally vague or misleading.

- It involves an important real-world context or mathematical context that has the potential to attract and maintain students' interest.

- It can be solved with a range of methods from informal to more formal. Its solution or solutions can be productively approached at several levels of sophistication.

- It has interesting extensions. Most rich tasks have interesting extensions, and these extensions are valuable for at least three reasons. First, they help the teacher accommodate individual differences within the classroom. Simpler versions of the task can be assigned to students having difficulties, and more complex extensions can be used to challenge high-achieving students who finish the initial task quickly. Second, allowing students to suggest extensions to tasks is a nice segue to problem posing, a process that has been associated with increasing students' learning. (See Goldenberg and Walter [this volume] for more information on problem posing.) Third, looking at problem extensions can often lead to students' making and verifying mathematical generalizations, two important skills that mathematically proficient students should have.

Forming Good Questions

A good question captures one's interest, starts mental activity, and may stimulate creative thinking. Given this potential, a teacher must carefully form some appropriate questions in advance as part of lesson preparation. In this preparation, he or she should pay particular attention to generating questions that promote students' ability to make generalizations, that provide hints for making progress on a task without giving away the solution path, and that stimulate higher-order thinking. These types of questions are the most difficult to form in the midst of a class session, yet they have great potential to enhance students' learning.

Class Organization and Lesson Structure

One of the decisions a teacher makes in planning a lesson is how the class will be organized for the lesson. Many choices and combinations of choices are available. Certainly the most popular lesson format in secondary school mathematics classrooms is the whole-class arrangement. However, having students work in small groups has been used increasingly in recent years, and other formats, such as student presentations and independent study, are used regularly by some teachers for either an entire lesson or part of a lesson. Any of these formats can be used successfully; their effectiveness depends, in large part, on how they are used. Because small-group instruction has been strongly advocated for greater use by many mathematics educators and because it has been used inappropriately in some situations, I give it special consideration in the discussion that follows. The focus on it should not be taken as a signal that it is the preferred method of teaching mathematics through problem solving.

The Role of Small Groups in Problem Solving

Including small-group work when teaching through a problem-solving approach can facilitate mathematical discussions. Small-group work presents opportunities for more students to verbalize their questions and thinking than whole-class instruction does. Further, for some students, participating in small groups may be less intimidating than engaging in whole-class discussions. Two important principles should be considered when making decisions about the use of small groups.

- Not every problem or task lends itself to small-group work. In general, for a problem having one primary solution path and a single solution, small-group work may degenerate to a situation in which one student in the group—often, but not always, the highest achieving student—solves the problem and explains it to the other students. Teachers can reduce the likelihood of this occurrence by using a variety of techniques (see, e.g., Artzt and Newman [1997]; Davidson and Worsham [1992]), including assigning unique roles for each student to assume within the group or insisting that every student in the group must be able to explain the group's solution to the task. When selecting tasks for small-group work, however, teachers can select from many rich tasks and so have no need to limit problems to those that have a predominant solution path and a single correct answer.

- Tasks that have a variety of reasonably apparent, viable solution methods and multiple solutions are good task choices for group work. Such tasks allow students to pursue solutions in different ways and then to describe their solution paths to their peers. This process demonstrates that generally many ways are available to solve a mathematical problem and provides practice in communicating orally about mathematics. Further, because multiple solutions to the task are possible, different students can contribute different parts to the total solution.

In closing this section, a point worth mentioning again is that what a teacher does within a chosen lesson organization is particularly important, and we discuss this role and these decisions next.

During the Lesson

Teachers make literally thousands of decisions each day as they teach their lessons (Good and Brophy 1996). They make some of the more important decisions early in the lesson when the tasks for the day are conveyed to students and they begin work. Although one cannot prescribe how to present a task, benchmarks can provide a useful basis for successful presentations.

Presenting Tasks

Obviously, an interesting task will motivate students to begin work on it. To make significant progress toward solving a problem and learning the mathematics within it, however, requires that students come to fully understand the task, that is, to know what is given and what is to be found or shown in more than a superficial way. When difficulties arise at this introductory stage and the teacher senses that students are beginning to lose interest, she or he can often help the students refocus on the task by asking direct questions about what is given and what is to be found. This questioning may include asking students to tell the meaning of various terms and phrases in the task or modeling the problem in some way using either symbols or actions. In the latter instance, the teacher is wise to draw attention initially to problem conditions and not to potential solution methods or paths.

One presentation strategy that some teachers have found effective is presenting a task in several parts, with early parts relatively easy to solve and subsequent parts more challenging. See Marcus and Fey in this volume for examples that use this strategy. This teaching strategy also attends to individual differences among students in the class by allowing slow workers sufficient time to complete at least the first part of the task and by providing high-achieving students with engaging work to do after they quickly finish the first part of the task. At some point in a lesson, a discussion of (a) the task, (b) its various solution paths, and (c) valid solutions is essential to ensure that the mathematics embedded within the task is brought to the surface and that every student develops an understanding of it. Questioning plays an important role in these culminating discussions.

Using Questions

Educators generally agree that students learn best from instruction when they are actively involved, that is, when they are mentally interacting with the ideas being considered. Asking questions is one way to promote intellectual involvement. Although questions asked by students are an important and productive part of every successful mathematics lesson, a teacher with a deep and thorough understanding of mathematics can pose questions that not only foster students' involvement but also lead directly to the development of important mathematical ideas and understandings—the "residue" ideas.

Some guidelines for teachers as they ask questions are the following:

- Encourage reasoned guessing, not savage guessing (Pólya 1945).

- Establish the norm that students' responses should include a rationale (Mason, Burton, and Stacey 1982).

- Always be aware of who is doing the thinking, the teacher or the student.

Teachers' questions that encourage students' thinking are especially important in conducting good lessons. The following questions are some that can be used to promote students' thinking:

- How did you decide on a solution method to try?

- How did you solve the problem?

- Did anyone solve it in a different way?

- How would you compare these solution methods?

- Which of the solution methods do you like best? Why?

- Can you tell me how you solved the problem without saying the answer?

- Does this problem remind you of any other problems you have solved?

- How can we change the problem to get another interesting problem?

- What mistakes do you think some students might make in solving this problem?

Clearly the preceding list of suggested questions is far from exhaustive, but it is indicative of the type of open-ended questions that cause students to think about, and reflect on, mathematical ideas.

Creating Classroom Climate and Developing Mathematical Dispositions

Classroom climate is shaped largely by the decisions a teacher makes about many lesson components, including the mathematical tasks considered, the amount of time devoted to investigation, the value placed on discussion, the treatment of incorrect answers and errors in reasoning, the placement of authority with regard to correctness, and so on. The teacher directly or indirectly controls all these factors and thus is a major determiner of classroom climate. I discuss a limited number of aspects of classroom climate here. See Rasmussen, Yackel, and King in this volume for a detailed discussion of social norms and classroom climate.

The way teachers react to students' responses and questions has a major influence on classroom climate. And classroom climate affects students' willingness to respond to questions, describe their thinking, share their solution methods, posit hypotheses, suggest generalizations, and, in general, participate in "doing" mathematics in the classroom. What kind of classroom climate is needed? Certainly the atmosphere to seek is one in which effort is valued and mistakes are recognized as a means to learn. An emphasis on giving reasons for responses and a focus on making sense of the mathematics are also necessary. As one would expect, developing such a classroom climate takes time. We emphasize here that how a teacher acts and reacts in front of a class communicates to students important notions about how mathematics is done and about the nature of mathematics. Consider the following three ideas:

- How a teacher solves a problem in front of the class is crucial. A teacher must do some acting as he or she solves a task for the class, as Pólya (1945) pointed out long ago. Because the task presented is often an exercise for the teacher, how she acts out solving it influences greatly what students think about how problems are solved in mathematics. As we all know, solving a mathematics problem involves advances and retreats, and moments of frustration and excitement, to name but a few of the cognitive and emotional components. A teacher should communicate these components to students while demonstrating a solution to a task, teaching students not always to expect a smooth march to a mathematical problem's solution. Accepting that difficulties are normal and that they should not be a cause for distress or quitting is a lesson that can have positive long-term effects. For this reason alone, teachers need to regularly solve problems in front of the class.

- A teacher should handle inappropriate solution methods and incorrect solutions that students bring forward in a way that conveys the idea that mathematics must make sense. That is, often the teacher can discuss an incorrect method or solution in a way that pinpoints a student's false assumption by showing that had the assumption been true, then the student's proposed solution method or answer would have been correct. Dealing with a student's idea in this respectful way casts a positive light on the student's response and is far preferable to a response that dismisses the proposed method or solution out of hand.

- Through questioning and modeling solutions, teachers can help students develop habits of mind that will be useful to them in all their mathematical studies. Consider the following questions: (1) Is the answer reasonable? (2) Did I recheck the steps taken to find the solution? (3) Is this problem related to other problems? (4) Can I change the problem to make it easier to solve? (5) Is another solution possible? Asking these questions of students or mentioning them aloud when solving a problem in front of the class suggests that these questions are reasonable for anyone to ask when solving a problem, possibly fostering their use by students whenever they confront a mathematical task or situation. In general, some of the attributes of classroom interaction that facilitate the development of a positive learning climate and desirable habits of mind are these:

  ➤ Learning mathematics as sense-making prevails.

  ➤ Reasonable guessing, as opposed to savage guessing, is valued.

  ➤ Sharing one's thinking is expected.

  ➤ Justifying one's assertions is the norm.

Focusing on Students' Thinking

The means available for assessing students' thinking generally involve questioning or interviewing, listening to students' responses, and carefully observing their written work. As previously mentioned, questions carefully prepared in advance can be of major help in generating the data about students' thinking that the teacher needs to proceed with a lesson in a productive manner. Observing students' written work while they are working on a task can also foster useful insights into students' thinking and into misconceptions they may hold. Given that time for observation is short, teachers should not feel compelled to examine the work of every student during the class period. Indeed, more benefit may be gained by looking at just a few papers, but each in some depth. Through experience, a teacher gains insight into what to look for and how to effectively deal with specific student responses that arise. Although successful methods of carefully attending to students' thinking and students' work are difficult to communicate, the value of these activities has been shown in several programs of research. For further discussion of listening to students, see the chapter by Driscoll in this volume.

After the Lesson

After a lesson has been taught, a teacher should take time to reflect on the lesson, thinking about how subsequent lessons can build on, and be linked with, the current lesson and previous lessons. The ideas learned in one lesson must be reviewed, extended, and linked with the ideas from other lessons. Connecting lessons in this way promotes students' learning—learning that can be represented as a meaningful network of ideas. Forming such a network of connected ideas is essential in developing a deep knowledge of mathematics (Hiebert and Carpenter 1992). In addition to logically connecting ideas among lessons, a teacher needs to consider students' work as part of the process of planning future lessons.

Examining and Taking Account of Students' Work

Students' thinking must be studied while a lesson is being taught, and students' written work should be carefully examined after a lesson has been taught. But what should be the focus of such assessments? The most obvious things to look for are students' misconceptions, error patterns, and other observations that fall under the umbrella of shortcomings. Students' strengths, however, are equally important to observe. These strengths might be in such areas as the ability to represent ideas geometrically or symbolically, to systematically organize ideas in table or graphic form, or to carry out complex procedures orderly and accurately. Although this type of assessment takes time, the teacher should remember that not every assignment must be graded. Similarly, when looking for data on students' knowledge alone, the teacher need not examine every student's paper.

The results of assessing students' work can be taken into account in several ways. First, establishing a good sense of students' thinking and students' knowledge provides the basis for choosing tasks that have a high cognitive demand but are still within students' reach. Second, specific knowledge about students can be used to structure appropriate questions for students that will stimulate discussion and draw out important connections among mathematical ideas, including ideas that may be in place but need to be made explicit, or ideas that need to be more fully developed. Finally, a working sense of the scope and depth of students' knowledge can be used to structure homework assignments that help overcome deficiencies and keep important skills and procedures at a high proficiency level. For further discussion of assessing students' learning and other important outcomes, see the chapter by Ziebarth in this volume.

A Final Note

The decisions a teacher makes when planning and implementing a problem-solving approach to mathematics instruction have a pronounced impact on the progress students make toward acquiring mathematical proficiency. If students are going to realize their mathematical potential, their teachers must be much more than "guides on the side"; they must be active, thoughtful decision makers prior to instruction, while teaching, and after teaching a lesson.

The author wishes to thank Sandra Pulver for the idea of the problem used in the number theory task.

CHAPTER 10

Social and Sociomathematical Norms in the Mathematics Classroom

Chris Rasmussen
Erna Yackel
Karen King

PAYING explicit attention to the social aspects of learning and teaching mathematics is a crucial component of creating a classroom environment in which students learn mathematics with understanding (Cobb and Bauersfeld 1995; Hiebert et al. 1997; NCTM 2000). The nature of the learning environment is especially important in those classrooms where students are communicating their mathematical ideas and strategies as part of an instructional approach that strives to develop mathematics through problem solving. In other words, attention to the social aspects of learning mathematics offers a way to bring together communication, reasoning, and problem solving, three main strands of the NCTM *Principles and Standards for School Mathematics* (2000). Marcus and Fey (this volume) devote specific attention to selecting tasks for a problem-based curriculum, and they, along with Grouws (this volume), note the equal importance of devoting specific attention to creating a learning environment in which these tasks are enacted. The purpose of this chapter is to take up this charge and to focus on social aspects of teachers' and students' creation and sustentation of environments that foster and promote learning mathematics through problem solving.

This work was supported in part by the National Science Foundation under grant No. REC-9875388. The opinions expressed do not necessarily reflect the views of the Foundation.

A common, and admittedly oversimplified, view of teaching mathematics through problem solving is that it is characterized by use of technology and small-group work. These aspects might be considered surface features of the classroom structure that can be captured by a photograph. By contrast, in this chapter our interest is in exploring the way students participate in on-going classroom events. We use actual dialogue from two different mathematics classrooms to explore such questions as "What is the nature of the discourse in the classroom as students go about the task of learning mathematics through problem solving?" "How do students interact with one another and with the teacher for purposes of learning?" "What characteristics typify students' interactions from a mathematical point of view?" These questions focus on social aspects of the classroom that relate specifically to the goal of learning mathematics. These aspects cannot be captured with a photograph. Instead, they require attention to the dynamic interplay between participants as classroom events unfold. We turn our attention to these social aspects in this chapter.

By illustrating and clarifying the interactive social aspects of explanation and justification, we intend to make explicit several elements of instruction that are often left implicit and that may even be outside the awareness of the students and the teacher. Our hope is that by doing so, we are giving you, the teacher, a means to think about your own teaching. What type of classroom environment do you wish to promote? How might you go about establishing that environment? What types of explanation and mathematical reasoning do you wish to foster in your students? How might you be proactive in doing so? We conclude with some insights and suggestions for ways in which a teacher might proactively support and develop an instructional approach in which mathematical explanations and justifications are typical features of the classroom learning environment.

Examples from the Classroom

We focus our attention on two aspects of the classroom and their significance for mathematics learning. One is developing a classroom environment that promotes explanation and justification as core aspects of students' activity. The second is the distinguishing features of mathematical explanations and justifications that can become the norm in a mathematics class.

Developing a Classroom Environment That Promotes Explaining and Justifying

In this section we present excerpts from two classes that were studying rate of change. Both classes were similar in that students' previous experiences had been traditional—they had not been expected to explain and justify their thinking. Despite this similarity in previous experience, these two classes exhibited sharply contrasting norms for students' explanations. In the first class, which we refer to as class A, students were neither obliged to explain their thinking nor expected to make sense of other students' explanations. In the second class, which we refer to as class B, they were so obliged.

In the following example from class A, the teacher was introducing a method for solving a rate-of-change equation. He began by writing the equation on the board and asking whether anyone could guess a solution. The intention of the whole-class discussion was for students to develop a "sense" for the method through illustration and pattern recognition. Because your students may be developing different mathematical ideas than those in this example, we intentionally omit the actual problem in which students were engaged, so that the reader can focus on the social aspects of this episode.

> *Joey:* Guess e^x?
>
> *Mr. P:* That gives us zero. That won't work. Try another guess.
>
> *Debra:* Try e^{2x}.
>
> *Mr. P:* Let's try. Let's figure that out. That seems OK.

The teacher writes an equation on the board and continues the discussion

> *Mr. P:* Doesn't work, does it?
> *Isabel:* How about e^{-x}?
> *Mr. P:* Don't give up so fast on e2x. Do you really want to give up so fast? So that gives us –e2x. That didn't work, did it? Do you really want to give up on this so fast?
>
> *Debra:* $-e^{2x}$?
> *Mr. P:* Yeah, then we get ...

This same type of exchange was repeated with four different equations. The point of the previous excerpt is not to criticize a well-intentioned teacher. In fact, the teacher was genuinely attempting to engage his class in dialogue. However, the episode clearly illustrates the nature of the expectations regarding explanations. At no point in the foregoing exchange, nor in the similar ones that followed, were students obliged to explain the reasoning behind their particular guesses. Neither the teacher nor the other students pursued the reasons someone thought a particular function was a solution, nor did the teacher invite other students to comment on the feasibility of any proposed solution. All that was expected was the guess, which was evaluated by the teacher without request for explanation (Rasmussen 2001).

Before discussing the example from class A, we invite the reader to reread the example from class A and to imagine how he or she might have responded to Joey's guess. In particular, if a teacher's intention is to promote a classroom learning environment in which students routinely explain and justify their thinking and try to make sense of other students' thinking, how might this dialogue have proceeded differently?

In contrast with the example from class A, the students in the next example, from class B, were expected to explain their reasoning, as well as to try to make sense of other students' thinking. The following excerpt begins partway through a whole-class discussion in which students were explaining their analyses of solutions to the rate-of-change equation

$$\frac{dP}{dt} = 0.5P\left(1 - \frac{P}{8}\right)\left(\frac{P}{3} - 1\right),$$

which was developed as a way to describe the rate of change for the population of fox squirrels in the Rocky Mountains. Moving beyond the problem given, the teacher asked the class what would happen if the initial number of squirrels were negative. "I know this question does not make sense for a population, but mathematically speaking, what if we were below zero?" After an initial response, the teacher remarked, "Jerry says it will increase. What do you think, Stan?"

    Stan: Umm (15 seconds later). Yeah, I don't know.

    Mr. Q: How are you beginning to think about it? Our initial starting population is negative. Granted this doesn't make sense to have a negative number of squirrels, but maybe there is a different situation where a negative value makes sense.

By asking Stan about his initial thinking, the teacher implicitly lets Stan know that he expects him to engage in the question posed and share his reasoning, however tentative. After a short wait, Stan begins to explain how he is thinking about the question posed.

> *Stan:* (15 seconds later) I guess it would increase.
>
> *Mr. Q:* Tell us about it.
>
> *Stan:* If you put a negative number in there, the first term, well, I guess it will decrease.
>
> *Mr. Q:* OK, tell us how you are thinking about it. As a class, we will think about it with you.
>
> *Stan:* OK. Well, the first expression, 0.5*P*, will be negative. The next one will be positive, and next one, that one will be negative. So I guess you are going to increase.
>
> *Mr. Q:* So you are going to increase. What do you guys think?
>
> *Joe:* So far it looks like everything is going to equilibrium.

After Stan explains his reasoning, Joe spontaneously frames Stan's remarks in terms of the behavior of the function with starting values below and above zero without being specifically called on. Joe's contribution is mathematically significant, as it begins to move the discussion from individual solution functions to collections of solution functions. (Unlike algebraic equations that typically have a finite number of solutions, a given rate-of-change equation can be solved by an infinite number of functions.)

Moreover, Joe's contribution and the entire excerpt illustrate that the students and the teacher acted in accordance with the normative understandings that students were expected both to explain their reasoning and to try to make sense of other students' thinking. These understandings, which were constituted through interaction early in the semester, contributed significantly to the climate of the classroom as one in which sense making and meaning making prevailed.

Mathematics educators call such normative understandings *social norms*. Social norms refer to those aspects of the classroom social interactions that become routine. As the course progresses, they become taken for granted and are no longer open to question. The students' and teacher's activity become implicitly regulated by these norms. Every class, from the most traditional to the most reform-oriented, has social norms that are operative for that particular class. What distinguishes one class from another is not the presence or absence of social norms but, rather, the nature of the norms that differ from class to class. The two classes from which we took the previous examples exhibited sharply contrasting social norms for students' explanations. In class A, neither the students nor the teacher expected others to explain their reasoning or to try to make sense of the reasoning of others. In class B, these expectations did exist for both the teacher and the students.

The previous examples illustrate a second crucial aspect of classroom norms, namely, the way in which they are constituted in action. Norms are ways of acting and interacting that become routine through ongoing participation. For example, as Stan and Joe engaged in explaining and making sense of others' contributions, they not only acted in accordance with these social norms but also contributed to sustaining them as routine. (Here we think of norms as being interactively constituted. This view is based on the symbolic interactionist perspective as adapted by Cobb and Bauersfeld [1995] for mathematics education. According to this perspective, we say that norms are not established once and for all but instead are continually negotiated and renegotiated through interaction. The significance of this perspective is that it accounts for subtle shifts that take place over time and also for differences that occur from one class to another even though the classes may have the same teacher or follow the same general instructional approach.)

Similarly in class A, when neither the teacher nor other students sought out explanations and justifications for their ideas, they simultaneously established and acted in accordance with the expectation that explanations and justifications of one's ideas are not required.

Initiating Social Norms

In the preceding discussion we used examples to clarify what we mean by social norms, to document those norms regarding explanations, and to illustrate how they are sustained. A question that we have not addressed so far is how such norms as those illustrated in class B might be initiated. We answer this question by considering an extended episode from the second day of class.

The teacher began the class with a brief statement of the expectations and obligations regarding class participation. These responsibilities included the expectation that students were to—

- develop a personally meaningful solution;
- explain and justify their thinking to their peers and to the teacher;

- listen to, and attempt to make sense of, the explanations and justifications of others; and

- ask questions and raise challenges if they did not understand or disagreed.

He concluded his remarks by saying, "We had some nice examples of that kind of participation from Shawn and Natasha last time." Specific statements about expectations are useful and often necessary. However, they are by themselves insufficient for establishing a classroom in which routines are regulated by those expectations. The students and teacher must come to act in accordance with the expectations. As exemplified in the following dialog, the next twenty minutes of the class was devoted to a dual agenda. On the one hand, the class was engaged in a mathematical discussion about rate-of-change equations intended to model the spread of a virus. On the other hand, the teacher paid continual and explicit attention to creating conditions that contributed to students' acting in accordance with the norms of explanation.

In the following episode we include only the teacher's remarks to emphasize the explicit attention he was giving to fostering social norms for explanation.

> *S:*
>
> *Mr. Q:* Okay, can you explain to us then why it was 1/14 times *I*? How did that sort of make sense as a way to express the change in the recovered population?
>
> *S:*
>
> *Mr. Q:* Please say that again.
>
> *S:*
>
> *Mr. Q:* What do the rest of the people think about that?
>
> *J:*
>
> *Mr. Q:* (To student S) Is that similar to what you were thinking?
>
> *S:*
>
> *Mr. Q:* Kinda. What about the explanation here? Did everyone understand what was said?

The effectiveness of the teacher's approach is indicated by the next student's remark.

> *G:* I didn't quite understand what he said.

> *Mr. Q:* So maybe you could rephrase it or say it a little bit louder so people can hear how you're thinking about it.
>
> *J:*
>
> *Mr. Q:* Anyone want to add to that explanation? Expand on it a little bit? Maybe you still have questions about it.

The episode continued in this manner for a total of twenty minutes. During this time the teacher gave almost no mathematical explanations himself. Instead, he used his position as authority in the classroom to direct the students as they offered explanations and asked questions. As the students did so, they were increasingly acting in accordance with the social norms regarding explanation that the teacher wished to foster. As this example suggests, when the teacher devotes explicit attention to developing social norms, students can and do freely offer mathematical explanations. Moreover, students can and do take on responsibility for attending to, interpreting, and evaluating other students' explanations.

Distinguishing Features of Mathematical Explanations and Justifications

The previous examples and discussion focused on social norms for explanation and justification and ways in which these norms can be initiated and sustained in the classroom. As Yackel and Cobb (1996) noted, the social norms that we have discussed— expectations that students are to explain their reasoning; listen to, and make sense of, other students' reasoning; and indicate agreement or disagreement—have little to do with the fact that the subject of instruction is mathematics. The class may have just as well been studying history, science, or social studies.

In contrast, let us examine those normative aspects of the class pertaining to explanation and justification that were specifically related to the fact that the subject of study was mathematics. For example, what constitutes a different mathematical solution, an elegant mathematical solution, an efficient mathematical solution, or an acceptable explanation? To clarify the distinction, the expectation *that* one is to give an explanation falls within the influence of social norms, but *what* is taken as constituting an acceptable mathematical explanation is particular to the discipline of mathematics. Likewise, the expectation *that* a student is to offer a solution only if it is different from those already offered falls within the realm of social norms, but *what* is taken as a mathematically different solution falls within the purview of the mathematical community.

Consistent with other mathematics educators, we use the phrase *sociomathematical norms* to differentiate between general social norms and those norms that are specifically related to the fact that the subject of study is mathematics. This differentiation between general social norms and sociomathematical norms is pragmatically and theoretically significant. Social norms relate to students' emerging beliefs about their own role in the classroom, whereas sociomathematical norms relate to students' emerging beliefs and dispositions specifically related to mathematics. Paying explicit attention to sociomathematical norms has the potential to foster desirable mathematically oriented beliefs and dispositions. (For more detail on beliefs, see Yackel and Rasmussen [2002].)

Similarly as in the discussion of social norms, we begin by offering two contrasting images of what constitutes an acceptable mathematical explanation in two different mathematics class-rooms. In the first excerpt, the teacher in class A was discussing a particular method for dealing with rate-of-change equations intended to describe the motion of a pendulum. In the course of this discussion, the teacher drew a picture of the situation, did some calculations, and concluded with two simplified equations. At this point one of the students in the class asked, "How did you get those two simplified equations?" The teacher's response was "Because that's the rule. Remember that you get the simplified equations by using $Ax + By$ and $Cx + Dy$, where the coefficients are obtained by taking derivatives."

Unfortunately, we never get to find out what this student's real question is. Is it a conceptual question? Is he simply having trouble following the procedure? We do not know. We do know, however, that because no one requested further clarification, the teacher's response, "Because that's the rule," was implicitly accepted as sufficient mathematical justification.

In contrast, rule-based or procedural explanations in class B were insufficient. In particular, explanations had to be grounded in an interpretation of the rates of change rather than as a rule to follow. The following example illustrates this sociomathematical norm. These excerpts stem from a whole-class discussion about the equation

$$\frac{dP}{dt} = 0.5P\left(1 - \frac{P}{8}\right)\left(\frac{P}{3} - 1\right),$$

which, as mentioned previously, was developed to describe the rate of change in the number of fox squirrels in the Rocky Mountains.

> *Mr. Q:* OK, so Jerry says that if the population gets above 8, they are going to start dying. Tell us why you made that conclusion.

> *Jerry:* Because some number greater than 8, over 8, is going to yield some number greater than 1, which 1 minus something greater than 1 is going to give you a negative number. And so something times a negative number is going to give you a negative number. So your slope is going to be negative.

Notice how Jerry's explanation was given in terms of procedural instructions. To facilitate a shift in the nature of the explanation, the teacher probed further into the meaning of what Jerry said in terms of rate of change and the context of the problem.

> *Mr. Q:* So if P is bigger than 8, like you said, maybe 8 million or 8 thousand fox squirrels, then this term here is negative, like you said, right?

> *Jerry:* Mmm hmm....

> *Mr. Q:* And so what does that mean for us? That means what? If this term is negative, that doesn't tell us anything in itself in relation to the rate-of-change equation.

> *Jerry:* The change is negative.

> *Mr. Q:* OK, so this part here is negative; is this part negative or positive?

> *Silvia:* Positive.

> *Mr. Q:* All right, if P is bigger than 8, certainly $8/3 - 1$ is positive, and so this is positive, and this is positive, so the rate of change, dP/dt, is negative. So that means dP/dt is negative, which means what?

> *Greg:* The population is reducing.

> *Mr. Q:* They're reducing, good. So the rate of change is negative; that means the population, the number of fox squirrels, is getting smaller, the population is decreasing. So the number of squirrels [i.e., the function $P(t)$] is decreasing.

As the discussion progressed, the teacher asked Dave how his group thought about the analysis. Dave's response reflects a shift from explanation as procedure to explanation in terms of the rate of change and the significance of the rate of change for the population.

> *Dave:* Well, pretty much kind of same as what Jerry was saying but just the opposite. In this case, it says the fertile adults have to be able to find other fertile adults to be able to increase. Well, if they don't, then the rate of change of that is going to be negative, which makes everything else negative, so it's decreasing.

Even though Dave prefaces his response with, "pretty much the same as what Jerry was saying," his response was given in terms of the situation and the meaning of rate and not in terms of procedural instructions, as Jerry's initial comment had been. This shift reflects the effectiveness of the teacher's efforts to promote explanations based on meaning rather than on procedures.

We presented the foregoing example to clarify and illustrate what we mean by the sociomathematical norm that explanations had to be grounded in an interpretation of the rates of change rather than in terms of rules to be followed. We also maintain that this example illustrates how the norm is constituted. Sociomathematical norms, like social norms, are constituted in interaction. As students act in accordance with a norm, they contribute to its ongoing constitution. Thus, we would argue that Dave's comments served to contribute to the constitution of the sociomathematical norm that they exemplify.

Conclusion

In this chapter we illustrated the nature of social and sociomathematical norms that foster meaning making, mathematical reasoning, and communication. The significance of this work is that it directs our attention to, and makes explicit the social aspects of, classrooms in which mathematics is taught through problem solving. These social aspects, in addition to instructional materials, the use of technology, and course content, are elements over which teachers at all grade levels can exercise control.

Teachers can begin to foster a classroom atmosphere of the type discussed in this chapter by inviting participation through such remarks and questions as the following:

- Tell us how you thought about it. That is what we are interested in.

- What do some of the rest of you think about what Jason just said?

- Did anyone think about that in a different way?

- That is a good question. Let us put that question out to the rest of the class. What do the rest of you think about it?

- Tell us why you are thinking that.

- I am not sure that everyone heard what you were saying. Say it again, please.

- Please say a bit more about that.

An important point to remember is that norms are regularities in the ways individuals interact. As such, the teacher alone cannot establish them. They are constituted and sustained through participation. Nevertheless, the teacher has the responsibility for their initiation.

We close this chapter by inviting you, the teacher, to once again consider the questions we posed previously about social aspects of your instruction: What type of classroom environment do you wish to promote? How might you go about establishing that environment? What types of explanation and mathematical reasoning do you wish to foster in your students? How might you be proactive in doing so?

Balancing Problem-Solving Skills with Symbolic Manipulation Skills

Cheryl Bach Hedden
Dan Langbauer

THE ROAD from teacher-centered instruction to a problem-based approach has been challenging, exciting, and frustrating at times. In the early 1990s, realizing that the mathematics curriculum we were using at our high school was disjointed and not at all based on the NCTM Standards, we decided to make a change. We moved to a curriculum that was centered on students' making sense of mathematics through problem-solving activities. Slowly we learned to change our teaching styles so that the students were the ones doing the mathematics while we were there to guide them. We wanted our students to be excellent problem solvers, but we also realized that they would confront hurdles—such as the SAT, ACT, and other standardized tests—in which they would need to have solid paper-and-pencil symbolic reasoning skills as well. Ours has been an interesting journey over the past ten years as we learned to balance our emphasis on problem solving with the concomitant need to practice decontextualized symbolic reasoning.

Teaching through problem solving has turned our past practices completely around. Rather than teach specific algebraic skills and then progress to story problems that use those skills, we start from interesting contexts and pose problems about those contexts. Initially, students use two tools to solve the problem, namely, graphs and tables. They begin by making graphs and tables by hand, then later use graphing calculator technology. After dealing with specific contexts long enough to be comfortable, students eventually learn to transform these problem-solving contexts into algebraic rules. From there they can also use symbolic reasoning to solve problems.

Linear Equations

The progression in which we develop linear equations is a good example. For over a month, students work with interesting linear situations in which they use graphs and tables, with or without technology, to solve problems. Students become very comfortable with the concept of rate of change because they see it recursively in a table and as slope on a graph. They also come to fully understand that the initial value in a problem context (for instance, the initial length of a bungee cord before being stretched) corresponds to the y-intercept, which in a table is also the y-value for which $x = 0$. They develop to the point where they can easily write linear equations for the contexts and can scroll down tables or trace along graphs to find answers.

Finally, after all that preparation, the moment of *symbolic reasoning* is at hand. Students are introduced to several methods of solving algebraic equations, and they start to practice their paper-and-pencil skills. For most students, though, we find that something interesting has happened. Since the problems are still embedded in context, students do not just blindly add numbers to each side or divide at random. For example, they continue to understand that, in $100 = 20 + 0.5W$, 20 might mean the initial length of a bungee cord in feet, where 0.5 is the stretch of the bungee cord per pound of weight added and 100 is the desired length. They understand that this abstract algebraic equation may really be asking how much weight is needed to make the bungee cord stretch to a length of 100 feet. So the number of students who make common algebraic symbol manipulation mistakes, such as $20 + 0.5W = 20.5W$, is greatly reduced. When asked, our students say that to add the initial length of the bungee cord to its rate of change would not make sense. The algorithm's step "Subtract 20 from 100, then divide by 0.5" makes sense to them because they can mentally picture that $100 - 20 = 80$ is the amount the bungee cord has yet to stretch, and that dividing by 0.5 will show how many pounds are needed because it stretches 0.5 feet per pound.

After students learn to manipulate variables using symbolic reasoning, more applications of technology open up as well. For example, solving such a system of equations as $3x + 5y = 65$ and $4x + 8y = 88$ can be handled in many ways. As a start, our students visualize the two equations as two intersecting lines, use symbolic manipulation to solve for y in each equation, then enter the "$y =$" form of the equations into their graphing calculators to create graphs and tables. So even as they use technology, they are still practicing symbolic manipulation. Later, they learn other methods for solving systems of equations that use matrices and linear combinations.

Learning at Different Rates

Even though many students learn symbolic reasoning quickly in problem-solving contexts, each child learns at a different rate. What is developmentally appropriate for one student may not be so for another. The good news is that students who do not easily learn to solve algebra problems through symbolic reasoning still have graphs and tables to fall back on. Since the sequence of "graphs and tables first, then symbolic reasoning" is embedded throughout our curriculum, all students have the opportunity to understand symbolic reasoning. We find it helpful to think of two students on a year timeline such as that in figure TS3.1.The first student required a relatively short time in which she used only graphs and tables, then was able to transition quickly into symbolic reasoning. The second student was introduced to paper-and-pencil methods at the same time as the first, but she used tables and graphs to validate her thinking for a longer time and did not become proficient at symbolic reasoning until later in the year.

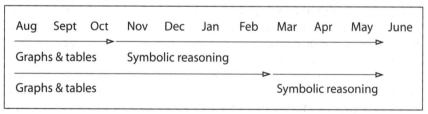

Fig. TS3.1. One-year timeline for students' development of symbolic reasoning

In our former way of teaching, students had to "get it now or forget it." They had no context to link with, nor any method other than symbolic reasoning to use as a backup for solving an equation. Now students can transition into more abstract thinking whenever they are ready. We do not expect mastery right away, but as students mature over their high school years, we want them to become equally proficient at solving problems with graphs, tables, or symbolic reasoning. To show that we value all three methods equally, we design assessments that require all three.

Multiple Approaches to Equations through Problem Solving

As we shifted from a teacher-centered approach to a problem-based approach, we also needed to shift our emphasis to match what we wanted students to value. One concept receiving greater emphasis is the development of the quadratic equation. In the first two years of our curriculum, students work informally with many situations involving parabolas on their graphs and tables. For example, they might look at the height of a ball that is thrown straight up from 1 meter off the ground at an initial velocity of 20 meters per second with the force of gravity pulling it downward as $H = 1 + 20t - 4.9t^2$. Using graphs and tables, students become expert at finding the zeroes (where the ball hits the ground) and the vertex (where the ball reaches its maximum height). Finally, in their third year they are introduced to the quadratic formula as

$$x = -\frac{b}{2a} \pm \frac{\sqrt{b^2 - 4ac}}{2a}$$

$$\underline{\hspace{3cm}}\qquad\underline{\hspace{4cm}}$$

vertex distance to the zeroes
(left and right)

As teachers, we are always amazed at how easily students understand this potentially difficult equation. During the preceding years, students have developed a comfort level with parabolas and see the quadratic formula as a natural extension of the pattern of "graphs and tables first, then symbolic reasoning." The same is true of factoring quadratic polynomials. Students easily make the transition from the zeroes they have found graphically to the factors they find with symbolic reasoning. For example, students see $y = x^2 - 3x - 10 = (x - 5)(x + 2)$ simply as a concave upward parabola with zeroes at 5 and –2 and a y-intercept of –10. Algebraic and geometric thinking constantly meld for our students because they are always using graphs, tables, and symbolic reasoning. We changed our focus from "know this equation" to "build this equation" by prompting students to make natural use of their prior problem-solving experiences with graphs and tables. This method has given our students stronger symbolic skills, especially in relation to quadratics, than we had seen previously.

However, we should reiterate that not all our students master the quadratic formula and factoring quickly. Some continue to validate their thinking with graphs and tables for a long time, but most students develop symbolic reasoning skill eventually. Here, too, we value all three methods equally on our assessments, thereby forcing students to practice thinking in flexible ways.

Although we are pleased with the skills our students learn in the problem-solving environment, we realize that at times in life they will be required to use symbolic reasoning in completely abstract situations. To prepare them for this eventuality, we use several different techniques.

First, embedded in our curriculum are ample opportunities for students to practice algebra in decontextualized situations. We assign such problems as homework, and students are expected to show and justify each step in their solution. In addition, they are often expected to make tables or graphs to validate their thinking. We emphasize these types of symbolic problems more strongly with students in their last two years of high school.

Second, at the beginning of class we use daily "warm-ups" that target symbolic reasoning often with decontextualized algebra problems. Good sources for these problems are SAT and ACT practice booklets and practice problems for college mathematics department placement tests. The students work on the warm-ups while we are taking roll and checking homework. Then several students are randomly asked to show their work on the board, and the class discusses the answers and techniques.

Looking Back

In looking back on the changes we have made as teachers over the past ten years, we realize that we still use many of our former techniques to teach and practice symbolic reasoning, but we have changed our emphasis. Skill with paper and pencil remains one of the "big three" in our classrooms, but it is given no more or less importance than solving problems with graphs and tables. When faced with a problem-solving situation and a student who just does not "get it" yet, we are empowered by having other tools available to help that student understand and solve the problem. We also take comfort in the realization that the student is likely to acquire skill with symbolic reasoning, as well as with graphs and tables, when the time is right.

CHAPTER 11

The Sound of Problem Solving

Mark Driscoll

A S THE previous chapters by Grouws and by Rasmussen and others illustrate, a teacher's role in a problem-based classroom is complex. Teachers must select and use good task sequences, ask good questions, structure lessons to ensure that the mathematical goals are achieved, create a classroom climate that enables students to learn through problem solving, and monitor learning as it takes place. Underlying each of these teaching responsibilities is the need for the teacher to listen to students—to their responses to problem-solving tasks, to their answers to questions, and especially to their problem-solving endeavors.

Over the past decade I have been involved in several professional development projects with written student work at their core. Typically, these projects provide teachers with rich mathematics problems that they can explore together and then administer to their students between sessions. Each time they meet, the teachers analyze their students' work on the problem that they themselves explored during the previous session, with a particular focus on analyzing the development of mathematical thinking in their students.

I recall being with one group of teachers as they looked at students' problem-solving work contributed by a middle-grades teacher named Carol. As the pieces circulated through the group at the table where I was sitting, two things were clear: (1) many students had made considerable inroads into the problem, as evidenced by their conclusions and partial conclusions; and (2) little of their thinking was revealed in what they wrote. Consequently, those of us looking at the students' work had little to talk about. Half apologetically, Carol said, "I know there is not much there to talk about. I wish you could have heard them as they worked on it, though. Ideas were flying."

I was aware that, although the particular problem was mathematically rich, even lending itself to numerous extensions, it did not invite written work that made the solvers' thinking transparent. This deficiency only compounded a common dilemma: that students do not readily write to describe their mathematical thinking, and they do so far less to describe their shifting attention, testing of assumptions, conjecturing, drawing of analogies— all examples of so-called "metacognitive" qualities, which are essential features of effective problem solving. These qualities also influence teaching through problem solving, conveying crucial information to teachers who want, for example, to gauge how well students can access relevant knowledge and bring it to bear on problem solving, or who want to help students sharpen their skills in monitoring and regulating their own cognitive processes— proven correlates of higher order mathematics learning (Stein et al. 2000).

Listening to Carol was illuminating for me and eventually inspired a revised notion of "student work" in our design of professional development programs. My colleagues and I have come to believe that, to be an effective catalyst for learning about students' mathematical thinking, the term *student work* should include what we hear as well as what we see. This chapter concentrates on the benefits to teachers of listening to students as they learn mathematics through problem solving.

A Surprise Gift

Two years ago, during a pilot test of professional development materials at one of our test sites, we received a surprising and welcome gift from a teacher and her students, a videotape that conveyed better than any number of words the value of listening to students. Listening is the focus of the particular unit being pilot tested by the teacher, but the gift tape brought our appreciation and commitment to deeper levels. In the unit, we ask teachers to have two or three students work on the Postage Stamp problem given on the next page, to audiotape the students' work on the problem, and to transcribe a short selection for use in discussion with their study-group colleagues. This problem leads to, and requires the use of, some important divisibility ideas from number theory, and it often elicits algebraic thinking in ways that surprise teachers We urge the teachers to treat it as an information-gathering, not teaching, experience. Thus, we call it a "listening interview."

Postage-Stamps Problem

The post office has only 5¢ and 7¢ stamps. By combining different numbers of 5¢ and 7¢ stamps, customers can usually get the amount of postage they need. For example, one 5¢ and two 7¢ stamps makes 19¢ in postage; two 5¢ stamps makes 10¢ in postage.

1. Which amounts of postage is it impossible to make using only 5¢ and 7¢ stamps?

2. Explain how you know that each of these amounts is impossible to make.

3. Explain how you know you have found all the amounts that are impossible to make (that is, tell how you know that all the other amounts of postage are possible).

This particular seventh-grade teacher approached the task differently. She sent three students into an empty classroom to work on the problem, along with a fourth student to videotape their work. Later, she used a taped segment for her study-group discussion and then sent the entire tape to us.

We consider the tape a gift because it shows youngsters working on a mathematics problem, for an extended period of time, with no adult intervention. Rarely do we get this fly-on-the-wall opportunity, and viewers of this tape cannot help but notice the great difference between what the students say and what they write in response to the problem.

Before reading on to the sequences from the transcript, work on the problem yourself and be aware of what factors drive and support your problem solving. You may, as colleagues and I do, find helpful Schoenfeld's (1985) description of the kinds of thinking that contribute to effective problem solving. According to this characterization, slightly adapted for our purposes, effective problem solving makes use of the following:

- *Heuristics,* for example, what strategies you decide on, what you wonder about, where you start

- *Control,* for example, what you notice, what you pay attention to, how you check assumptions, how you monitor progress, how you decide to change course, how you know you are finished

- *Beliefs,* for example, what assumptions influence your approach, what you suspect will be true about the problem

- *Resources,* for example, what knowledge and skills you can bring to bear, what tools and information you can apply

Next read the following excerpt from the students' discussion, which begins right after the three students systematically try out the amounts up to twenty-two cents. As you read it, "listen" to what the students are revealing about what they are wondering about, what they notice and pay attention to, how and how well they are monitoring progress, and so on.

S2: What about 23?

S1: Twenty-three, you can't do. Twenty-four?

S2: Yes, you can do 24. You can do 24—it's 14 + 10, so two of each stamp.

S3: You guys, I don't want to list them all.

S2: Well, what are we supposed to do? I don't get that.

S1: I mean, I think you just . . . get the examples of it . . . ; you can't really. . . .

S2: Let's go up to 40.

S3: You can make a pattern, can't you?

S2: Six, 8, 9, 10, 11.

S3: The thing's that, are you sure you can't do 18?

S2: Eighteen, 14, 5.

S1: You can't, unless you can subtract, because you can do 28 and then take away 10.

S2: It's not. Explain. OK, well, let's go up to 40, you guys.

S1: You can't do 24.

S2: Twenty-four—yes, you can.

S1: I am, like, not thinking today.

S2: Twenty-four.

S1: Twenty-five, 26.

S2: Twenty-six—wait, wait, wait.

S1: Twenty-six, you can. . . .

S2: Twenty-six—how?

S1: Three times 7 is 21, plus five is 26.

S2: Yeah, yeah, yeah. You can make 27—yes, you can.

S1: How can you do 27?

S2: Twenty and 7.

S3: Twenty-eight?

S2: Yes, that's divided by 7. . . . Twenty-nine, I think you can do that.

S1, S3: No, you can't.

S2: Fifteen plus 14.

S3: How are you doing that?

S1: Okay, I know!

S2: Thirty, you can do. . . .

S1: Thirty-one. . . .

S2: Yes . . . 21 + 10. Thirty-two, yeah, no. . . . Seven plus 25 . . . I think you can do every number after 23.

S1: Well, let's see.

S2: Thirty-three is 28 plus 5.

S3: Thirty-four is 24 plus 10.

S2: Yeah, you can do all of them after that.

S1: Well, I mean, let's make sure, let's . . .

S2: Thirty-five, of course you can, 36 . . .

S3: You guys, if you can do 26, you can do 36.

S2: Yeah, exactly.

S3: What about 38 though?

S2: Wait—we can do 24, 25, 26. We can do them all, because if we can do. . . .

S1: After 23. . . .

S2: After 23, we can do them all.

S1: That's why it's a good thing we were going to try to go to 40.

What did you hear in the dialogue? Even in print form, the fast, almost frenetic pace of early teenaged conversation comes through, but so do some other qualities. Listening to the three students as they proceed, one notes their shift from fearing that they will have to "list them all" and go on forever, to suspecting that by the time they reach the number 40, they will be able to reach some kind of conclusion. Although they seem to be noticing that various combinations of 5s and 7s yield a consecutive string of numbers after 23, they do not make any particular effort to organize their information. However, they start to pay attention to what the number 10 can do for them in reaching a final conclusion. And they appear to build steadily toward a convincing argument that they can "do them all." Lastly, what previous knowledge is of help to them is not very clear. It seems more than computational facility and appears to involve the ability to break up whole numbers into linear combinations of other whole numbers.

Most, if not all, this information gleaned from listening can be useful to a teacher wanting to help students hone their problem-solving skills and develop a deeper understanding of the mathematical ideas embedded in the solutions. Arguably, the students' conversation reveals a lot of fruitful mathematical thinking, with the potential for becoming even more powerful and fruitful. Next,

read the following sequence. When they start to write a response
to the third part of the problem, the students struggle to construct
a convincing argument that, in the words of one of them, puts it
"in a nutshell."

> *S2:* How about we write, because we can write the number 24,
> we can write each number that has a 4 at the end of it
> because we can make 10.
>
> *S1:* Once you get to a number that ends in any number, you
> can just add 10. So to put that in a nutshell. . . .
>
> *S3:* *N* plus 10 equals *N*. . . . This is too easy. . . . That's not the
> formula.
>
> *S2:* *N* plus 10 equals *N*; *N* is not the same as *N* plus 10.
>
> *S3:* *X* equals *x.*
>
> *S1:* Once you have 29 + 10 equals 39. . . .
>
> *S2:* Hang on, because you can do everything, if you are able to
> write a number that has. . . .
>
> *S3:* I think you're making this a little too complicated.
>
> *S2:* If you're able to make a number that ends in anything. . . .
>
> *S1:* Ends with any of the numbers from 1 to 10, well, from 1 to
> 9. . . .
>
> *S2:* Ends in 1 to 9. . . . You can obviously make the number in
> the next tenths. . . .
>
> *S1:* Going up by increments of 10.
>
> *S2:* Hang on, watch this. . . .
>
> *S3:* Alright, so once. . . . After, all numbers, I need a way to
> word this.
>
> *S2:* It's really easy, but hard to write, you need to like. . . .
>
> *S1:* Once you've found a number that ends in any of the num-
> bers from 1 to 9. . . .
>
> *S2:* From 0 to 9. . . .
>
> *S1:* That will work too, but, okay, anything from 0 to 9. Once
> you find a number that works, which just happens to be
> from 23 and beyond, it works.
>
> *S3:* That's a lot of work, though.
>
> *S1:* You have to try to put it in a nutshell.
>
> *S3:* I'm sure you can, because you have to explain it. After
> you've reached 23, you can reach every other going up by
> increments.

What does a listener hear in this segment? First, one hears an
almost painful struggle, suggesting how difficult it is, particularly
for middle-grades students, to craft a convincing mathematical
argument that will cover an infinite set of numbers. (The segment
may also imply that wording a convincing argument is not a good

group task.) Second, one hears at least one possible line of thinking about explanation being eliminated, one that seems as interesting as the explanation the students do choose to write: When S3 attempts to use a letter as a generalized number to come up with a shortcut, she sounds like she is crafting a recursive rule—a very interesting tangent, but something she quickly drops when S2 tells her that "N is not the same thing as N plus 10." Not surprisingly, her effort never gets reflected in the group's written response. To a teacher wanting to help young students learn to craft convincing mathematical arguments and to use symbolism to make algebraic generalizations, this kind of listening data can be invaluable.

With the permission of the teacher and students, we use this videotape in our revised version of the professional development materials (Driscoll et al. 2001). We ask users to watch and listen, and to reflect on the information that listening to students can reveal about their problem solving and mathematical thinking—information that their written work often does not reveal. We also ask teachers to imagine themselves sitting with the students and to determine active-listening, inquiring questions they might ask the students, presumably spare enough so that the flow of investigation is not destroyed. Thus, when S3, early on, asks, "You can make a pattern, can't you?" one might step in to ask what "making a pattern" means. Later, when S3 asks S2, "How are you doing that?" one might slow the action to prod S2 to try to answer that question.

Learning to Listen

The fly-on-the-wall opportunity represented by the Postage Stamps videotape is rare. Listening to students in an ordinary classroom is a challenging skill that develops through effort and in stages. However, teachers can take steps, beginning in staff development sessions, by which they can practice listening to and understanding their own thinking and the thinking of their colleagues. A productive means for understanding one's own thinking is reflective writing, particularly after a mathematics investigation. Borassi and her colleagues (1999) recommend focused writing assignments using specific prompts. For example, after their teachers in a professional development program had engaged in a mathematical exploration,

> the participants were asked to (a) reconstruct in detail the key components of the activities they had experienced, (b) write down what helped/hindered

> their learning in each of these components, ... and
> (c) share and discuss what they wrote with the rest
> of the group. (p. 73)

This kind of structured reflective writing, not a common feature of mathematics professional development, can sharpen an individual teacher's focus on mathematical thinking and lay the foundation for listening to others and inquiring into their thinking. Interactions with colleagues, as they relate how their thinking progressed during mathematical investigations, provide fertile opportunities for practicing listening. Often, listening to colleagues is easier than listening to students in the classroom, where many other distractors can get in the way. One teacher expressed this fact in the following way, referring to the part of our professional development sessions in which teachers work on mathematics together, and to his letting the experience of listening to other teachers influence his classroom behavior:

> Just hearing that it was about the thinking, more
> than just doing the problems. Seeing how people
> think ...and really, when you're with the kids, when
> you think they might be totally off-track, you start
> to tell them, "No, you're doing it wrong." With other
> teachers, I feel they probably know what they're
> doing. So instead of just not even looking at (a stu-
> dent's) idea, I try to now accept more, other ways of
> getting to the answer.

We have found that, whether directed toward colleagues or students, to be most effective, listening needs a focus—an answer to the question "Listening for what?" In one professional development program (Fostering Algebraic Thinking Toolkit [Newton, Mass.: Education Development Center, NSF grant number ESI-9819441]), an algebraic-habits-of-mind framework is used to guide the teachers' listening. Teachers are asked to listen for indicators of three habits of mind: (1) building rules to represent functions, (2) abstracting from computation, and (3) doing-undoing (Driscoll 1999). In another project, a teacher-enhancement project (Building Regional Capacity Project [Newton, Mass.: Education Development Center, NSF grant number ESI-9819445]), in which special attention has been given to mathematical problem solving, the developers have adapted Schoenfeld's (1985) description of the kinds of thinking that contribute to effective problem solving. The categories of heuristics, control, beliefs, and resources are used to develop the following set of prompts for teachers to use when they themselves do mathematical problem solving with colleagues and for them to adapt when they listen to students as they solve problems.

- What did you notice when you started the problem?
- What did you decide to try?
- How did you organize information?
- What did you pay attention to as you proceeded?
- What did you suspect was going to be true, and why?
- What did you wonder about—at different points during your work?
- What changes in thinking occurred, and why?
- What knowledge was helpful to you?

This same framework was applied earlier in this chapter in the analysis of what a listener might hear in the work of the three students on the Postage Stamps problem.

Factors Influencing Listening

In our experience, three factors influence the quality and the outcomes of the listening, if circumstances allow the teacher to listen and if he or she chooses to do so:

- The teacher's overarching beliefs and assumptions about the nature of mathematics learning and teaching
- The teacher's skill and experience in listening
- The teacher's intentions and objectives in listening on this particular occasion

These factors emerged clearly in one professional development project (Linked Learning in Mathematics Project [Marquette, Wis.: Marquette University, NSF grant number ESI-9619336]) (see Driscoll, Moyer, and Zawojewski [1998]; Driscoll, Foster, and Moyer [1999]). As one of their obligations in the program, a group of participating middle school and high school teachers conducted a "listening interview" of two or three students working on the Carnival Bears problem and wrote a paper based on a few segments of the taped interactions.

Carnival Bears Problem

Connie, Jeff, and Kareem went to the circus. They saw bears do tricks. Three brown bears and 3 black bears did one of the tricks. At the beginning of the trick, the 3 black bears were on the left side of a long mat divided into 7 squares, and the 3 brown bears were on the right side. Each bear had its own square with an empty square in the middle. The bears could do only two different types of moves:

1. they could *slide* onto the next square if it was empty, or

2. if the next square was not empty, they could *jump* over one other bear to an empty square.

The black bears moved only from left to right, and the brown bears moved only from right to left. When the trick was over, the bears had switched places. All the black bears were on the right side, and all the brown bears were on the left.

1. The bears needed 15 moves to switch places. Explain how they did it. How many moves were slides? How many moves were jumps?

2. What is the smallest number of moves that 5 black bears and 5 brown bears need to switch places? Explain how to do it. How many moves would be slides? How many moves would be jumps?

3. If 20 black bears and 20 brown bears were involved, how many slides would be needed? How many jumps would be needed? How many moves would be made altogether? Explain how you got your answer.

4. Pretend that someone told you how many black bears and brown bears did the trick. Explain how you could figure out how many *slides*, *jumps*, and *moves altogether* the bears needed to switch places.

As with the Postage Stamps problem, you should work through this problem and track your thinking before reading on.

The thoughtful work of the teachers in preparing and writing their papers propelled our own thinking about factors that influence listening. We present two examples to illustrate this effect. You should know two things about the examples. First, we have, for the purposes of brevity, paraphrased what the teachers wrote, although the essential messages have not been changed. Second, the teachers were all given the same instructions: they were told that they could ask questions during the listening interviews but that the purpose of the questions should be to elicit and understand students' thinking, not to teach. This instruction derived from a core purpose of the project, to increase teachers' understanding of how algebraic thinking develops in students.

Even in these two examples, one can see that our instructions were filtered through teachers' sense of a teacher's role when students are solving mathematics problems.

Sharon's example

This excerpt is right after they did it with three bears on each side. Now they had to do it for different numbers of bears. They had moved the bears successfully and were now looking at the worksheet to see what might happen for other numbers of times. I tried not prompting them. I deliberately did not use the word *pattern* because I wanted to see how they'd progress if I didn't introduce this leading word. I guess if they got stuck, I might have jumped in, but I didn't have to.

S1: Do that again with the bears. I keep getting stuck right here. I did it once but I don't know how to do it again.

S3: You have to slide this one and then jump that one.

S1: What?

S2: Slide and then jump!

S1: Oh, yeah, yeah. Okay.

S2: Okay, we got it. Now what do we do?

S1: I didn't get it yet. This is so stupid.

T: You did get it. Move those, and you're there.

S1: Oh, yeah.

T: Read the next part of the problem.

S2: We don't have enough bears to try it.

S1, S2: (Reading) What is the smallest number of moves that 5 black bears and 5 brown bears need to switch places?

S1: Can we figure it out without using bears?

S3: Let's write all of the moves down and see.

T: See what?

S2: See if there is a pattern.

I was so excited to see them begin to look for a pattern without leads from me. We've talked a lot in class this year about patterns, but you never know how much they're taking in and making a habit.

Alex's example

I wanted to see how efficiently the students could solve the problem. My strategy, which shows up in this excerpt, was to question and guide a bunch in the beginning to make sure the students saw the complete picture and had a sense of totality about the problem, and then to sit back and watch them work. I am convinced that patterning and generating rules are not intuitive approaches that students take and that you have to let them know it is expected of them.

T: Okay, you've read the problem. Do you understand what you need to do?

S1: Yes.

T: Did you notice how many moves this first problem will require?

S1: Fifteen.

T: Let's look at the other side.
(Students read.)

T: Okay, what do you have to do on this side?

S3: Explain how we did it and determine the number of slides and jumps needed.

T: If that is the goal, then it would be a good idea to keep track of the different moves involved. Right?

S3: Right.

T: Here are some chips for you to use to figure out the sequence of moves if you want to. You don't really have the space to work with the chips for the 20-and-20-bears problem. Would that be practical to try, though?

S2: No.

T: Why not?

S1: That's too many moves probably.

T: So, what kinds of things should you do before you get to that point?

(Silence)

T: You know you have to keep track of the slides, jumps, and total number of moves. Why do you think all that is important?

S1: Because there might be a pattern.

T: Sure! Perhaps even a formula or a rule that you can come up with. Right?

This exchange made all the difference, I believe. From this point on, I didn't have to get as involved, since they saw that patterning and generation of a rule were parts of a logical and sequential process. They moved through the problem pretty quickly, and pretty much all I needed to do was ask a few "why" and "what does that represent" questions.

Although Sharon says she was prepared to intervene, she did not do so; thus her listening interview came closer to what we had in mind for that assignment than Alex's did. He intervened pre-emptively, for reasons he clearly articulates, and reportedly started listening only when the students were on the pathway he wanted for them. No doubt, the kinds of purposeful questioning Alex exhibits would be useful in many teaching situations. However, at least in this segment, his listening appears to fit squarely in a category that some call "evaluative listening" (Davis 1997), that is, listening for something in particular rather than listening to the speaker.

The Role of Questions in Listening

As the examples of Sharon and Alex illustrate, a teacher's questions help shape the kinds of responses the teacher will hear. Different questions have different purposes, and some are much more effective than others at uncovering students' thinking. Over the course of one professional development project (Driscoll, Moyer, and Zawojewski 1998), we developed a taxonomy of questioning intentions on the basis of classroom observations of participating teachers. Figure 11.1 shows an adapted version of the taxonomy, with real examples from the teachers.

At various points in a teacher's day, every one of these intentions may guide questions. Our point in laying out the taxonomy is not to discredit any particular category. Instead, we recommend that teachers become more aware of their intentions behind questions and seek some balance across the categories in their regular practice.

Both Sharon and Alex use questions in the interview segments they submitted. In his segment, Alex's questions appear to lie mostly in the "Orienting" intention category. In her segment, Sharon asks one question, which appears to lie in the "Clarifying" category and leaves her in a listening posture. Generally, we think that questions seeking clarification and, as in the last two categories in figure 11.1, questions inquiring into students' thinking are conducive to fruitful listening. In all three of these categories, the questions aim to reveal the thinking of the students and, at least temporarily, put aside any other agendas the teacher may have.

Question Type	Examples
Managing Intended to help set students on task, get their work organized, and the like	*Who's in charge of writing it down?*
Clarifying Intended to request information from the student when the teacher is not clear about what the student meant or intended; also to help the student clarify the question	*The problem mentions the word **perimeter**. Do you know what perimeter means?*
Orienting Intended to get students started or keep them thinking about the particular problem they are solving; may suggest ways to focus on the problem; may also be used to orient the student toward the correct answer or away from the incorrect answer	*Have you thought about using a table?*
Prompting mathematical reflection Intended to prompt mathematical thinking that the student, not the teacher or textbook, owns. Questions may ask students to reflect on and explain their thinking; encourage them to understand others' mathematical ways of thinking; or have them extend their thinking about the mathematics in a problem.	*Can you explain why the two of you reached different conclusions?*
Eliciting algebraic thinking Intended to prompt a particular kind of mathematical thinking: to ask about what statements are "always" true, about nth terms, about finding patterns and looking for what changes; to suggest working forward and backward; to ask students to justify generalizations	*What does this number in the equation represent?*

Fig. 11.1. A taxonomy of questioning intentions

Conclusion

In engaging with students as they learn mathematics through problem solving, one can listen passively or actively; one can listen to hear what one wants to hear or expects to hear (e.g., listening to determine whether students will see the need for organizing data in a table), or one can listen with the intention of understanding students' thinking (e.g., listening as an assessment effort to guide instruction.) Arguably, good mathematics teachers do all kinds of listening at different times for different purposes. The impact of consistent, purposeful listening, especially in a problem-based classroom, can be a powerful way to elicit and understand students' deeper thinking and, perhaps, to propel them toward a more generalized way of thinking. That outcome would seem an ideal teacher accomplishment: to understand deeply the mathematical thinking that students bring to solving a problem and to help them push that thinking further.

CHAPTER 12

Classroom Assessment Issues Related to Teaching Mathematics through Problem Solving

Steven W. Ziebarth

A TEACHER who decides to teach mathematics through problem solving will need to make changes in curriculum tasks, instructional methods, and classroom norms, as other authors in this volume have pointed out. These changes will be possible only if students are also assessed and graded in ways that reinforce the importance of the new tasks and teaching methods and that are consistent with the new classroom norms. In this chapter, we consider classroom assessment as having two major goals. One is to monitor students' mathematical understandings, skills, and problem-solving abilities so that teachers can appropriately plan and guide instruction. The other is to evaluate students to assign a grade. These goals are not mutually exclusive, and they are both important in classrooms where mathematics is taught through problem solving.

One purpose of this chapter is to illustrate how classroom assessment can and should be expanded when one adopts a teaching-through-problem-solving approach. A second purpose is to address some fundamental assessment issues that teachers must consider when they teach mathematics through problem solving.

Assessment That Supports Teaching and Learning

As Hiebert and Wearne and others in this volume have noted, teaching mathematics through problem solving expands the teaching-and-learning focus from skill mastery alone to the development of a deep understanding of important mathematical ideas. The traditional assessment practices used to assess skill mastery do not assess understanding well. Assessments of students' mathematical understanding must come from multiple sources, including carefully chosen questions, group observations, whole-class conversations, writing in journals and reports, in-class and take-home assignments, portfolios, and projects (Glaser 1990; Silver 1992; Silver and Kenney 1995). For much of this assessment, teachers need to be adept at listening to and observing students as described by Driscoll (this volume).

To illustrate how assessment should expand, let us compare a traditional approach used to assess a topic commonly found in a beginning algebra course with an approach more consistent with teaching mathematics through problem solving. Consider the following task:

Solve $y = 180 - 60x$.

This task mainly requires procedural recall. The only process information that this task elicits is restricted to checking the steps the student takes to complete the task. Having students solve problems like this one does little to assess their understanding of linear equations. One way to get more assessment information from such tasks is to ask related questions that focus on understanding. The teacher could ask students to solve the equation in more than one way, to explain the meaning of the numbers in the equation, or to give a real-life application that the equation might model. Goldenberg and Walter (this volume) suggest other ways to pose problems to make them more useful in teaching and assessing for understanding.

Another approach to designing tasks that assess understanding is to begin with a context and build the assessment questions around it. For example, mathematical equations similar to the foregoing one arise in the following situation, but students are required to think more deeply.

Many people like to buy popcorn to munch on during a movie. But movie theater popcorn is often very expensive. The manager of a local theater wondered how much more she might sell if the price was lower. She also wondered whether such a reduced price would actually bring in more popcorn profit. One week she set the price for popcorn at $1.00 and sold an average of 120 cups per night. The next week she set the price at $1.50 and sold an average of 90 cups per night. She graphed a linear model based only on these two points to predict number of cups sold at other possible prices. Find the equation of the linear model.

(Example derived from Coxford et al. [1999, p. 246])

To solve this problem, a student needs to demonstrate an understanding of such terms as *graph, linear,* and *model* and the ability to work among verbal, graphical, and symbolic representations. Although the problem, as stated, requires only the equation of a linear model, such related questions as the following can provide the teacher with additional evidence about whether students have made sense of the popcorn situation.

Assume that your linear model provides a good estimate of the number of cups sold at a particular price.

a) Explain what the slope and intercept of the model tell about the prospective number of popcorn cups sold at various prices.

b) Write and solve equations or inequalities to answer the following questions: What price results in an average daily number of 150 cups sold? What price results in an average daily number of fewer than 60 cups sold? What number of cups sold is predicted for a price of $1.80 per cup?

c) Using the graph or rule that relates price to average daily number of cups sold, make a table that shows how popcorn price is related to revenue. Explain what the pattern in that table tells about the relation among price, number of cups sold, and revenue. Solve the following equation and inequality, which are similar to those about popcorn price and number of cups sold. Use three different methods to solve them:

table, graph, and reasoning with the symbolic form itself. Show how each answer could be checked.

$$9 + 6x = 24; 1.5x + 8 < 3 + 2x$$

Together, these questions require students to demonstrate an understanding of the context and the ability to apply and solve linear equations. For instance, in part (a) students are asked to interpret the meaning of slope and intercept. In part (b), they write and solve equations or inequalities given values or ranges of one variable. In subsequent parts, they are asked to find patterns, read tables, solve the problem using multiple methods, and explain their thinking and solution methods. Additional questions could extend the problem to solving systems of equations and to other applications. Such a multipart problem also has the potential to be used in a variety of assessment modes: a paper-and-pencil task to be completed individually by students in homework or on an examination, the basis of a pair or group investigation, an individual interview problem, or even the core of a small project. Depending on which of these modes is used, the focus of the teacher's feedback to students can be on their individual understanding and problem-solving abilities exhibited in each question or, more holistically, on how well they completed the entire problem.

Resolving Practical Issues

Adopting new assessment techniques consistently ranks as one of the top concerns for teachers as they shift to teaching through problem solving (c.f. Ziebarth [1998; 1999]). In this section, I discuss some practical assessment issues that teachers face as they shift instruction toward teaching through problem solving. My approach is not a typical one with specific examples of how to use rubrics, portfolios, journals, and so on. Many practical guides are available from which readers can choose as they develop these assessment techniques. (Titles of some resources that I have found particularly useful are provided in the list at the end of this chapter.) My approach is to respond, often in the words of teachers and students, to four questions that seem to resonate with teachers as they make this shift:

1. How can I effectively use more open-ended assessment techniques in my classroom?

2. How can I help my students learn to accept a broader view of assessment?

3. How can I assess students as they learn in groups?

4. How can I assemble all the assessment information to assign a letter grade, and how can this information be communicated to students and parents?

How can I effectively use more open-ended assessment techniques in my classroom?

The examples presented previously illustrate that some context and question variations in an assessment task can yield more information about students' mathematical understanding than others. These variations usually require making the task more open-ended, and that adaptation in turn requires adjusting scoring techniques. Teachers often use rubrics as a way to assign "partial credit" on open-ended problem-solving assessment tasks. Here, a high school teacher describes his rationale for using rubrics.

> Often they [students] can have the wrong answer, but most of their thinking is correct. We didn't used to give points for this. We looked at answers and marked them right or wrong. With students explaining their answers, I gain so much more insight into how they think. And surprisingly, how they think is often correct. Or at least, they have some valid reasoning that just needs a little guidance. And ...[I] know exactly what to fix about their incorrect thinking.

Rubrics, checklists, and other organizational and recording tools are useful for evaluating all sorts of assessment materials. Here, for instance, is a sample rubric for student journals:

> *Scoring Rubric for Journals*
>
> 5—work for all investigation problems (done in class, to date) and reflections present, labeled, and easy to find and follow
>
> 4—most class work and reflections present, labeled, and easy to find and follow
>
> 3—some missing class work or reflections, teacher needs to work to find and follow student work
>
> Below 3 is unacceptable.
>
> (Fey et al. 1996, p. 71)

To reduce demands on their time, some teachers bring students into the scoring and recording process. For example, one teacher requires students to keep a notebook to help organize their homework, and students exchange their notebooks and complete the grading form given in figure 12.1.

How can I help my students learn to accept a broader view of assessment?

Students will need to adjust their view of assessment when they first experience teaching through problem solving. However, our research suggests that getting students to accept a broader view of assessment is not as difficult as it may seem at first, especially when teaching and assessment expectations are well aligned with the norms of the classroom. When students are regularly expected to make sense of mathematics in problematic contexts, they then accept as natural that during assessments they will be expected to explain their thinking, make conjectures, or discuss the reasonableness of a solution. In short, students' expectations about assessment are part of the classroom norms described by Rasmussen, Yackel, and King (this volume).

Assessment can be either written or oral in a problem-based classroom. Here, a student describes in general terms the expectations for written work in his classroom:

> You have ... to give complete sentences. You have to be specific. Explain yourself. You have to make it to where the person can understand as if they have never seen the problem in their life.

Another student echoes these expectations in greater detail as she responds to a problem-solving task in which a moving speedboat uses up its gasoline (note: the tank has 18 gallons to start). She contrasts what is expected of her on this assessment as compared with that in a previous course.

> I've never really had to explain what the "meaning" [of the terms] is, like, as much as I have to right now. I have to write ... a lot of words. Maybe two sentences, but all I'd have to do, like, last year would [be to] say "18" would be the gallons of gas to start out with. You didn't have to go into as much detail, and then all I would have to do [is say] the –2 means it's subtracting 2 gallons from every mile or whatever. But ... in our [current math class] we have to explain it more and make sure that the reader knows what you're saying....

Many teachers in problem-based classrooms assess their students' communication and problem-solving skills through oral presentations, as the student in the following dialogue explains.

Notebook and Class-Participation Grade Sheet

Directions:

Grader:

      1. Write your name and the owner's in the space provided below.

      2. Circle one score for each of the criteria.

      3. Calculate the total, and write it in the space provided below.

      4. Return notebook and this sheet to the owner.

Name of grader: _____

Whose notebook are you grading? _____

Neatness	Sloppy		Average		Excellent
	1	2	3	4	5
Organization by dates	No dates		Some		Perfect
	1	2	3	4	5
Dividers	None		Not labeled		Labeled
	1	2	3	4	5
Vocabulary	None		Half	Most	All
	1	2	3	4	5
Classwork	None		Most		All
	0	2	6	8	10

Total _____ (30 points possible)

Owner:

      5. Make sure the grader added your points correctly above.

      6. Score your participation in class on the basis of classwork done.

      7. Add your participation points to your notebook points.

      8. Indicate if you believe your notebook grade is unfair and you wish

         [Ms. Jones] to regrade it by circling PLEASE REGRADE below.

Participation:	None		Not labeled		Labeled
	1	2	3	4	5

Total Including Participation: _____ (35 points possible)

PLEASE REGRADE

(Turn in this sheet with your notebook.)

Ms. Jones reserves the right to change any score on this grade sheet.

Fig. 12.1. Notebook and class-participation grade sheet

S: Generally, we'll take the assignment from ... the previous day, and we'll go over that, step by step, problem by problem. Sometimes, he has us take overheads and write problems and our answers to them and then present them to the class.

I: Are you pretty comfortable doing that?

S: Yes. At first I was, like, whoa, because I am not a public speaker, but you know, it just becomes routine after a while.

Assessment in a problem-based classroom can also be done in a group format, as discussed in the next section.

How can I assess students as they learn in groups?

For group assessments, students are usually required to tackle large problems or extend their thinking about previously completed individual homework, as a student describes in the following comment:

> Every ... month we have group projects where we have this big piece of paper and each group is assigned a question that we did for homework, and we have to write it out and do a presentation. And most of our homework is done in groups. It's not individualized. It's mostly together, and everyone's putting forth the information. And I think that's beneficial, because that way some of the people that don't understand it—as long as they asked questions, they can understand it and do good in class.

One issue that teachers who use group problem solving must resolve is how to balance group and individual accountability. Various ways can be used to address this issue effectively, depending on the teacher's pedagogical preferences and the guidelines in the school or district. One teacher who has struggled with this assessment issue offers the following ideas:

> One of my more successful group structures is to give a group homework quiz on selected problems. I give each group one premade cover sheet divided into workspace for four selected investigation problems. One person is responsible for (re)writing out a complete solution for that problem. (I tell them I check handwriting!) They can help [one another] and should not allow the person in charge of a problem to submit less than perfect work, since each person's grade will depend on it. I staple each individual homework to the group cover sheet before col-

lecting it. I now have only one paper to grade per group. Each person then gets a composite grade, for example: 60% group quiz part + 40% individual homework completion. This model achieves several things: (1) material independence and common goal (one quiz), (2) personal independence (one person in charge of each question that the entire group will get a grade for), and (3) individual responsibility (homework grade).

Sometimes teachers who are experiencing common difficulties with assessment profit a great deal from working together, as seen in the following conversation between the author and a classroom teacher:

I: When I was in [your colleague's] class, I noticed she had an evaluation sheet she used as she observed her groups, and she said you were the one who designed that sheet. How did that come about?

T: Well, there was a time when kids were preparing to do a presentation, and I noticed immediately that some kids weren't doing anything ... I want them all chipping in and to see it as a group effort, ... so I let them know I'm going to come around and I want to see that everybody is doing something. So on this sheet it allows me to quickly give them a 1–4 rating, 1 being the least and 4 being the best, of how well they are using their time. Are they just sitting there doing nothing—well, that's a 1, and if they're actively taking their information and doing the written part of the assignment, then they score higher in the use-of-time category.... On the next day I may be looking at other categories you saw at the top of the sheet, like creativity, the accuracy of their work, and did everybody present. That's all part of group responsibility, and I have some things that I can quickly average and record in my grade book. Then I can show students why they got the grade they did if they really want to see it.

In another interview, a teacher describes how she combined group work with interview techniques to assess group dynamics and individual mathematical understandings. This idea was also suggested by one of the teacher's colleagues.

> When students test, they get the grade of their test of
> how many they missed ..., but then ... they have to
> explain it [their work] to me [in an individual interview].
> ... If you talk to one person in the group, they not only
> tell you about their answers, ... but they tell you about
> the group chemistry. Say something like "Student A
> showed me how to do this," and now you know that this
> group is functioning. But ... the same person won't say
> that if he is sitting or standing right beside them. And so
> I have gone to interviewing my students because (1) I get
> the [individual] accountability and (2) I get to learn a lot
> about the groups.

With the wide variety of assessment information—written and
oral, individual and group—used by teachers in a problem-based
classroom, constructing a useful summary of a student's performance is not a simple task. Some aspects of this issue are
addressed in the next section.

How can I assemble all the assessment information to assign a letter grade, and how can this information be communicated to students and parents?

The following is an example of a somewhat complex assessment and grading system that a teacher developed for his problem-
based classroom. He allocates 25 percent each for the following
major assessment components: (1) written responses to problems
completed during classroom investigations, (2) sets of homework
problems, related to those investigations, that comprise several
levels of difficulty and include "exact content of the investigation"
along with "ones that look interesting," (3) tests involving at least
two types: one is a pretest used as review, and the other [is] an
in-class test; and "the results of the two are averaged, and I make
it clear that 25 percent of their grade is from tests," and (4)
quizzes drawn from two parallel forms provided in the curriculum, from which he chooses the form that "is most appropriate."
Additionally, students are required to construct and continuous-
ly update a "Toolkit," which is a type of notebook where important class notes, formulas, definitions, and examples of functions
and graphs are kept up to date for daily reference and possible
use in one of the four major assessment components. Finally, as
part of a comprehensive semester assessment, students are
required to keep a "best work" portfolio for which they select
items from each of the major assessment components. The portfolios are presented to parents and other teachers on various
occasions.

Teachers' use of methods designed to assess understanding has been found to be associated with their students' increased learning. In a study involving forty ninth-grade teachers who used a curriculum that supports teaching through problem solving, Schoen and his colleagues (2001) found that teachers of students with the greatest average growth in student achievement used the widest variety of assessment techniques including group observation, written and oral reports, take-home examinations, and journals. Teachers with the greatest growth in achievement were also more likely to use open-ended quizzes and examinations, and they based a higher percent of their grades on purely academic factors, such as quizzes, tests, and student projects, rather than on students' effort or attendance. The average grading weights used by the ten teachers (of forty in the study) whose students had the greatest growth in achievement are shown in figure 12.2.

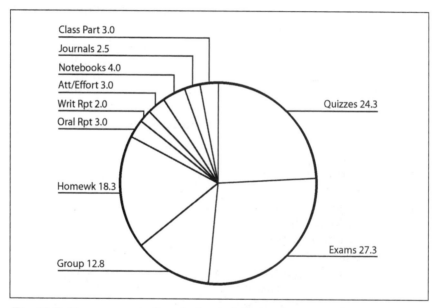

Fig. 12.2. Mean percent of grade for each factor for ten teachers with greatest student achievement (Schoen et al. 2001)

As teachers broaden their assessment and grading practices, they must articulate the changes to parents in a timely manner. Parents, like their students, will often be unfamiliar and perhaps uncomfortable with new assessment practices that support teaching mathematics through problem solving. Many teachers send letters to parents explaining the assessment system (c.f. Fey et al. [1996]). Some have also found innovative ways to communicate through e-mail exchanges or by posting assignments, problems, solutions, and activities on their Web sites. Daily-grade updates are becoming easier for teachers to produce on request, as one teacher recently described to me:

> All my grades are at home, and they are on my computer at school. I do have a computer-generated grade book ....They [students and parents] can see their grades any time they want after school.

For a more detailed description of how another teacher communicates with parents, see Sosenke (this volume).

Summary

In this chapter, I have emphasized the importance of aligning assessment with the goals and methods of teaching mathematics through problem solving. I have described some ways to move toward that alignment by extending and opening up traditional assessment tasks. I have also used the experiences of teachers and students to discuss possible ways to resolve four important assessment issues: managing more open-ended assessment, helping students accept a broader view of assessment, assessing students who work in pairs or groups, and assigning grades.

An important message in this chapter is that most teachers require time and effort to become comfortable with the assessment required for teaching mathematics through problem solving. For students, however, the assessment transition is usually not problematic, provided classroom norms are appropriately focused. In that situation, students view the alignment of assessment methods with other classroom norms as a natural occurrence.

Additional Practical Assessment Resources and Guides

Bright, George, and Jeane Joyner, eds. *Classroom Assessment in Mathematics: Views from a National Science Foundation Working Conference.* Lanham, Md.: University Press of America, 1998.

Bush, William, and Anja Greer, eds. *Mathematics Assessment: A Practical Handbook for Grades 9–12.* Reston, Va.: National Council of Teachers of Mathematics, 1999.

Bush, William, and Steve Leinwand, eds. *Mathematics Assessment: A Practical Handbook for Grades 6–8.* Reston, Va.: National Council of Teachers of Mathematics, 2000.

Charles, Randall, Frank Lester, and Phares O'Daffer. *How to Evaluate Progress in Problem Solving.* Reston, Va.: National Council of Teachers of Mathematics, 1987.

Danielson, Charlotte, and Pia Hansen. *A Collection of Performance Tasks and Rubrics: Middle School Mathematics.* Larchmont, N.Y.: Eye on Education, 1997.

Danielson, Charlotte, and Elizabeth Marquez. *A Collection of Performance Tasks and Rubrics: High School Mathematics.* Larchmont, N.Y.: Eye on Education, 1998.

Romberg, Thomas, ed. *Reform in School Mathematics and Authentic Assessment.* Albany: State University of New York Press, 1995. (See, especially, chapter 3.)

Schoenfeld, Alan, Hugh Burkhardt, Phil Daro, Jim Ridgway, Judah Schwartz, and Sandra Wilcox. *Balanced Assessment for the Mathematics Curriculum.* White Plains, N.Y.: Dale Seymour Publications, 1999. (Three volumes—middle, high school, and advanced high school; two packages for each level)

Stenmark, Jean Kerr, ed. *Mathematics Assessment: Myths, Models, Good Questions, and Practical Suggestions.* Reston, Va.: National Council of Teachers of Mathematics, 1991.

Wilcox, Sandra, and Perry Lanier, eds. *Using Assessment to Reshape Mathematics Teaching: A Casebook for Teachers and Teacher Educators, Curriculum and Staff Development Specialists.* Mahwah, N.Y.: Lawrence Erlbaum Associates, 2000.

Teachers Working with Parents:

A Crucial Component of a
Problem-Based Mathematics Classroom

Fanny Sosenke

THE REALIZATION that I needed the support of my students' parents to accomplish my goal of teaching mathematics through problem solving did not happen overnight. When I was hired to teach seventh and eighth grades in a progressive school in Cambridge, Massachusetts, I was very enthusiastic about the prospect of teaching in a problem-based classroom. One of our premises was that eliminating tracking would help us teach all our students meaningful mathematics through problem solving. However, even though we tried to keep parents informed, the concerned telephone calls started to come. Most of our students' parents, whose main experience in school mathematics was direct instruction in tracked classes, did not understand how teaching mathematics through problem solving and eliminating tracking were beneficial to their children. Then we realized that keeping the parents informed was not enough. Parents are an important piece of the puzzle in a classroom where problem solving shapes mathematics instruction.

We decided to take a proactive rather than a reactive approach to parents, to work with them, not only by keeping them informed but also by educating them. We thought that by sharing our beliefs regarding mathematics learning and teaching, as well as by giving parents resources for helping their children grow as mathematics learners, we would be more likely to succeed at developing a community of problem solvers. In this article, I describe the ways in which I regularly touch base with the parents of my students in three main areas. (For examples of resources that parents can use at home with their sons and daughters, see the references for teachers at the end of this chapter.)

1. *Keeping parents informed of curricular decisions*

At the beginning of a unit, as well as before a special project or activity, I send home with each student a letter that includes some or all of the following components:

- The mathematical goals of that unit, project, or activity

- The nonmathematical goals of the unit, such as awareness of social issues, emphasis on leadership skills (e.g., the fact that students will be expected to make presentations in class), and development of cooperative learning skills

- The activities in which the students will engage in the unit

- Some guidelines for how to help students succeed in the unit or project

2. *Sharing my beliefs about mathematical learning and teaching, and the tools and strategies that I use to implement these beliefs in the classroom*

I accomplish these outcomes in the following ways:

- At the beginning of the year I send parents a letter describing my expectations for the course.

- I send parents articles supporting my beliefs about teaching and learning. See the references for parents at the end of this chapter and the NCTM Web site (http:// www.nctm.org) for some examples of good articles. The themes of some of these articles are the place of calculators in the mathematics classroom, the advantages of cooperative learning, and the advantages of using manipulative materials with secondary school students.

- I conduct parents' workshops, in which parents learn about the foundational role of problem solving in learning and doing mathematics. These workshops may have a specific theme or a general one. For example, one specific theme I have used is number sense, through which parents learn what it means for a student to have strong number sense, what activities we do in the classroom to develop students' number sense, and what parents can do to support us in this goal. An example of a more general theme is problem solving. In this workshop, parents get a general idea of the kinds of activities their students engage in, of the rationale for cooperative learning and how it works, of our emphasis on justifying ideas, and in general, of what can be expected in a problem-based classroom.

3. *Providing guidelines for how to support their children in becoming problem solvers*

The following are three examples of areas that I address:

- How to help students with homework

- How to continue our problem-solving journey during summer vacation

- Suggestions for resources, such as software and books, that can be purchased or checked out of the library

I strongly believe that ongoing communication with parents is crucial to the success of teaching mathematics through problem solving. Even though this communication could be seen as just "another thing to do," the response I have received from my school administrators and from the parents is so positive that it makes the extra effort worthwhile. But the biggest reward for me is the change I see in my students when they recognize that we are "all in this together."

References for Teachers

Ford, Marilyn S., Robin Follmer, and Kathleen K. Litz. "School-Family Partnerships: Parents, Children, and Teachers Benefit!" *Teaching Children Mathematics* 4 (February 1998): 310–12.

Involving Families in Mathematics Education: Readings from "Teaching Children Mathematics," "Mathematics Teaching in the Middle School," and "Arithmetic Teacher," edited by Douglas Edge. Reston, Va.: National Council of Teachers of Mathematics (NCTM), 1992.

Kliman Marlene. "Beyond Helping with Homework: Parents and Children Doing Mathematics at Home." *Teaching Children Mathematics* 4 (November 1999): 140–46.

Oakes, Jeannie. *Multiplying Inequalities: The Effects of Race, Social Class, and Tracking on Opportunities to Learn Mathematics and Science.* Santa Monica, Calif.: Rand Corporation, 1990.

O'Connell, Susan R. "Math Pairs: 'Parents as Partners.'" *Arithmetic Teacher* 40 (September 1992): 10–12,

Peressini, Dominic D. "What's All the Fuss about Involving Parents in Mathematics Education?" *Teaching Children Mathematics* 4 (February 1998): 320–25.

Reys, Barbara. *Elementary School Mathematics: What Parents Should Know about Problem Solving.* 2nd ed. Reston, Va.: National Council of Teachers of Mathematics (NCTM), 1999.

Williams, Luther. "Help Children Succeed in Math and Science." *PTA Today* (March 1991): 16–18.

References for Parents

Burns, Marilyn. *What Are You Teaching My Child?* Sausalito, Calif.: Math Solutions Publications, 1994. Videotape.

———. *Math: Facing an American Phobia.* Sausalito, Calif.: Math Solutions Publications, 1998.

Calculators—What Is Their Place in Mathematics Classrooms?" *NCTM Dialogues*, May/June 1999.

Campbell, P. *Math, Science, and Your Daughter: What Can Parents Do?* Newton, Mass.: Office of Educational Research and Improvement, U.S. Department of Education, and WEEA Publishing Center, Education Development Center, 1992.

"Tracking." *NCTM Dialogues*, November 1998.

National Research Council. *Everybody Counts: A Report to the Nation on the Future of Mathematics Education.* Washington, D.C.: National Academy Press, 1989.

Paulos, John A. *Innumeracy.* New York: Vintage Books, 1990.

www.geocities.com/fannysosenke. World Wide Web.
   Author's Web site, source for various types of letters and guidelines for homework.

CHAPTER 13

Phasing Problem-Based Teaching into a Traditional Educational Environment

Larry Copes
N. Kay Shager

YOU MAY want to try to teach mathematics through problem solving but are working in a traditional teaching environment that seems incompatible with these ideas. We believe that these realities can indeed coexist, although you may need to phase in the new practices gradually. What determines the pace with which you try out new ideas? Perhaps the easiest answer is "Make changes as you are comfortable with them," but the most comfortable stance could be not to change at all. So we suggest an alternative: "Make changes when you are only slightly nervous about them." The extent of your nervousness will be determined not only by how well you think you are teaching but also by the anxiety levels of your students, colleagues, administrators, and students' parents.

Here we address five of the many dimensions of teaching you will be considering: (1) articulating the mathematics, (2) structuring class sessions, (3) sources of problems, (4) working in groups, and (5) changes in the teacher's role. These dimensions of teaching through problem solving are intertwined; success in phasing in one dimension will allow you to progress more easily in other areas.

Articulating the Mathematics

What mathematics are you trying to teach in a lesson? An easy answer, such as "linear equations," is too vague. We find that being more specific helps us teach better, for example, "Linear equations have straight-line graphs," or "Linear equations model constant-rate growth," or "The balancing method is one way of solving a linear equation."

How might you phase in a more specific articulation of the understandings you want to develop? Begin by studying your current textbook. Study other texts, too, including materials from college or in-service courses, to understand the ideas more deeply by seeing them from different viewpoints. Study more mathematics to see the ideas in a broader context, even if you will not be teaching it. (E.g., Does knowing that a linear transformation defined on a vector space preserves lines deepen your understanding of linear equations?) Your articulation can improve through the rest of your career. Later in life, your "better" summary of the foregoing outcome might become "Arrow diagrams and working backward can be used to solve equations that arise in predicting the result of linear growth."

As you become more comfortable articulating the important ideas you want students to understand, you can begin to consider not only content goals but also what you are teaching about mathematical processes. For example, you might articulate the goal "Mathematical modeling is useful but not an entirely algorithmic process" for the same lesson as the content goal above.

As another example, the topic of the day in a traditional curriculum might be the formula for finding the area of a parallelogram. You could write your goal as "The area of a parallelogram is LW." Better, however, would be "The area of a parallelogram can be found by multiplying the length of one side by the length of an altitude to that side." Even better might be "One of several ways of finding the area of a parallelogram is to multiply the length of any side by the length of an altitude to that side." To teach to this last goal, you will have to plan for students to see more than one way to determine the area. For example, you could ask them, without any introduction, to find the area of the shape in figure 13.1 in as many ways as they can. This approach can accomplish several process goals, such as "More than one way can be used to solve at least some mathematics problems," "Different degrees of precision in recording data can lead to different answers," and "Looking at a problem from a different point of view can help solve it!"

Articulating the mathematics is important whether you are teaching in a traditional or a problem-based way. Articulating content goals that include specific process goals, however, leads naturally to the question of how to accomplish those goals. How

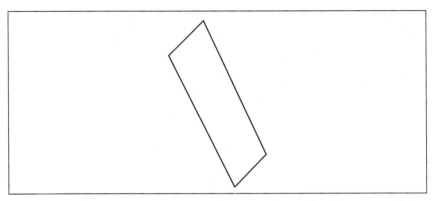

Fig. 13.1. Without any introduction, have students find the area of this shape in as many ways as they can.

can you move your traditional classroom toward a problem-based environment in which students might learn more about both mathematical content and mathematical processes?

Structuring Class Sessions

In many U.S. mathematics classrooms, we first tell students how to solve a particular type of problem, next show them some examples, and then have them practice on more problems of that type. Many content and process goals, however, can be taught more effectively with a different structure: one in which we first give students a problem that they do not know how to solve, then let the mathematical ideas arise as needed to solve that problem. As Stigler and Hiebert (1999) report, class sessions in Japan are often structured this way.

So how might you phase in this change in how your class sessions are structured? At first, you might just pose a problem that you will later use as an example, then go on with your lesson. Gradually let students have more time to think about the problem and to discuss it with a neighbor or in a small group. Eventually, you hope to arrive at something like the SPOSA model of problem-based teaching:

Set the context. Remind students in a sentence or two of what they have been doing in recent class sessions, and if needed, set the stage for the new problem.

Pose the problem, defining any terms that might not be understood by some students. (Be especially sensitive to students who do not understand English well.) Start the students working in their groups.

Observe and listen to students while they work. Decide which students you will ask to present what, and make some tentative notes on the points that you want to arise during their presentations or in your concluding comments. Observe students' presentations, creating as much safety as you can for students to critique one another's ideas and ask questions.

Summarize, with the help of the class, what has been done and the mathematical points that have arisen, using the mathematical goals you articulated. Introduce vocabulary for the new concepts.

Assess the learning and the lesson. For the remainder of the class period, have students assess their learning through writing about it or beginning work on follow-up problems. These problems should not just reiterate the ideas being taught, but rather, should build on them. Work on extensions of the problems can serve as homework. Meanwhile, you can make quick notes about what went well and what changes you will make the next time you teach the problem.

For example, suppose you are introducing vertex-edge graphs. In planning, you search for a problem that will engage students. You look several sections ahead in your own textbook, through other textbooks, and on the Internet. You get ideas and reject them. Finally you settle on an idea and work hard to phrase it carefully, hoping that it will be successful enough to use again. And you ponder all the ways you can think of to approach the problem.

S   This problem is the introduction to this topic, so students have done no earlier work on the topic to connect with. However, you might say a little about painting lockers and the importance of efficient planning to pique students' interest in the problem context.

P . Here is your problem, adapted from Coxford and others (1999, pp. 250 ff).

> You have a summer job painting lockers in a school building. On one floor, the lockers (shown by the thick lines in fig. 13.2) are located in the hallways along the walls around eight classrooms and along an outside wall.
>
> Because you are moving bulky equipment, the lockers in the center hall must be painted one row at a time.

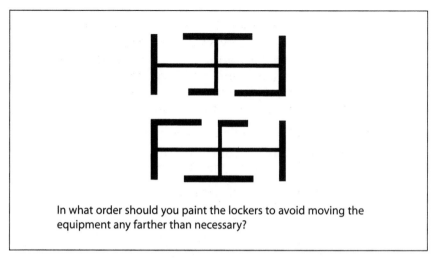

In what order should you paint the lockers to avoid moving the equipment any farther than necessary?

Fig. 13.2. Locker configuration for locker-painting problem

After students have read the problem, you might make sure they know what the word *bulky* means and understand why the equipment should not be dragged back and forth across a hall.

O As groups work, observe how they represent the problem in various ways. When they present their ideas to the full class, observe how well both the presenters and the audience members exhibit understanding of previously encountered ideas.

S Introduce the terminology *graph, vertex, edge, degree, Euler circuit,* and so on, to help with the discussion. With your students' help, articulate the ideas you are trying to teach: "Movement from one place or task to another can often be modeled by vertex-edge graphs," "A graph has an Euler circuit if and only if all its vertices have even degree," "A good problem-solving technique is to look for patterns in simpler problems," and so on. Pose extension problems, such as, "But why are the degrees of vertices related to Euler circuits?" or "What if you wanted to touch every vertex exactly once instead of every edge exactly once?"

A You might give out note cards to the students and ask them to write a sentence or two about what they learned and about what remains confusing to them. Meanwhile, make your own notes of what you would do differently next time and how well various students demonstrated understanding of the mathematical ideas, facility at problem solving, and skills in doing group work.

Even though at first you may designate particular class periods as "SPOSA days," you can let the distinction fade as you begin using the SPOSA techniques more frequently. To aid in teaching both the content and process goals of the mathematics you have articulated, such problem-based structures as SPOSA begin by posing a problem. Where do such problems come from if you are using a traditional curriculum?

Choosing Problems

You can start by going to your textbook. Look over the examples and the exercises. Or later in the textbook, find a problem that could promote thinking about several topics. If your curriculum comes with auxiliary materials, consult them for performance assessments or extension problems. Some published standards—from both NCTM (2000) and individual states—have good examples. Talk with colleagues in your school, your district, or your state professional organization; some of them may have collections of good problems. Occasionally you will find a good problem in a puzzle book or problem collection, perhaps on the World Wide Web. A growing database of rich problems is found at Copes (2003).

You may be tempted to use a problem just because it is fascinating, but the most important selection criterion is that the problem will carry the mathematics you want to teach. When you find a fascinating problem that you think will engage your students, study it until you can articulate what mathematics, both content and processes, it involves, and then file it away for when you are teaching those ideas.

For example, suppose that you want to teach these content goals with understanding.

- In a linear growth function, the amount of change is the same in each equal interval of the domain.

- In an exponential growth function, the amount of change in an interval of the domain is a constant multiple of the amount of change in the previous interval of equal length.

- Exponential growth is more dramatic overall than linear growth, even if the initial changes are smaller.

A problem that might serve well for teaching these goals is the two-job problem:

You have been offered two summer jobs. One begins at $5.50 per hour and increases by 10 cents per hour each week that you remain on the job. The other also begins at $5.50 per hour and increases by 1 cent per hour the first week, 2 cents per hour the second week, 4 cents per hour the third week, 8 cents per hour the fourth week, and so on, the amount of your raise doubling each week. Which job will pay you more for the summer?

In a problem-based classroom, this problem can also help in teaching some process goals, such as these:

- Several ways can be used to solve a mathematics problem.

- Real-life problems are often ambiguous, and solving them requires making assumptions.

What if you want to teach a particular idea and have no relevant rich problems in your storehouse? For example, you may be working with a curriculum that emphasizes basic skills, just as many standardized tests do. You can nonetheless phase in rich problems by enriching some of the problems that are part of the curriculum. For some examples, see Goldenberg and Walter (this volume) and Becker and Shimada (1997). One of the easiest and most effective ways to do so is to ask students to solve a problem in as many ways as they can. Such a challenge can lead to a deepening of their mathematical understanding as students see different perspectives on the same idea and make connections with other ideas. It can also help students who otherwise "freeze up" when they cannot remember "the right way to solve this problem."

For example, a paraprofessional, working with two children who were bored with a drill-and-practice worksheet, simply wrote at the top, "Work these problems in as many ways as you can." One of the previously disenchanted students stayed with the worksheet for about twenty minutes. The other was engaged with the problems for an hour and a half, working each problem in several ways, not necessarily including the way the teacher had taught. Even the leanest of problems can be enriched to become more engaging and to foster the deeper understanding that comes through multiple perspectives.

Besides selecting good problems, an essential component of problem-based teaching is observing and listening. You can make observations if the class is working in a traditional way, but usually you can observe and hear more, and the students can learn more, if they are working in groups. How do you phase group work into a traditional environment?

Working in Groups

To phase in group work, you might begin by reading and by attending professional development workshops. If you or your students are uncomfortable with having the class work in groups, you might build comfort by having pairs of students in adjacent seats work together on a focused task for only a minute or two at a time. Later, you can group three or four students occasionally, again for a few minutes at a time. As you extend the amount of time that students work in groups, you might assign roles to students until all are in the habit of contributing. You can also articulate—preferably with the help of the class—rules for group work.

Parents, students, and administrators will need reassurance that students' grades will not be lowered by working in groups. We suggest that you continue to assign grades to individual students rather than groups, but as students acquire skills in group work, you might gradually introduce a group-participation part of their grade. Its weight may increase over grading periods from, say, 5 percent to 15 percent. This grade shows that you believe in the value of learning group skills. You can emphasize that the group-participation grade is based on notes you make as you circulate around the classroom while students are working in groups.

You can begin group work even though you have had little experience using this format. But you will be happier if you build up your trust in the group process as well. Gradually take more time to help students address difficulties with working together. When students ask you for answers or hints to mathematical questions, try to avoid responding directly by deflecting their questions to their group members.

Problem-based teaching in a traditional setting begins with articulating mathematics and then finding appropriate problems to be used in a SPOSA-like class structure, usually with students working in groups. Your teaching will be most effective, though, if you also alter your role in the classroom. (See the chapters by Grouws and by Rasmussen, Yackel, and King in this volume for other perspectives on the teacher's role.)

The Teacher's Role

In a traditional environment, a teacher acts as a dispenser of knowledge. A more effective role for you might be described as a manager of investigation teams. Imagine that you are employed by a company or governmental agency, and you supervise teams of employees whose work is to solve various problems that come your way. What would your job entail?

Some of your tasks would be similar to what you probably already do, such as assigning problems to teams, evaluating the workers, and dealing with your supervisors. Other managerial aspects that you might find to be less familiar in a traditional educational environment may have to be phased in over time.

- **Good managers avoid micromanaging.** Begin to trust the student groups to organize their work, to think creatively, and to self-correct their ideas. Gradually you can intervene less and less, until you are focusing only on helping the groups work more effectively. When groups make presentations to the class, increasingly withhold your judgment, letting other students critique each presentation before you ask clarifying questions.

- **Even the best managers do not know the outcomes.** In business, money would be wasted if teams worked on problems that managers could already solve. In education, though, you can indeed solve the problems yourself. If you work toward more and more openness, however, you cannot really anticipate all methods and outcomes. As you learn to resist students' manipulations to get you to show them a solution, and as you encourage them to think creatively yet critically, they will begin to produce ideas you have not anticipated—ideas that you can then use to bring about deep understanding.

- **Good managers are experienced investigators.** Although you may be increasingly surprised by the outcomes, you are experienced in problem solving. You can offer suggestions, not to give omniscient "hints" but to provide good thinking strategies. "You know, the problem seems pretty complicated to me. I often find it helpful to work on a simpler problem first. Have you tried that?" Or "Do I remember that you reported on a similar case before?" Or "I believe I heard that the group over there had an idea about that. Why don't you send a representative over to find out if I heard correctly?" "Are you trying to say that this is a method to trisect every angle? Do the rest of you agree?"

- **Good managers hold workers accountable.** Pick individuals or groups to present their ideas to the entire class. Increasingly, part of the grade you give each student should reflect your assessment of that student's contributions to group work.

- **Good managers give appropriate praise and encouragement.** You cannot very well praise students for being "on the right track" while you are in the role of not knowing how to solve the problem. You can, however, praise good thinking and cooperation when you see it. You can also encourage students to learn from mistakes and to persevere despite setbacks.

- **Good managers are not the center of attention.** As you observe group work and presentations, begin sitting down or kneeling as much as possible to remove attention from yourself. Consciously try to disappear from students' awareness. Try to suppress the desire to be the focus of attention. Move toward letting students be more independent thinkers and learners.

- **Good managers take a long-term perspective.** Become more familiar with the entire curriculum and where the problem you have just assigned lies in that context. Become aware of the extent to which you must transcend the focus on solving this particular problem and build students' problem-solving and group skills so that they can deal successfully with the mathematics that lies ahead. Think more about the students' life spans and of how important the process skills and habits of mind will be in those lives.

- **Good managers manage.** They do not manage the individuals' thought process, but they manage the groups of workers so they work productively. Begin focusing on doing all that you can to help the groups function well together. Keep control of the working atmosphere so that individual workers feel confident that they can contribute and so that nobody distracts others from working. Think more about also controlling the order of group presentations so that students get ideas from one another.

Synergy

As you change your role and the structure of your class sessions, you loosen your control over students' thinking, so they will be generating ideas that you had not thought of before. As a good manager, you are enthusiastic rather than threatened, and you ask questions until you and the students better understand the proposed ideas. This questioning deepens your own understanding of the mathematics and helps in your articulation of the mathematical content and process goals. In the future, you will understand more deeply the foundational ideas, so that you can choose or generate rich problems that get at those ideas. Over time, you build your students' confidence and engagement so that your role and the structure of the class can be adapted to support learning through problem solving.

Some progress can be made in a term, and a good bit can occur over a year. Your own mathematical understanding, however, continues to deepen as you work with students for many years. And your skill as a manager of investigation teams grows as well, so that you and your students continue to learn in increasingly rich environments.

CHAPTER 14

Teaching Low-SES Students Mathematics through Problem Solving:
Tough Issues, Promising Strategies, and Lingering Dilemmas

Sarah Theule Lubienski
Jean Stilwell

D ATA from the National Assessment of Educational Progress indicate that students of low socioeconomic status (SES) are in particular need of opportunities to increase both their understanding of mathematical concepts and their problem-solving skills (Lubienski 2002). This book proposes teaching mathematics through problem solving as a means of addressing this need. Other chapters discuss the general benefits of, and strategies for, teaching mathematics to all students through problem solving.

This chapter assumes that beneficial outcomes can occur when teaching mathematics through problem solving, but it also acknowledges that teachers of low-SES students can face special challenges when implementing this approach. We believe that teachers are better positioned to help students learn important mathematical concepts and skills if they are aware of the special strengths and needs of their students and possess strategies for meeting their students' needs. However, discussing the strengths and needs of particular student groups is difficult, even controversial, because characterizing differences between groups of people can validate harmful stereotypes. The distinctions to be discussed are, of course, generalizations about groups and will not hold true for all individuals in those groups. However, avoiding all discussion of such differences can make teachers, and their students, the victims of blame and frustration when their attempts to move away from traditional teaching methods are met with students' struggles and resistance. (This chapter uses the term low SES to mean students whose parents have relatively limited formal education, income, and occupational status. This group includes some Caucasian students, as well as disproportionate numbers of students from various ethnic groups, including African Americans, Hispanic Americans, and students for whom English is a second language. Although this chapter focuses on low-SES students, likely, some of the strategies discussed here will be useful to teachers of other students as well.)

The purpose of this chapter is to bring some of our struggles and successes to light so that other teachers can learn from them. As we begin, we introduce ourselves and discuss how our experiences come together in this chapter. We then summarize Sarah's research, highlighting some of the challenges that her lower-SES students faced when learning mathematics through problem solving. We then describe a lesson taught by Jean, followed by a conversation between Sarah and Jean, as a way of illustrating some of the ways in which Jean has attempted to address the challenges raised in Sarah's research.

As a faculty member in mathematics education at Iowa State University, Sarah studies equity issues in relation to reform-oriented mathematics teaching. In a recent study, she identified SES-based differences in students' reactions to learning mathematics through problem solving (Lubienski 2000a; 2000b). Her study highlights challenges that teachers of low-SES students can face when moving toward problem-based mathematics instruction.

Jean has been a mathematics teacher for twenty-four years, including fourteen years in her current location, Patrick Henry High School in Minneapolis, Minnesota. The majority of students at Patrick Henry are African American, Hispanic, or recent Liberian or Hmong immigrants, with 74 percent of the students qualifying for free or reduced-price lunch. With funding from a National Science Foundation grant, Jean spent the past three years as a mentor to Minneapolis-area teachers who were beginning to implement an integrated, problem-centered curriculum (Fendel et al. 1997). Like Sarah, Jean acknowledges some special issues relating to teaching mathematics through problem solving in this setting. Jean's years of teaching experience have also given her much practical wisdom that helps her address these issues.

Sarah Discusses Her Research

After earning a master's degree in mathematics, I began a doctoral program in mathematics education at Michigan State University. During my course work there, I read about teachers who perpetuated inequities by using rote-based methods with low-SES students, whereas teachers of higher-SES students emphasized higher-level problem-solving skills (see, e.g., Anyon [1981]; Means and Knapp [1991]). I heartily agreed with critics who stated that teachers simply must raise their expectations of low-SES students.

At that time, I also worked on an NSF-funded curriculum development project that created sixth- through eighth-grade problem-centered mathematics materials. Having pilot tested the sixth-grade materials for one year in a middle-class school, I was ready to begin a year of pilot testing the seventh-grade materials in a more socioeconomically heterogeneous school (and to study the results for my dissertation). I, myself, was from a lower-SES background, yet I had excelled in mathematics. I was confident that other low-SES students could succeed when given a teacher who had an understanding of the current reform movement, a strong mathematics background, and high expectations for students.

During my teaching, I tried to avoid being the main authority for knowledge in the classroom and to have students learn through solving problems and discussing their ideas with me and one another. I avoided telling students whether their ideas were correct, instead encouraging them to think for themselves about which ideas were reasonable. I saw SES-related patterns in students' experiences with some aspects of this approach. (For more information about the pedagogy and curriculum used, see Lubienski [2000a; 2000b].) Whereas the higher-SES students tended to have confidence in their abilities to make sense of the mathematics problems and whole-class discussions, many lower-SES students said that they were "confused" by the open nature of the problems and conflicting ideas in the discussions; they desired more specific direction from the textbook and from me as their teacher. More lower-SES students said they were unsure of what they were supposed to be learning, and many said they wished I would just tell them "the rules" so they could have more time to practice them.

The contextualized problems in the curriculum often engaged the lower-SES students, who tended to delve into the contexts and consider a variety of real-world variables in solving the problems. Yet in doing so, these students sometimes missed the intended mathematical point. As one example, in a pizza-sharing problem designed to help students learn about fractions, several lower-SES students became concerned about who might arrive late to the restaurant and who would get "seconds." These students were sophisticated in their consideration of multiple, real-world variables, but they did not encounter the intended ideas about fractions.

Although some disparities in the lower- and higher-SES students' experiences were attributable to prior mathematics achievement, this explanation was not complete. The patterns I saw in my classroom are consistent with class cultural differences identified in sociological literature. (See Lubienski [2000a; 2000b] for an extended discussion of this literature.) Some of the pertinent results are discussed in the following paragraph.

Working-class jobs tend to require obedience to authority and conformity to routines, whereas middle-class occupations generally involve more autonomy. This effect is thought to carry over into child rearing, where more working-class parents tend to be overtly directive, whereas middle-class parents are more likely to use discussion and questioning when instructing their children. Some scholars connect lower-class cultures with the belief that outside forces, such as other people or luck, control one's fate, as well as with lower self-esteem in relation to school. These beliefs can combine to constrain some students' problem-solving efforts. Moreover, some scholars have linked lower-class cultures with more contextualized ways of knowing. Working-class children may become engrossed in mathematical contexts, such as shopping, used in school but still not gain the intended mathematical knowledge.

Again, in making these comparisons, one should remember that they involve broad generalizations about groups, and one cannot assume that such claims hold true for individual group members. Still, this literature suggests ways in which both instruction centered on discussion and the abstraction of mathematical ideas from contextualized problems could pose obstacles for some lower-SES students. However, it also confirms the need for many lower-SES students to become more confident mathematical problem solvers. Fortunately, some teachers have been persistent in their attempts to implement problem-centered approaches with lower-SES students. Jean is one such teacher, and we can learn from her experience.

Sarah recently visited Jean's classroom to examine her instructional methods, and the following narrative describes what she saw. A condensation of a dialogue between Jean and Sarah follows.

A Portrait of Jean's Classroom

It is a particularly hot day in May. Before students arrive for their freshman-level mathematics class, Jean distributes a folder and a basket containing protractors, rulers, and calculators to each of seven tables in her classroom. The folders are Jean's mechanism for collecting and returning students' daily work and grades. As students enter, they justifiably complain about the heat and locker-room smell of the classroom. Only twenty of the twenty-six enrolled students are present today. Jean knows that suspensions and mental health issues account for some of the absences. Several of the students present are recent immigrants with limited English proficiency.

As a "warm up," Jean places questions regarding the definitions of *corresponding* and *proportional* on the overhead projector. Students answer the questions in their journals, using their unit study guide to help them. Jean developed the study guide, which contains questions, phrases, and words followed by blank lines to prompt students to write important definitions and ideas throughout the unit. (Examples of writing prompts in the study guide include "Counterexample," "Why are triangles special?" and "Proportions: How I solve them.") As students work, Jean circulates and notes which students brought their textbooks to class.

Jean uses student absences the previous day as a rationale for summarizing what was learned. With questions from Jean, two students explain that they made shapes with straws to learn that quadrilaterals collapse but triangles do not. Jean explains how this discovery led to the side-side-side triangle congruence theorem.

Jean begins today's lesson on the angle-angle similarity theorem. At the overhead projector, Jean uses a protractor to draw a 40-60-80 triangle. She then tells students to draw a horizontal line at the bottom of their papers and instructs them to use that line as a base to build a triangle with 40- and 60-degree angles. Students must then compare their triangles with others made at their table to see whether they are similar or congruent. When some students have difficulty getting started, Jean offers explicit reminders about how to use the protractor. As students work, Jean regulates some overheated students' visits to the hallway drinking fountain.

When students are finished comparing their triangles with those of others at their table, Jean directs a brief discussion of whether the students' triangles are similar or congruent to one another. During the discussion, Jean has a tense confrontation with a student, Rodney, who does not want to wait until after the discussion to sharpen his pencil. Although larger than Jean and very persistent in his efforts to walk past Jean toward the pencil sharpener, Rodney eventually backs down and returns to his seat. The discussion continues. With a prompting question from Jean, students agree that the triangles are similar but not congruent because, as several students call out, "They aren't the same size." "OK!" says Jean.

Jean then tells students to make another triangle with 30- and 60-degree angles. The students again make their triangles. "Are they similar or congruent to each other?" asks Jean. A few students call out "similar." At Jean's prompting, several students trace their triangles on transparencies and overlay them on the overhead screen, revealing an array of similar triangles. After working to get students seated again, Jean asks students to turn to the "Why are triangles special?" prompt in their study guide. She remarks, "It's a waste of time to do the activity if you don't catch the meaning of the activity." After three students describe how they know when two triangles are similar, Jean summarizes their comments by writing the following on an overhead transparency: "To get similar triangles, you need to have ONLY corresponding equal angles OR proportional sides." Students write this statement in their study guides.

During the final minutes of class, Jean assigns four homework problems involving finding missing side lengths of similar triangles. Jean completes the first problem with the students, using questions to remind them of what they know about similar triangles and proportional sides. Students conclude, "Oh, this is easy," as they hurry to try the next problem before the bell rings.

A Dialogue about Jean's Teaching

Sarah: When you first began teaching through problem solving, how did your students react?

Jean: During the first two years, my students asked for "real math." But after having problem-centered instruction for a few years, they stopped asking. I actually think that students and parents here are more open to new things than those in more affluent districts. (The trend for high-SES parents to actively resist educational reform has been documented elsewhere, e.g., in Rothstein, Carnoy, and Benveniste [1999].) Still, I have to work hard every day to get students to focus. There are two particular struggles that my students face with their new roles in the classroom.

First, my students want a teacher who takes charge of the classroom. They complain about teachers who do not have an orderly classroom, but they will not help them get that order—student resistance is very active here. So for these students, there are extra challenges when trying to move toward the teacher's being less directive and the students' taking on a stronger role in the classroom. For example, when a student is presenting ideas to the class, I must constantly push the class to pay attention to that student.

Second, many of my students have low self-esteem. These students think it is a bad reflection on them to struggle with a problem, so it's better to not even try. I have worked hard to create an atmosphere in which it's OK to struggle. I try to build up students' feelings of competence by setting attainable, yet challenging goals for their learning and by providing nonjudgmental feedback. Notice that in the triangle lesson every student did try to build a triangle, and they got something out of it in terms of vocabulary.

Sarah: These two issues are consistent with the struggles I saw with my low-SES students. I began teaching through problem solving, expecting students to be enthusiastic participants. Many students did find the problems interesting, but they wanted more specific direction from me. They also missed the validation they previously received when they got 98 out of 100 problems correct on a worksheet.

I'm wondering about some of the strategies you have used to address these issues. I noticed that you gave students more direction during the triangle lesson than was suggested in the teacher's edition of your textbook. For example, the book suggests letting each group choose its own angles, but you specified the angles to be used.

Jean: Yes, and I modeled how to draw the triangle, reminding them how to use the protractor. I even told them to begin by drawing the line across the bottom of their paper. I sometimes add more structure so that students can focus on the meaning of what they are doing instead of being distracted by extraneous details. Also, you might have noticed that the lesson in the book introduced the angle-side-angle idea, as well. We did not get to this, but we covered the main idea of the lesson, which was my goal.

I used to stay closer to the teacher's guide, but I found it didn't give enough structure to students who were struggling with their behavior and with the mathematics. I have tried to add a predictable structure to each lesson. I begin with a warm-up, which I use to reinforce previous learning and/or set the stage for new lessons. I also sometimes use it to prepare students for the Minnesota Basic Standards Test, which my students must pass in order to graduate. The day's lesson begins with something concrete for them to explore, and then we move to the abstract. Like yesterday we created shapes with straws, today we drew triangles, and then we moved to the angle-angle similarity theorem. The concrete experiences give students something to refer to.

Sarah: Is the study guide another adaptation you've made? It seems to help address the issue of students' focusing on the contexts of the problems instead of abstracting the intended mathematical ideas from problem explorations.

Jean: Yes, and the study guide is particularly important for this unit because of all the vocabulary involved with learning about similarity.

Sarah: I noticed that you have a detailed grading system. I'm wondering if this system helps fulfill students' desire for direction and affirmation from the teacher. I also continue to wonder whether teachers should fulfill this desire, as opposed to promoting more student self-direction and intrinsic motivation. Can you say more about how you handle grading and assignments?

Jean: I'm still working with many of my students on how to come to class ready to learn. So I give students points for the warm-up, having their book with them, completing class work, and doing their homework. All this information is recorded daily on a chart in their folder and is then totaled to give students a weekly grade and a current estimate of their quarter grade.

The teacher's guide suggests having students discuss homework at the beginning of class. I've found that to be problematic, because several students will not have done the work, due to absences, needing help with it, or other reasons. I don't want to tempt students to simply copy others' solutions. I give bonus points to homework that arrives on time, but I always accept late work. I have found that my students need to know they can always raise their grade, and they need to see their own effort as directly and fairly linked with their grade. This is one reason why I've moved toward more individual accountability and fewer group assignments than the teacher's guide suggests.

At the end of each unit, there's a test. I let them use their study guides on tests, which is another way in which their work pays off. Students also have portfolios, and I give them specific writing prompts for their end-of-unit portfolio entries. Finally, we have a "problem of the week," which allows students to explore more open-ended problems. I use these problems as a way to explicitly teach problem-solving skills and metacognitive strategies. For example, the first part of each write-up is the student's explanation of the problem in his or her own words.

Sarah: So you explicitly teach your students about problem solving, in addition to teaching through problem solving. (See Lubienski [1999] for more details about this distinction.) Although the trend in the past decade has been toward the integration of these two aspects, you give your students time to focus explicitly on problem-solving skills, apart from the regular curriculum. This makes sense in light of the struggles I observed in my classroom.

Something that troubled me as I was doing my study is the fact that I was in the school only part of the day to do the research. I felt disconnected from the rest of my students' lives. Are there things you do that go beyond class time?

Jean: I've found that my students need to know that I care about them or I cannot instruct them. For example, if Rodney and I did not have a relationship based on caring and trust, I could not have confronted him in class like I did. My students are not looking for a buddy, but want a teacher who is caring, firm, and fair.

A primary way I show that I care is by giving students support to help them complete and understand their work. I do after-school tutorials with pop and cookies each Wednesday. Many of my students can't ask for help from their parents at home, and some have incredible commitments outside of school. For example, I have one Hmong eleventh grader who is married, and it is her responsibility to go home and cook for about twenty people and to run the household. She also works at [a fast-food restaurant]. The support I give to her and other students during and after school is absolutely essential. We hear much talk about raising expectations of students, but high expectations are not enough. Students must be supported so they can meet those expectations.

Sarah: How do you handle dilemmas of how much support is too much? In my teaching I strongly resisted giving in to students' desire for more structure and more direction because I trusted that more open-ended methods would ultimately serve my students better. I continue to be haunted by the knowledge that higher-SES students are more likely to be taught critical thinking skills, whereas lower-SES students are more likely to be taught obedience to rules their teachers give them. Are you concerned that by adding support and structure for your students, they are not becoming independent mathematical problem solvers?

Jean: Yes, this is an issue. However, I view this as a long-term process. Students' becoming independent problem solvers is an end goal, not something I can simply assume from the beginning. I gradually diminish the explicit support I give as students develop the confidence and skills they need to learn mathematics through problem solving. By the third year, their problem-solving, discussion, and group-work skills are improved, and that's encouraging.

Teaching my students through problem solving is not easy. A strength of the new reform-oriented curricula is that I can actively involve heterogeneous students working from bell to bell. These curricula do not make math a ladder. Students who struggle with basic skills can and should still engage with important ideas, such as why two triangles have the same shape.

Discussion and Conclusion

Many of the issues that Sarah identified in her research are similar to those faced by Jean. For example, Sarah's research suggests that low-SES students can face particular difficulties when moving away from a direct-teaching model. Jean addresses her students' desire for teacher direction and affirmation by using predictable lesson sequences, adding structure to help students focus on the problems' main points, and by laying out for her students clear expectations that include a grading scheme explicitly linking students' daily efforts with grades.

Sarah's research also suggests that some low-SES students need help in abstracting the intended mathematical ideas from contextualized problems. Jean points out the benefits of contexts—they give students something concrete to build on. However, she also uses tools, such as the study guide, to help students identify the main mathematical ideas after their problem explorations, and she gives students explicit support so they can accurately describe and record those ideas.

Many of the strategies that Jean has developed are consistent with others reported in the literature as being particularly useful for low-SES, as well as ethnic minority, students. Examples include her emphasis on building a supportive relationship with students, conducting individualized tutoring sessions, building from what students know to what they do not know, connecting new ideas with meaningful models or contexts, and making the desired classroom norms explicit. (See, e.g., Ladson-Billings [1995]; Fuson et al. [2000]; Silver, Smith, and Nelson [1995]; and Delpit [1988].)

The need for such strategies points out the vital importance of the role of the teacher when teaching low-SES students through problem solving. Moreover, Jean's observation that her students need several years to develop problem-solving and discussion skills indicates the importance of teacher collaboration across grade levels, so that students are given consistent support in adapting to their new roles. This collaboration appears to be particularly important for secondary schools containing many low-SES students who have been taught with traditional methods in the past.

However, many questions remain that researchers and educators must continue to address. For example, despite students' frustrations, to what extent is it beneficial to push for an open-ended problem-solving environment, as opposed to providing additional structure for struggling students? How might adapting instruction for lower-SES students, even for a limited time, perpetuate inequities, because teaching lower- and higher-SES students with different methods produces different mathematical outcomes? Our hope is that this chapter supports and stimulates teachers who are looking for help for low SES students that goes beyond simple admonitions for holding high expectations for all students. We acknowledge that the struggles they face in teaching through problem solving are different in some ways from those faced by teachers in more affluent districts. In addition to those discussed here, issues involving absenteeism, crime, student health care, school funding, and parental involvement—just to name a few—are different for teachers in low- and high-poverty schools. We do not raise these issues to validate the approach of those teachers who teach low-SES students only basic computational skills through rote methods. We discuss these issues to help teachers identify and address the difficulties that they and their low-SES students can face as they move toward more meaningful, problem-centered mathematics instruction.

Who Says They Can't Do Algebra?

Mary Jo Messenger
Emma Ames

TEACHING a mathematics course that is firmly based on problem solving, collaborative work, and journal writing to ninth-grade students who are not fully prepared to study regular algebra is a challenge even for two teachers with more than sixty years of combined experience. Such a course, however, can be extremely important for these students' development of conceptual understanding and problem-solving skills, and it can foster a sense of unprecedented satisfaction in them and in their teachers.

In this article we describe some of our experiences with this kind of class: characteristics of the students, our classroom philosophy, suggested classroom-management techniques, some of the activities we used, and the importance of using technology in the class. In addition to those practical matters, the most important thing that we hope to communicate is our belief that this approach to teaching not only can give these marginal students real understanding and skills but also can profoundly and positively affect their attitudes toward their study of mathematics and toward themselves.

The Students: Marginal Preparation, Poor Learning Habits

The students in these three classes consisted primarily of lower level ninth- and tenth-grade students with weak basic skills and poor social skills—students considered by some to be incapable of significant mathematical thinking. The students were of a variety of races, with more than half being African American.

About one-third were special education students, and several were nonnative speakers of English who were also enrolled in ESOL classes. In general, the students had had difficulty in previous mathematics classes, as well as in other subjects. Support at home was inconsistent, or not even present at all, for many of the students, but most of them attended school regularly.

Because of their less-than-successful background in mathematics, these students typically had not played a positive, active role in their own learning. For example, many students simply expected the teacher to show them every detail of a solution procedure. Also, early in the class, the few students who did venture to suggest ideas found it hard to convince their group to have confidence that their ideas were worth considering. Other students were only too quick to say that the work was too hard, that they were stupid, that they could not do mathematics or algebra, and so forth. Some students misbehaved by showing off or getting other students to fool around. By providing a diversion, these students refocused the attention of the other students and could thus avoid feeling inferior and frustrated because they could not do the mathematics. Because of these old patterns in the students' behavior, we had to work hard both at establishing different social norms and at holding back to allow students sufficient opportunities to understand the mathematics and to become better problem solvers.

Classroom Philosophy: Emphasizing Problem Solving without Ignoring Basic Skills—and with High Expectations

Like many other teachers and school systems, we faced the philosophical issue of whether to use traditional mathematics curriculum and instruction or problem-based curriculum and instruction in our classes. Although we recognized the need for these students to continue to work on basic skills, we also wanted them to have rich problem-solving experiences that would allow them to strengthen their conceptual understanding, gain confidence in their mathematical abilities, and acquire the skills needed to collaborate with others—all while using the graphing calculator to solve meaningful problems. Moreover, we had to prepare our students to pass the Maryland State High School Assessment. This test, for which students are expected to use graphing calculators, emphasizes conceptual understanding in solving real-world problems.

To meet all these expectations, we used two different textbooks. One was used for working on basic skills and was the resource for most homework assignments. The other was used for rich problems. This book presents a problem situation and then leads solvers through a carefully developed sequence of questions that allow them to learn mathematics, often using tables, graphs, and symbols. We believe that this hands-on, collaborative approach is essential for teaching meaningful mathematics through problem solving to the types of students in these classes.

This combination of textbooks and instructional approach allowed us to focus on mathematical understanding through problem solving, collaborating, communicating, and using technology while still providing some work on the fundamental manipulative skills with which the students needed continued practice. Another fundamental tenet of our philosophy for these classes was high expectations for the students. We believed—and, after teaching these classes, now believe even more strongly—that these students, in spite of their weakness in symbol-manipulation skills, could indeed learn to do significant mathematical thinking. Because these students had generally been less than successful in previous mathematics classes, we are convinced that our firm belief in their ability to succeed in this class played an important part in laying the groundwork for their success.

Classroom Management: Structure, Organizational Skills, and Communication

Structure and routine were very important for these classes, which ranged in size from ten to twenty-two students. We set the firm expectation that students were to be in their seats with paper, pencil, textbook, and graphing calculator on the desk when the bell rang. We also established set routines for checking homework and for the way in which we conducted the problem-solving activities.

Another type of structural support came from regular access to peer tutors and special education assistants. Problem-solving experiences involving collaboration are crucially important for understanding, but students at this level often have difficulty working in a small group without an adult or older student to guide them and help them stay on task, boost their confidence, and work through the areas that might frustrate them. Having students work in pairs was a strategy that also worked well for us as we taught these classes. This practice was especially helpful at the beginning of the course, when the students were learning how to work collaboratively.

Communication with others is implicit in good group work, but we also structured the classes to offer many other opportunities for reflection and communication. Classroom routines included time for students to reflect on what they learned from the activities and for them to communicate their ideas to their classmates, both orally and in writing, through class discussions, oral presentations, and individual journals.

We firmly believe that problem-solving and thinking skills are strengthened by this kind of reflection and communication, which formed an integral part of these classes. This idea can be illustrated by the students' journal responses following an investigation in which the students collected heart-rate data before and after exercising. After collecting the data, the students created box plots, first by hand and then by using their graphing calculators. One of the major points that the students identified in the discussion of this activity as they examined the different graphs was the fact that to be able to make a valid comparison, the two box plots had to be drawn on the same graph with the same scale. When students did this activity by hand, they drew the box plots separately and did not use the same scale. When they plotted the data on the calculator, however, and turned two plots on at the same time, the scale was the same. The resulting discussion was quite animated. Most of the students, but not all, seemed to understand the importance and implications of using the same scale for comparison.

In addition to allowing us to assess the students' understanding of concepts, the various modes of communication also allowed us to assess the students' feelings and attitudes. We knew that both this type of class and our expectations of the students were different from what they had experienced in previous mathematics classes. Because one of our goals was to help improve the students' attitudes toward mathematics, determining how they felt about this experience was very important to our assessment of the effectiveness of the class. Journal entries such as the following show how some of the students reacted.

> In my earlier math classes only the smart people talked and answered questions, so I just sat there, did what I needed to do and left. This class is fun. We talk more, stand up, and everything.

> My last math class was nothing but work. As soon as we were done, we just handed it in. We did no group work. We did everything by ourselves. And

we did a lot of worksheets, and I sat at a desk by myself.

I liked this class period the most because I found myself doing well and not giving anyone any problems. I was not bored, but for the first time I was actually having fun in math. I had accomplished much since when I had left. I don't know what everyone else feels about this class, but I am just happy on how I had improved. I liked the group thing, and maybe that's one of the reasons I worked good.

These methods of conducting the classes did not turn the students into fully motivated, eager learners in every class session. However, conducting the classes as we described in this section was extremely helpful to the students.

Sample Activity: Problem Solving with Cable TV

What kinds of activities did we do in the classes? One activity from our regular textbook supported students' learning by putting the mathematics in the context of television viewing. The context of the situation was the percent of audience share for both major network programming and cable television beginning in the year 1982. Students were given the following information.

Trends in network and cable television audience shares can be modeled by the following linear equations:

Major Networks: $Y_1 = 75 - 2.5X$

Cable: $Y_2 = 5 + 2.5X$

Here, X stands for years since 1982, Y_1 and Y_2 stand for percent of audience share.

The students were then asked the following questions:

Write symbolic equations and inequalities that can be used to answer each of the following questions about the relationship between cable and network audience shares.

a. When will the network share fall to 25 percent?

b. How long will the cable share remain below 50 percent?

c. When was the network share double the cable share?

Students were allowed to answer these questions using what they thought was the easiest method. They also had to write what their solutions meant in the context of the problem. Requiring this explanation is very important for students at this level because it requires them to show they understand that the symbols relate to each other and have meaning in a real-world situation. Students were then asked to further demonstrate their understanding of the symbols in this situation by writing questions corresponding to several symbolic equations and inequalities, including the following:

$$75 - 2.5X = 40,$$

$$5 + 2.5X \geq 20,$$

and

$$75 - 2.5X = 3(5 + 2.5X).$$

This activity is an example of the type of work that the students were doing when they started to solve linear equations and inequalities; the questions in the activity led students to be able to solve a system of equations. Although in our skill work during the year we worked on solving symbolic algebra equations, this particular lesson gave meaning—at least for many students—to something that still caused many of them difficulty. This activity also allowed students to see that algebra is useful beyond school.

The Importance of Technology

Teaching this course to these students would not have been possible without the graphing calculator. From the very beginning, the calculator offered the visualization that gave extra support to students with poor English skills. The value of looking at a problem in alternative ways—through tables, graphs, and equations—was constantly reinforced by the use of the graphing calculator. For our students, many of whom could not do basic arithmetic at a level necessary for traditional algebra, the calculator was an essential tool that allowed them to focus on solving the problem at hand and not be held back by their arithmetic skills.

Our assessments showed that the various capabilities of the calculator (e.g., graphing and producing tables of values) gave the students a means to understand the mathematical concepts while compensating to some extent for their weak symbol-manipulation skills. Furthermore, they were often aware of this understanding and proud of themselves for attaining it. These facts proved to us that the philosophy behind, and the practices in, this class did make a crucial difference in both what students could do and how they viewed their own ability to do mathematics.

Summary

Our work with these classes demonstrates that, with a problem-based approach supported by collaborative learning, graphing calculators, communication, and practice on basic skills, even students who would not ordinarily be considered ready to study algebra can indeed learn to do significant mathematical thinking. This approach also allowed these students to gain confidence, to become enthusiastic about mathematical ideas, and to experience a fundamental, positive change in attitude toward their own study of mathematics. A corollary to this change in attitude, we believe, was students' improved self-images as a result of real success in this mathematics class—a first for many of the students.

Although this approach was not uniformly successful with all students and although individual students still had bad days as well as good days, we know of no approach that is as successful with this level of students. The results in our classes meant not only that the students' achievement and attitude improved significantly but also that we as teachers found great professional satisfaction in reaching these students.

We have not achieved the vision of the NCTM Standards in a single year, but as we reflect on the following quote from *Principles and Standards for School Mathematics*, we believe that we are headed in the right direction:

> Students are flexible and resourceful problem solvers. Alone or in groups and with access to technology, they work productively and reflectively. . . . Orally and in writing, students communicate their ideas and results effectively. They value mathematics and engage actively in learning it (NCTM 2000, p. 3).

CHAPTER 15

Teaching through Orchestrated Problem Sequences in Russia

Nina Shteingold
Nannette Feurzeig

THIS chapter presents one approach to teaching mathematically gifted students in Russia, an approach in which students are taught mainly through solving problems. Some students who show a high interest in mathematics are gathered into one class, usually called a *math class*. Neither the curriculum nor the teaching style is the same in any two of these math classes; however, certain trends and commonalities are present. Although the math class approach is somewhat different in structure from typical U.S. problem-based approaches described in this volume, many of its elements may be useful to U.S. teachers.

A math class usually lasts for the two or three final years of high school, ninth or tenth through eleventh grades. Most students who enter a math class have spent the previous year attending an after-school *math circle*. (Not all math circles are associated with math classes; for a different type of math circle, see Fomin [1996].) The math circles associated with math classes are intended to help students develop a certain attitude toward mathematics, a certain style of communication about mathematics, and some habits of mind useful in solving problems. Not everyone who attends a math circle becomes a student in a subsequent math class, and not all math class students are former math circle members. Still, the math circle is an important stage in teaching

The writing of this chapter was supported, in part, by the National Science Foundation, grant number ESI-0099093. The opinions expressed are those of the authors and not necessarily those of the Foundation.

mathematics through problem solving. The next section describes the math circle and gives an example of study problems. The third section describes how a math class is organized and taught. The main and the unique part of teaching and learning mathematics in a math class takes place in a course that we call Mathematics through Problem Solving. The fourth section gives specifics of this course, with examples of study problems. The final section describes some strengths and weaknesses of students taught primarily through problem solving.

The Math Circle

Usually the teacher who plans to form a math class conducts a math circle during the previous year. For example, a teacher who plans to teach a three-year math class would start a math circle for eighth graders. Many Moscow students who have participated in a city math Olympiad receive invitations by mail, but any student may come to a math circle meeting even after it has started.

Math circles usually meet once a week for two hours. The meetings are very informal. The teacher is assisted by several mentors, who are older high school students or undergraduate mathematics majors; these mentors are usually current or former math class students. At every meeting, a list of problems is given to each student; the students work on these problems in groups or individually, raising hands as soon as they have solved one. The teacher or one of the mentors comes to discuss the student's solution.

The problems are often puzzlelike and require no mathematical knowledge outside the traditional mathematics program. An example of problems, translated from Shen (2000), for one meeting of a math circle for seventh graders is given in figure 15.1.

The following are some of the important features of math circle problem sets:

- **Short questions.** For example, no "...if yes, show how; if no, explain why" types of questions are used.

- **Simple vocabulary.** For example, problem 1 includes the concept of *congruence* but does not use the terminology.

- **Proceed from easier to harder problems.** Note how problem 2 requires deeper geometrical thinking than problem 1.

- **Problem extensibility.** For example, in consideration of the student's level and interest in problem 1, the mentor might request a proof that the parts are really identical,

1. Can you cut the shape in picture 1, which is made of three squares, into two, three, and four identical parts?

2. Can you divide in two equal parts both a rectangular piece of bread and a round piece of cheese by a single straight cut (see picture 2)? If yes, in how many ways? (The cheese on the bread cannot be moved.)

3. All faces of a $3 \times 3 \times 3$ cube are painted. Then the cube is cut into 27 small $1 \times 1 \times 1$ cubes. How many among these small cubes have—

   • no colored faces?

   • one colored face?

   • two colored faces?

   • three colored faces?

   • four colored faces?

4. Inside a 1×1 square are 105 points. Prove that among these points are two that are no more than 0.2 apart.

5. How would the inner diameter of a ring change when the ring is heated? See picture 3.

6. Can you cut the horseshoe in picture 4 into six parts with two straight cuts (the parts cannot be moved between the cuts)?

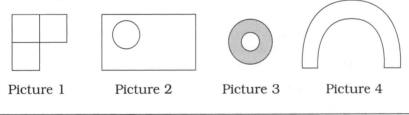

Picture 1   Picture 2   Picture 3   Picture 4

Figure 15.1. A math circle problem set

ask whether another way exists to cut the shape, or offer another shape to dissect. Also, a student interested in problem 3 may be asked what happens with a cube of different dimensions ($4 \times 4 \times 4$, for example, or even $n \times n \times n$). A student who gives a correct solution to problem 4 may be asked whether the problem can be made stricter, for example, by using fewer points, a smaller distance, or a larger square.

- **Broad assortment of approaches.** For example, problem 5 is a physics problem rather than a mathematics problem. It requires a mental experiment: What happens if we have a disk instead of the ring? When students do not know what technique the next problem will require, they must be alert, ready to use their whole arsenal. They perceive every problem as a new adventure.

- **Attractiveness of problems.** Many problems look like puzzles.

Mentors do not teach general problem-solving techniques. Students acquire various techniques in the same way that they learn to solve problems, without explicit teaching. Exposure to mathematical culture also takes place along the way, as adults and students talk about problems. For example, problem 2 does not ask for a proof, but a student who offers "no" as a solution is asked to explain why. The explanation is pursued until the student has presented a complete, although not necessarily formal, proof. Gradually the student learns that any answer is expected to include either a solution or a proof that no solution is possible. Thus, students in a math circle slowly develop a sense of what solving a problem means; they learn to explain their solutions clearly. The main goals of a math circle associated with a math class are to expose students to mathematical culture and to develop their general interest in problem solving rather than to teach them new mathematics topics.

The year spent in the math circle does not directly teach students the content essential for entry into a math class, but the experience offers them the opportunity to attack an assortment of nonstandard problems at the appropriate level of difficulty and to "invent," and thus acquire, a variety of problem-solving techniques. Thus the students experience the pleasures of solving problems and of communicating about them—they feel what it means to do mathematics. The year of conducting a math circle is also important to the teacher, who uses it to become familiar with the majority of the future math class students and to set the tone of communication with them.

The Math Class

In early spring, all participants in a math circle are invited to apply to a math class that their teacher is forming. Students outside the math circle may also apply. The teacher selects students and forms the class. The students in this class study all subjects together during their remaining math class years, usually three, less often two or four years. During these years, students take about three hours of algebra and two hours of geometry per week, which is the same as, or even a little less than, students in non–math classes usually take. The content and pedagogy are usually traditional. Regular textbooks are used; the teacher presents new concepts; the students are responsible for class work and homework, and they write tests and receive grades.

But the students also take another math subject, usually for two two-hour sessions each week, taught by the teacher who formed the math class. We refer to this subject as Mathematics through Problem Solving, and the classes are completely different. Content varies from one class to another, usually including some topics from algebra followed by calculus. No textbooks are used. Instead, the students work on a series of problem sets created by the teacher, sometimes with the help of mentors. Each set includes definitions and problems on a particular topic. Some problems are required, as being necessary for moving on to later material; others are optional. Each student receives the same set. The next set of problems is given out when most of the class has completed most of the required problems in the current set. The school year includes about thirty of these sets.

In class and at home, students study the definitions and solve the problems. During class, a student who has solved a problem presents the solution to the teacher or to one of the assisting mentors, orally or in writing. The mentor points out any holes, circular arguments, or other difficulties, sometimes mentioning a different path to the solution. The student continues working on the problem and discussing it with the mentor until a full solution is reached. The tone of these discussions is generally not that of an examination but is more like a discussion between two colleagues. Meanwhile, the other students in a classroom are solving problems on their own. The atmosphere in a classroom is very similar to that of the math circle.

A math class is usually referred to as "the class of [the founding teacher]." The relationship between the teacher and the students is close; it is less formal than in conventional classes and often lasts well beyond the students' school years. Graduates of math classes often become mentors in subsequent math classes of their teachers. Usually, each math class mentor works with several students, but each student works primarily with a single mentor; mentor-student connections deepen across time. The informal atmosphere in the classroom and the close teacher-student relationships reduce the need for grades as assessment tools. The progress of any individual student is known—to the teacher, to the student's mentor(s), and to the student—through many conversations, discussions of problems, and the teacher's record of all problems solved by that student. Tests are usually take-home tests that serve more as a review of material learned and an opportunity to make new connections among the concepts learned than as an evaluation of students' knowledge. The need for a grade as part of an individual student's high school record is generally met with an A. Although students are relieved of the pressure of grades, they feel a different constant pressure, namely, that many problems remain to be solved. No student is likely ever to solve all the problems in all the sets.

Teachers rarely, if ever, assign homework or set deadlines for solving all problems of a set. Students work on the same set of problems, submitting solutions at different times to different mentors, yet cheating is not an issue. Sometimes, a pair of students work on a problem and present it together, and each student receives credit.

Mathematics through Problem Solving: An Orchestrated Problem Sequence

Because Mathematics through Problem Solving consists almost entirely of students solving problems on their own, good problem sets are essential to the course. To be useful for students with various abilities, the problem sets must be designed very carefully. Rather than just collections of problems, they must be problem *sequences*, in which each problem has its own important place in the orchestration of students' learning. The problem sets generally enable the student to move from one problem to the next without requiring great leaps of insight. The progress and style of the problem sets for a class vary with the mathematical tastes of the teacher and the strengths of the particular class.

The example of a problem set given in figure 15.2 is our translation, with slight edits and shortening, of an actual set (Shen 2000). Students received it toward the end of eighth grade. This problem set was their first exposure to complex numbers.

The following are some essential features of all math class problem sequences:

- **Minimal introduction.** Only definitions and some important reference information are included. Occasionally an example is included for clarity.

Complex numbers

Complex numbers are expressions of the form $a + bi$, where a and b are real numbers, and i in as imaginary number for which $i^2 = -1$. Complex numbers can be added and multiplied by multiplying out and combining like terms.

1. Calculate:

   (a) $(2 + 3i) + (7 - i)$,   (b) $(2 + 3i)(7 - i)$,   (c) $(1 + i)(1 - i)$,

   (d) $(2 - 3i)(3 + 2i)$,   (e) $(4 + 3i) - 3(2 - i)$.

2. Calculate:

   (a) $(-i)^2$,   (b) i^{10}.

3. Calculate:

   (a) $(1 + i)^{10}$,   (b)' $(1 - i)^{10}$.

4. Calculate $(1 + i)^{101}$.

5. Find two complex numbers such that their sum and product are both equal to 2.

6. Find x such that $x(1 + i) = 1$. (Here and below, x is a complex number.)

7. Find x such that $x(2 + 3i) = 3 - 2i$.

8. Find x such that $x(1 + i) = 3 + 4i$.

9. Optional. Find x such that $x(2 + 3i) = 5 + 4i$. (Hint: Look for $x = a + bi$; construct a system of two equations with unknowns a and b.)

10. Optional. Calculate $1 + i^2 + i^3 + \cdots + i^{100}$.

11. Optional. Calculate $\left(\sqrt{3} + i\right)^{30}$.

12. Optional. Find x such that

    (a) $x^2 = 2$,   (b) $x^2 = -2$,   (c) $x^2 = 2i$.

13. Optional. Find x such that $x^2 = 1 + i$.

14. Optional. Find x such that $x^2 + 2x + 2 = 0$.

15. Optional. Find all $x = a + bi$ such that $x^3 = 1$.

Figure 15.2. A math class problem set

- **Low entry level.** Students usually begin working on a sequence by themselves, without any introduction from their teacher or mentors. Because each student must be able to start the work independently, the problems at the beginning of each sequence are relatively simple.

- **Gradual increase in difficulty.** Each problem in a sequence has its own place and its own value. Subsequent problems are more difficult; to solve them, students must use what they have learned from previously solved problems. This gradual increase in difficulty characterizes the problems within a set and also the collection of problem sets across the life of the math class.

- **Maximum clarity.** Teachers do everything possible to avoid ambiguity, keeping the text of problems as short and clear as possible so as to save students' energy and keep them motivated. This clarity ensures that students are solving exactly the problem the teacher means them to solve; its result may be needed for solving subsequent problems.

- **Many multilevel problems.** On the surface, a multilevel problem looks very specific, asking for a concrete answer, a number, or a yes-or-no response. Any student who finds and justifies that concrete answer gets credit, but the problem also offers the opportunity to discover or formulate a more general fact or rule. Problems 2 through 4 are examples. Any student who calculates i^{10} will discover the periodic nature of the sequence $i, i^2, i^3, \ldots$, but nothing in the problem statement requires the student to report this discovery. Problem 5 is another example. While solving this problem, a student may figure out that, given the sum and product of two complex numbers, it is always possible to find the two numbers. Such problems not only allow a multilevel approach, in which both strong and average students can learn from the problem, but also teach a student to be always alert for more general facts than a problem explicitly states. Some students develop such a habit in a couple of years; others seem to possess it from the beginning.

- **Generally nonstandard problems.** A student approaching a problem usually has not yet learned a method for solving it. The student is challenged to create a method or an algorithm; such a requirement is definitely a nonstandard problem. See problems 4 through 8 in figure 15.2 for examples.

- **Limited use of terminology.** New concepts or definitions are introduced only when they are needed, or even a little later. For example, in this sequence, students manipulate *conjugates* without yet knowing the term.

- **Clearly stated but multiple approaches.** A problem, if possible, should be stated in a way that requires an exact and clear answer but allows multiple representations or approaches to solving it. Similarly, if the goal of a problem sequence is for the student to discover a general fact or to develop a concept, this goal should allow different ways of achieving it. Shen (2000) says (our translation), "A theorem can be decomposed into a sequence of problems, so that a student, solving these problems, jumps from stone to stone and finally reaches that theorem's statement. We try to place more stones than necessary, so that there are different paths in the same direction."

Strengths and Weaknesses of Students Taught Exclusively through Problem Solving

Students who are taught mathematics through problem solving have many strengths. Generally they do not fear attacking a problem; they are good at understanding a posed problem, and they can actively use a variety of problem-solving techniques that they have learned implicitly along the way. Their knowledge of mathematics is very solid and active. Math class teachers avoid rushing students in their problem solving, because doing so would reduce their enthusiasm and interest as well as make their knowledge less solid. As a result, the process of learning mathematics by solving problems is slower than learning by explanation.

Usually a student presents a problem's solution to the mentor in a conversation. During the first few years, in particular, math class teachers prefer this approach. It not only allows for more individual attention and for correcting students faster and more appropriately to their levels and styles but also enables mathematical communication between a student and a mentor to be informal without leading to bad habits of incompleteness or approximation. As a result, the ability of math class students to solve problems often exceeds their ability to communicate their solutions in written form.

Also, as students develop their problem-solving abilities, they more and more prefer to solve problems themselves rather than read or listen to someone else's solutions. Later, in more traditional classes, this disposition may slow down students' learning and restrain their ability to read and write about mathematics.

Math class teachers use different methods to compensate for these potential weaknesses, including the following:

- Providing occasional lectures, in which students listen to a short, logically complete mathematics presentation and are then asked to write it down. The written texts are jointly checked and corrected by a mathematics teacher and a language teacher for mathematical accuracy and completeness and for the clarity and quality of the language (classes of A. Shen [2000]).

- Reviewing and then discussing papers for a Russian mathematics and science journal, *Quant* (classes of Pushkar and Checkanov as described in Russian by Davidovich et al. [1998]). (See http://www.nsta.org/quantum/ for information about *Quant's* American sister journal, *Quantum*. *Quantum* was published for twelve years and was as lovely as the *Quant* that Russian students enjoy. Unfortunately it was discontinued, but the Web site still offers access to its archives, which can be useful to readers of this chapter.)

- Facilitating independent study of mathematics books suggested to students by their teacher or mentor. Students then either discuss what they have learned with the mentor or present it to the class, or both. Such independent study happens in many math classes during students' last two years of schooling.

Students who learn mathematics through problem solving come out with important strengths and some potential weaknesses. Of course, not all the students, and not even most of them, become mathematicians. However, we believe that the few years spent in a math class have major influence on all math class students, and not only in forming the foundations of their mathematics knowledge or in shaping their thinking. Author Shteingold was a math class student, and she sees herself largely as its product. She feels enormous gratitude toward the teachers and the mentors who taught her. She considers herself extremely lucky to have experienced the pleasure of studying mathematics through problem solving in a math class.

A Tale of Two Cities

Margaret L. Kidd

AFTER teaching mathematics through problem solving in a girls' college preparatory academy for three years, I relocated to a school whose student backgrounds and resources were at the opposite end of the spectrum. Using the same instructional materials, I attempted to teach through problem solving in the second setting even though the students were academically at risk. This tale relates the experiences I had in both of these schools.

Background

About seven years ago, the teachers at my school began teaching mathematics through problem solving. This high school admitted into the ninth grade only young women who scored in the top 30 percent on the Education Research Bureau test. Virtually all the girls attended a four-year college or university after completion of their studies at the academy. The girls were conscientious students whose parents were very involved in their education. The parents not only contributed financially to their daughters' education but contributed emotionally as well. The parents were always available to the teachers and sometimes were more involved than the teachers would have preferred. In such a setting, few, if any, discipline problems occurred. Completed homework and class participation were all but assured. In addition to the annual tuition, each girl was required to purchase a laptop computer and a graphing calculator and to bring each of them to class daily. Rarely did a student forget to do so.

After teaching at the high school level in Dallas, Texas; Vallejo, California; and New York, New York, for ten years, Margaret Kidd is presently working full time on a doctorate degree in mathematics education at Teachers College, Columbia University.

That situation was ideal in comparison to the one in which I subsequently found myself. In the second school, I tried to teach in the same way with the same instructional materials to a very different clientele. These students had been socially promoted for years, and many functioned at a sixth-grade level even though they were in the ninth grade. One of the feeder middle schools had been without a full-time mathematics teacher for two years. Because of the politics of the district, those students had been "instructed" by a succession of thirty-day substitute teachers. The substitutes who had some mathematical background simply taught topics that they liked, whereas those with no mathematical training oversaw study halls. Other feeder schools provided TAG (Talented and Gifted) programs and taught a type of algebra in the eighth grade. These circumstances assured that no body of knowledge was common to all students.

Additionally, school administrators decided to make all classes heterogeneous and to start all ninth graders in the first year of the course regardless of their backgrounds. Discipline and classroom control were almost uniformly impossible throughout the school and were especially difficult in the mathematics classrooms because of the high level of difficulty of the content. Parents and guardians were involved in varying degrees. Most were either not involved in their children's lives or were so disheartened by their children's behavior that they frequently asked for advice from the teachers on rearing their children. As a result, calling parents to enlist their help regarding their child's schoolwork was ineffective. Some parents were advocates for their children, but their concerns were not always rooted in the reality of their child's abilities. Ninety percent of the students did not intend to continue their education past high school. Many openly stated that they would not even finish high school. Because of the system in place, summer school was an option that many of them found very attractive. One student even told me on the first day that she was going to go to summer school and, therefore, was not going to do anything in my class.

Teaching Experiences

A typical class at the academy was one in which the girls came in, took out their supplies, and after a word of reminding, started comparing their homework with that of other students at their table. They spent about ten minutes working together while I took attendance and wandered around the room checking that the students were on task. Most days a question arose that all the members of one group could not answer. So a girl from another group explained her answer using the overhead projector. Almost all the students were engaged in the discussion. After all the students were satisfied that they understood the homework, I spent approximately fifteen minutes discussing with them what they were going to do in the day's activity. At that point, they worked on the activity for the rest of the ninety-minute class period. I simply walked around the room and clarified points or challenged groups to delve further into the problem. Toward the end of the class period, I asked questions to assess how well students understood the work they did that day. I assigned homework early in the period so that those students who finished the activity early had something to work on.

The general climate of the classroom was one of active work and quiet talking. Each student brought her supplies each class period, including her calculator, textbook and computer. The girls discussed problems with their own group or walked over to other tables to seek or offer clarification of a point. Occasionally the conversation turned to what was taking place on the weekend or what the dress of the night would be. After all, they were teenaged girls! However, students got back on task fairly quickly with simply a raised eyebrow from me. They understood that if they did not finish the class work during the period, they had to do it at home before starting their regular homework. The work had to be completed, or they would stay with it as long as it took to understand it. When it came to presentations either to explain a topic to others who did not understand it or as a formal assessment, the students had few problems. Most had no qualms about getting up in front of the class with overhead marker in hand to give an explanation, sometimes taking over for me to explain a point in another way.

Contrast this environment with that in the second school. I quickly learned that any homework I assigned would not be done by any but the very few brightest and most motivated students. And the students had no expectation that homework should be done. The culture did not support homework in any fashion. The textbook was much too "heavy" for these students to carry back and forth to the locker or home. In fact, many textbooks were left in the classroom or simply stored in a locker after the first day. The students did not have pencils, let alone calculators! They also thought that the school should provide any necessary binder paper. In general, students thought they should not have to bring with them into the classroom anything that had anything to do with mathematics. When calculators were needed for class, each student borrowed a calculator with an assigned number from the classroom set and each battery compartment was checked upon collection.

The atmosphere in the classroom was chaos. I would laugh when I was told I had to teach in such a way that I could maintain the students' interest. I could not even get them to appreciate the fact that they were in a classroom, let alone that I was standing in the front of the room speaking to them. Usually, I would take a small group—somewhere around a third of the students—and teach them in a small circle. With the assistance of these students, we could get the rest of the students to keep the loud talking and screaming across the classroom down to a level at which we could hear one another. I tried to adapt the rich problems and emphasis on sense making that had worked in my previous school, but I normally did direct teaching. I often paraphrased the textbook because on average, the students read at about the sixth-grade level. I gave extra worksheets for practice and review. It saddened me to realize that many of these students were not even willing to entertain the idea that they could succeed.

Sometimes the ninety-minute block seemed interminable. The "saving grace" was that I taught only three classes each day. Each lunch hour and every day after school, a few of the students came in for small-group or one-on-one tutoring. These students were ones who wanted to do well and who knew that they could not "make waves" during class without fear of retaliation outside of school, which, in fact, did happen on a number of occasions. Those who wanted to learn worked well in groups, with a great deal of discussion among them. Time did not allow for presentations, however. The assessments were straightforward, with the students being able to test on a concept as many times as they needed to show competence. The reading levels and depth of thinking required by the curriculum's open-ended authentic assessments were too high for these students.

Results

At this point, one would probably predict that the academy girls did well on standardized testing and that the urban students did poorly. Well, the first part is correct. Virtually all the academy girls took the PSAT and SAT tests. Their average score in previous years was 1170. With the introduction of teaching through problem solving at the school, these test scores went up, but the improvement was not statistically significant. Although this outcome disappointed the teachers, the parents were satisfied that their progeny were not "harmed" by this new way of teaching.

Interestingly, the girls asked how I "managed to get questions [from their curriculum] on the PSAT"!

The urban students were required to take the new SAT9 Test. I "just knew" that the results would be disastrous when many students only took a fraction of the time allotted to complete the test. I was completely surprised when these same students scored much higher than the students at the other two high schools in the city, in which only traditional mathematics was taught. I believe the fact that my students had been exposed to a new way of doing mathematics had had a positive impact on them. The facility they now had with the calculator eliminated the silly arithmetic mistakes they had made previously. By simply being in the same room with students who were discussing different ways of solving practical problems, their consciousness had gradually absorbed the idea that mathematics had uses other than for homework. After a semester in this environment, being able to use mathematics to solve problems went from being a foreign concept to being one that was commonplace. For those students who were interested in learning, being able to solve problems in ways that made sense to them translated into solving more problems on the standardized test even though the problems were presented in a different way. The other students seemed to have derived value in observing classmates who were engaged in problem solving.

In typical mathematics classes, these students were required to sit quietly and read or to answer questions on paper. In my class, they were encouraged to be active in their learning. They had to discuss their ideas with, and defend their ideas to, others, so they had to have a pretty good understanding of the problems. The solutions to these problems required the students to work with their friends and to use more than one representation, not just algebraic symbols. They had to understand the problem well enough to know what type of mathematics was needed; they could not tell what was needed from the title of the section! After some time, they no longer simply quit when the first strategy they tried was not correct. Additionally, these problems frequently took more than one class period to complete, so mathematics learning continued over a number of days. I came to the conclusion that the best way to teach mathematics is through problem solving. Such an approach not only does not hold the very capable students back in any way, it somehow cuts through the roadblocks that other students create for themselves and gives them ways to solve problems that lead to better learning.

Section 4

Research

Teaching Mathematics through Problem Solving:
Research Perspectives

Mary Kay Stein
Jo Boaler
Edward A. Silver

T HE AUTHORS of previous chapters in this book have treated many important issues germane to teaching mathematics through problem solving. Our task in this chapter is to bring a research perspective to the topic. In so doing, we hope to complement what the other chapters offer regarding *why* one might want to teach mathematics through problem solving, *how* one might select and use worthwhile problems to do so, and *what* teachers might need to know, understand, and do to use this approach successfully.

Providing a research perspective on this topic is a daunting task. On the one hand, extensive literature is available on mathematical problem solving. Problem solving has a long history in the mathematics curriculum (see Kilpatrick [1985]; Stanic and Kilpatrick [1989]; see also D'Ambrosio [this volume]), and it has been the focus of considerable research activity. The 1970s and 1980s were particularly productive times, with a consolidation of research on the ways problem-solving activities can support students' learning. Such research continued with somewhat less intensity through the 1990s and beyond. In the space available, we cannot review and summarize all the various studies, but an interested reader can find many excellent reviews of this corpus of research on mathematics problem solving (see, e.g., Charles and Silver [1989]; Lester [1980, 1994]; Schoenfeld [1992]; Silver [1985]; Suydam [1980]; Wilson, Fernandez, and Hadaway [1993]). Another topic worthy of attention is research on mathematical problem posing (see, e.g., Silver [1994, 1995]; Silver and Cai [1996]).

On the other hand, the task is also daunting because very little of this vast research base has explicitly investigated the kind of instructional approach advocated in this volume. Research on mathematics problem solving has generally been prompted by a desire to understand the nature of problem solving as a process and to specify some ways to help students acquire proficiency as problem solvers. The instructional implications of much of this research directly pertain to the teaching *of* problem solving and teaching *about* problem solving. Yet the chapters in this book propose ideas related to teaching *through* problem solving. Although this perspective is not new in the mathematics education literature (see, e.g., Branca [1980]; Silver, Kilpatrick, and Schlesinger [1989]; Wilson, Fernandez, and Hadaway [1993]; Wirtz [1976]), far less research has been conducted from this perspective.

To accomplish our task, we decided to focus on research conducted in the 1990s. During the past decade or so, the development of mathematics curriculum and teaching standards spurred the development of new curriculum materials and innovative pedagogical approaches in the United States and abroad. These developments have afforded researchers opportunities to study mathematics taught through problem solving more extensively than was possible in earlier times. Our aim in this chapter is to examine this research base to investigate a simple but important question: What do the findings from research suggest about the feasibility and efficacy of teaching mathematics through problem solving?

In answering this question, we have divided the chapter into two sections that correspond to the different kinds of studies that have been conducted. In the first section we consider research that has been conducted on recently designed curricular programs that teach mathematics through problem solving and that have been implemented by teachers with varying background and experience. Such studies are important because they give us information on the large-scale implementation of curricula that have been written to infuse problem solving throughout instructional programs in realistic situations of varying teacher expertise. (Curriculum materials do not represent the *only* way to infuse problem solving into classroom instruction; however, they do arguably represent the most visible and systematic attempt to do so over the last decade.)

In the second section of the chapter, we review some studies that have considered the *particular* ways that problem-solving approaches are enacted in classrooms. Such studies, that include extensive classroom observations, are important because they provide information on the different factors that are emerging as central to the effectiveness of problem-solving approaches. We now have sufficient evidence in mathematics education to know that problem-solving approaches can result in high and equitable achievement but that such achievement requires a range of factors to be in place. As we move through the chapter exploring these different factors, we shift from the question "How does the use of curriculum materials that embody teaching mathematics through problem solving affect students' learning of mathematics?" to an equally important question, "What happens inside classrooms where problem-solving approaches are used effectively?"

How Does the Use of Curriculum Materials That Embody Teaching Mathematics through Problem Solving Affect Students' Learning of Mathematics?

Since the mid-1990s, a number of innovative mathematics curricula have been developed that embody many aspects of teaching mathematics through problem solving—presenting students with complex, open tasks, often in "real world" contexts, with the intention of encouraging the development of deep conceptual understanding through engagement in mathematical thinking, reasoning, and problem solving. The impact of these new curricular materials has been studied in recent years, sometimes through longitudinal analyses of students' learning within a particular curriculum and sometimes through contrasts of classes taught using the innovative, problem-solving oriented materials with those taught using more conventional curriculum materials. (We reviewed the following among studies that contrast innovative middle school and secondary school curricula and instructional materials with more traditional approaches: Boaler [1997, 2002]; Boaler et al. [2002]; Huntley et al. [2000]; Riordan and Noyce [2001]); and Thompson and Senk [2001]); findings similar to those summarized here have also been reported in studies of innovative curricula at the elementary school level, e.g., Fuson, Carroll, and Drueck [2000]; Riordan and Noyce [2001]; Schoenfeld [2002].)

Learning, in these studies, has generally been measured through students' performance on standardized tests that target procedural fluency—the kind of outcome normally expected from conventional curricula—as well as students' performance on assessments that probe their conceptual understanding, problem-solving capabilities, and facility with communicating their thinking and reasoning—the kinds of outcomes that standardized tests do not usually measure well but that are important goals for students' learning in innovative curricula. Some research studies have also paid attention to affective outcomes, such as students' dispositions toward mathematics, by administering questionnaires and interviews that probe students' attitudes toward, and beliefs about, mathematics.

Despite the differences in grades and curriculum studied, and even the methodologies employed, these different research projects have produced a number of consistent findings. The first is that students taught using reform curricula, compared with those taught using more traditional curricula, generally exhibited greater conceptual understanding and performed at considerably higher levels with respect to problem solving (Boaler 1997; Huntley et al. 2000; Thompson and Senk 2001). Second, these gains did not come at the expense of those aspects of mathematics measured on more conventional standardized tests. Compared with students taught using conventional curricula, students who were taught using reform curricula performed at approximately the same level on standardized tests that assessed mathematical skills and procedures (Boaler et al. 2002; Riordan and Noyce 2001; Schoenfeld 2002; Thompson and Senk 2001). The differences that occurred were usually not significant, and some showed the students in the reform classes doing slightly better, whereas others showed the students in the traditional classes doing slightly better. In general, across the various studies, students tended to do better on assessment tasks that covered topics and approaches about which they had had the opportunity to learn. For example, students in the Core Plus Mathematics Project (CPMP) outperformed others on tests of algebraic concepts set in real-world contexts, but students taught using more traditional textbooks outperformed those in the CPMP on tests of algebraic skills set in questions without contexts (Huntley et al. 2000).

Studies that have considered students' attitudes and beliefs in different curriculum programs have also produced a fairly consistent finding: students taught using problem-solving approaches are more likely to have positive and broad attitudes about mathematics. One of the limitations often associated with conventional mathematics instruction, in which students typically learn to repeat standard procedures but rarely are given opportunities to work on more complex problems, is that students come to regard mathematics as a meaningless collection of rules that need to be memorized (Schoenfeld 1992; Boaler 1997). Research evidence suggests that when teachers and curricular materials do pay attention to developing conceptual understanding and applications, students tend to see more uses for mathematics and to regard mathematics as more of a "doing discipline" (Treffers 1987, p. 60), as being connected with "sense-making" (Resnick 1989), and as affording more opportunities for using their own thoughts and ideas (Boaler et al. 2002).

An emerging insight from these curricular studies is that students who learn and practice symbolic skill manipulation in the context of meaningful problem settings may learn such skills in a qualitatively different way than do students who are taught skills in a more direct, sequenced, and structured manner. We need further investigations to understand more about the *forms* of knowledge and understanding that students develop in different approaches, and about the ways their knowledge relates to the curricular materials from which they work, because early studies suggest that students do not simply develop more or less knowledge in these different approaches but acquire knowledge, beliefs, and understandings that differ in important ways.

The results that have been recorded from different studies, relating to both attitude and achievement, are important because they show that large numbers of teachers with varying levels of expertise and experience have managed to use new curricula without an accompanying drop in students' achievement on tests of skills, and with many gains in students' achievement on tests of conceptual understanding and problem solving. Other research, however, suggests that curriculum materials alone do not make the difference between effective and ineffective teaching and learning. In our judgment, one of the limitations of studies that compare curriculum approaches without studying the teaching and learning within classrooms is that they often neglect what is arguably the most important dimension of the process—the ways in which teachers and students enact the curriculum in the classroom. The decisions that teachers make each day as they implement different approaches are essential to the success of any curriculum. Thus, studies that include the details of teachers' actions in classrooms provide an important complement to those that look across large numbers of classrooms.

In the next section we review a number of studies that conceptualize learning as an interaction of curriculum, teachers, and learners (Ball and Cohen 1999) and that examine particular instructional decisions and actions, as well as students' behavior, in teaching mathematics in innovative ways. These studies provide an important complement to the large-scale, curriculum-based studies that we have already considered, fostering important insights into effective teaching of mathematics through problem solving. The next section of our chapter explores what we believe is arguably one of the crucial research questions for the next decade: What happens inside classrooms in which problem-solving approaches are used effectively?

What Happens inside Classrooms in Which Problem-Solving Approaches Are Used Effectively?

In detailed studies of teaching practice inside classrooms, researchers have considered factors that affect the success of mathematics taught through problem solving. In the QUASAR project, a multiyear national study of middle school mathematics reform in economically disadvantaged communities (Silver and Stein 1996), students' achievement was found to be linked with instructional practices. In schools in which instructional practices were observed to be more problem-oriented and student-centered, students' improvement was greater on a periodically administered assessment consisting of open-ended tasks that measured problem solving, reasoning, and communication in a range of middle school topics than it was for students in schools in which the instruction was observed to consist primarily of routine, skill-driven practices (Stein and Lane 1996; Stein, Lane, and Silver 1996). Furthermore, students in schools characterized by reform practices showed no decay in their abilities to perform calculations over the course of the project as measured by district-required standardized achievement tests. Moreover, despite historical trends showing that the achievement gap between racial groups tends to grow wider during the middle grades, this outcome did not occur in schools in which teachers used innovative approaches to mathematics instruction. In fact, the achievement gap grew no wider in most schools and was reduced in some (Lane and Silver 1999). Furthermore, students in these schools outperformed a national sample of similar students on mathematics tasks from the National Assessment of Educational Progress (Silver and Lane 1995).

In addition to this set of findings concerning broad differences in students' learning, the QUASAR researchers collected and analyzed observations of more than 300 lessons to examine more subtle differences in teachers' instructional practices. The QUASAR teachers were trying to teach in ways that reflected many of the ideas in the NCTM *Standards* documents, including the use of intellectually challenging mathematics problems on a regular basis. When their attempts to teach mathematics in this way were analyzed, several findings emerged. The more challenging the instructional task, the harder it was to implement as intended. In particular, tasks that required students to engage in "doing mathematics" (e.g., such activities as making and testing conjectures, framing and solving problems, or looking for patterns) were most apt to decline into other, less cognitively challenging forms of thinking, such as routine calculations or unsystematic and non-productive exploration. In an initial study, students were observed to actually engage in the intended cognitive processes during the implementation of only 38 percent of "doing mathematics" tasks (Stein, Grover, and Henningsen 1996).

Follow-up studies focused on the characteristics of classrooms in which task complexity was either maintained or declined. Henningsen and Stein (1997) found that when students' engagement was successfully maintained at a high level of cognitive demand, numerous support factors were typically in place, including (a) the selection of tasks that built on students' existing knowledge, (b) the teacher's scaffolding of students' thinking, (c) the modeling of high-level performance, and (d) sustained pressure for students' explanation and meaning making. Factors associated with instances in which task complexity declined included (a) classroom-management problems, (b) too much or too little time devoted to task enactment, (c) lack of students' accountability for accurate and coherent explanations, and (d) a shift in focus from thinking processes to finding the correct answer.

In another study, this one at the high school level, Boaler (1997) monitored approximately 300 students, as they went from age 13 to 16, in two schools that employed very different mathematics approaches. In this three-year study of students' learning, Boaler found that students who had learned through open-ended projects developed more flexible and adaptable forms of knowledge and understanding than did those students who had learned through more traditional methods of teaching. These attributes resulted in the project students' outperforming more traditionally taught students on a range of different assessments, including the national examination. In addition to producing higher attainment, the project-based approach also produced more equitable outcomes; no differences in achievement by social class or gender were noted at the school using open-ended projects, but significant differences developed at the school in which students were taught more traditionally, with girls and students from working-class homes attaining less (little ethnic diversity existed at either school).

The reasons for the high and equitable attainment achieved by teachers in the project-based school extended beyond the curriculum materials they used. Boaler found that part of the reason that the project-based approach produced more equitable outcomes was that the teachers paid attention to teaching students *how to learn* in a more open way. Lubienski and Stilwell (this volume) point out that using an open, problem-solving approach is complex and that some enactments of open approaches can disadvantage students who are not prepared to work in such ways. At the project school Boaler studied, the teachers strove to ensure that the approach was accessible to all. For example, the teachers always spent time introducing each problem and having discussions with the students about what the problem entailed; they never left students to read and interpret unfamiliar texts. When the students started at the school, the teachers gave them more structure and support that they gradually withdrew over time. The teachers spent time discussing the aims of projects and the characteristics of "good work," and they gave students the criteria that would be used to assess work. The teachers worked hard and used particular methods to make the approach equitable, and these efforts were shown to be central to the effectiveness of the problem-solving approach they used and the elimination of inequalities (Boaler 2002).

A third study that considered different teaching approaches by examining classroom interactions was conducted by Hiebert and Wearne (1993). They studied six second-grade classrooms, two of which used a nontraditional approach that involved students' working on longer problems, looking at mathematical relationships, and describing and explaining alternative strategies. The researchers found that the classes working in a more open way showed higher levels of performance at the end of the year as compared with classes using a traditional textbook. Although this study was conducted at the elementary school level, the ways in which the teachers encouraged understanding seem to pertain in important ways to those teaching higher levels of mathematics. The researchers found that high performance on the part of students was related to the particular types of questions teachers asked, and they identified nine types of questions that differed in the amount of self-explanations and descriptions of cognitive strategies that they elicited. Hiebert and Wearne also found that students who learned the most were those who spent more time on each problem, with the additional time being used by students to describe the strategies they used and explain why those strategies worked.

These different studies—at elementary, middle, and high school levels—all included extensive classroom observations, enabling the researchers to provide information not only about the broad impact of curricular approaches but about the ways in which problems were used in the classroom and the important teacher actions that affected students' learning. These teacher actions included (a) scaffolding of students' thinking; (b) a sustained press for students' explanations; (c) thoughtful probing of students' strategies and solutions; (d) helping students accept responsibility for, and gain facility with, learning in a more open way; and (e) attending to issues of equity in the classroom. More detail related to these different factors is presented in other publications; we have been able only to summarize some findings here, but we have done so to illustrate the importance of the *particular* ways that teachers implement problem-solving approaches. The research amply demonstrates that the teacher's actions and reactions in the classroom affect the kinds of learning opportunities available to students, and this outcome is no less true when teaching through problem solving than in other modes of mathematics instruction.

Analyses that record particular teaching interactions in classrooms are also important because they provide a level of detail that is needed by other teachers who wish to implement problem-solving approaches. Conversations among teachers who are working to implement problem-solving approaches, as well as reciprocal observations of lessons, are also extremely important opportunities for teachers' learning. Historically, teachers in the United States have had few opportunities to learn from one another, both because teaching has developed as a private craft and because schools have not provided time or opportunities for teachers to work together nor to observe one another's lessons (Stigler and Hiebert 1997). The future is promising, however, as different versions of "lesson study'" become more commonplace and the field moves to greater recognition that the detailed practices of classroom teachers matter (Lampert 2001). Along with the evidence of effectiveness that is beginning to emerge from the large-scale curricular studies, the findings from more fine-grained studies of classroom implementations should provide a clearer and more complete picture of how and under what conditions problem-solving approaches lead to improvements in students' learning.

Many questions remain concerning the implementation of problem-solving approaches, including the following: How do effective teachers plan or "design" problem-solving lessons? How do they use curricular guides? How do they anticipate students' responses to a planned lesson? and How do they prepare to "work with" these responses? Much also is to be learned about the ways that teachers can effectively teach procedural skills in the context of problem-based forms of instruction (see Hedden and Langbauer [this volume]; Messenger and Ames [this volume]). Lessons that encourage a variety of ideas, solution strategies, and forms of representation have the advantage of engaging students in thinking and learning to justify and reason. However, they also have the disadvantage of not converging neatly into a common core of knowledge that all students share and should know—especially not in any predetermined time frame, be it a lesson, a grading period, a year, or simply in time for a high-stakes test. Making sure that all students eventually reach some clarity and closure on important mathematical ideas and algorithms is not trivial in this form of instruction (National Research Council 2001). The limitations of learning mathematics solely through instruction devoted to hierarchically ordered skill practice are well known; so too we suspect that limitations, risks, and challenges are inherent in learning mathematics primarily through problem solving. Much remains to be learned about how to teach mathematics through problem solving in ways that enhance the learning of all students.

Discussion and Conclusion

The largest and most consistent database on students' performance in the United States suggests that the vast majority of instruction in this country focuses almost exclusively on teaching algorithmic procedures for routine problems (Fey 1979; Stigler and Hiebert 1997; Stodolsky 1988). Additionally, large-scale assessments repeatedly show that U.S. students are not very good at tasks that demand that they think, reason, or solve problems in sustained and rigorous ways (Silver and Kenney 2000). Together, these findings suggest that students, by and large, do not have the opportunity to experience problem-solving approaches to instruction and, not surprisingly, are not very deep conceptual thinkers, nor do they perform well when confronted with problems that truly require solving.

In this chapter, we have summarized some research studies suggesting that students who have had the opportunity to work on problem-solving approaches tended to perform as well as—or better than—those who have worked traditionally. As important as these large-scale curricular studies are, they inevitably mask differences in the manner in which individual teachers implement problem-solving approaches. Thus, we have argued that research on problem solving should focus on the details of classroom implementation in addition to studying student outcomes associated with the adoption of particular curricula.

The importance of understanding more about instruction, in addition to broad curricular differences, is echoed in a recent review of research on mathematics teaching and learning in grades K–8 written by a distinguished group of mathematicians, mathematics educators, research scientists, and teachers (National Research Council 2001, p. 315):

> Labels make rhetorical distinctions that often miss the point regarding the quality of instruction. Our review of the research makes plain that the effectiveness of mathematics teaching and learning does not rest in simple labels. Rather, the quality of instruction is a function of teachers' knowledge and use of mathematical content, teachers' attention to and handling of students, and students' engagement in and use of mathematical tasks.

The studies reviewed in this chapter have given us some information on the nature of instruction that supports effective problem solving—including the role played by tasks, teachers, and students. The chapters in this book also make an important contribution, adding to our knowledge base of the ways in which mathematics can be taught well through problem solving. For example, some chapters focus on ways to select and set up good problem situations (e.g., Marcus and Fey [this volume]); others consider the importance of listening actively to students (e.g., Driscoll [this volume]); others consider the ways in which productive sociomathematical norms can be established in classrooms (Rasmussen, Yackel, and King [this volume]); and others consider the development of productive habits of mind through problem solving and teacher modeling (e.g., Levasseur and Cuoco [this volume]).

And so we return to the question stated at the outset: What do the findings from research suggest about the feasibility and efficacy of teaching mathematics through problem solving? The research evidence reviewed herein suggests both the feasibility and efficacy of such approaches. More conventional approaches to mathematics teaching may appear to be easier to implement, but their consequences for students' learning are well documented—

too many students are left out, disengaged, and unable to use much of the mathematics they learn. Research evidence suggests that the extra time, effort, and resources required to teach mathematics through problem solving effectively are well worth the effort if one's goals for mathematics education include students who understand mathematical concepts, are willing to tackle challenging problems, and see themselves as capable of learning mathematics. The research reviewed in this chapter suggests that we have good reason to think that teaching mathematics through problem solving can help achieve those goals.

To be sure, many challenges arise when using such an instructional approach effectively, including the need for teachers to develop a solid and flexible understanding of the mathematical terrain through which their students will navigate. Teachers will need considerable support, including good curriculum materials and strong professional development, if they adopt this approach. Thus, the extent to which our research-based knowledge of effective mathematics instruction advances students' learning will depend on a range of factors—not least of which is the support that states and school districts provide for teachers' learning. States, districts, schools, and teachers have the obligation to wrestle with, and articulate their goals for, students' mathematics learning and to provide the kind of professional development that is needed to support their teachers so that they can effectively help all students learn to think and reason *through* problem solving.

Section 5

Bibliography

Bibliography

Anyon, Jean. "Social Class and School Knowledge." *Curriculum Inquiry* 11 (spring 1981): 3–42.

Artzt, Alice F., and Claire M. Newman. *How to Use Cooperative Learning in the Mathematics Class.* Reston, Va.: National Council of Teachers of Mathematics, 1997.

Ball, Deborah L. "With an Eye on the Mathematical Horizon: Dilemmas of Teaching Elementary School Mathematics." *Elementary School Journal* 93 (March 1993): 373–97.

Ball, Deborah L., and David Cohen. "Developing Practice, Developing Practitioners." In *Teaching as the Learning Profession: Handbook of Policy and Practice,* edited by Linda Darling-Hammond and Gary Sykes. San Francisco, Calif.: Jossey Bass Publishers, 1999.

Becker, Jerry P., and Shigeru Shimada. *The Open-Ended Approach: A New Proposal for Teaching Mathematics.* Reston, Va.: National Council of Teachers of Mathematics, 1997.

Blume, Glendon W., and David S. Heckman. "What Do Students Know about Algebra and Functions?" In *Results from the Sixth Mathematics Assessment of the National Assessment of Educational Progress,* edited by Patricia Ann Kenney and Edward A. Silver, pp. 225–77. Reston, Va.: National Council of Teachers of Mathematics, 1997.

Boaler, Jo. *Experiencing School Mathematics: Teaching Styles, Sex, and Setting.* Buckingham. U.K.: Open University Press, 1997.

———. "Learning from Teaching: Exploring the Relationship between 'Reform' Curriculum and Equity." *Journal for Research in Mathematics Education* (July 2002): 239–58.

Boaler, Jo, Karin Brodie, Rachel Chou, Hermione Gifford, Victoria Hand, Kristen Pilsner, Emily Shahan, Melissa Sommerfeld, Megan Staples, Judy Strauss, Sean Whalen, and Toby White. "Stanford University Mathematics Teaching and Learning Study: Initial Report—a Comparison of IMP1 and Algebra 1 at Greendale School." 2002. www.stanford.edu/~joboaler/. World Wide Web.

Borasi, Raffaella, and Judith Fonzi. "Introducing Math Teachers to Inquiry: A Framework and Supporting Materials for Teacher Educator." Forthcoming.

Borassi, Raffaella, Judith Fonzi, Constance F. Smith, and Barbara J. Rose. "Beginning the Process of Rethinking Mathematics Instruction: A Professional Development Program." *Journal of Mathematics Teacher Education* 2, no. 1 (1999): 49–78.

Branca, Nicholas A. "Problem Solving as a Goal, Process, and Basic Skill." In *Problem Solving in School Mathematics,* 1980 Yearbook of the National Council of Teachers of Mathematics (NCTM), edited by Stephen Krulik and Robert E. Reys, pp. 3–8. Reston, Va.: NCTM, 1980.

Bransford, John D., Ann L., Brown, and Rodney R. Cocking. *How People Learn.* Washington D.C.: National Research Council, 2000.

Brooks, Edward. *The Normal Elementary Algebra: Containing the First Principles of the Science, Developed with Conciseness and Simplicity, for Common Schools, Academies, Seminaries, and Normal Schools.* Philadelphia: Sower, Potts, 1871.

Brown, Stephen I., and Marion I. Walter. *The Art of Problem Posing.* 2d ed. Hillsdale, N.J.: Lawrence Erlbaum Associates, 1990.

Brown, Stephen I., and Marion I. Walter, eds. *Problem Posing: Reflections and Applications.* Hillsdale, N.J.: Lawrence Erlbaum Associates, 1993.

Brownell, William A. "The Place of Meaning in the Teaching of Arithmetic." *Elementary School Journal* 47 (January 1947): 256–65.

Brownell, William A., and Verner M. Sims. "The Nature of Understanding." In *Forty-fifth Yearbook of the National Society for the Study of Education: Part I, The Measurement of Understanding,* edited by Nelson B. Henry, pp. 27–43. Chicago: University of Chicago, 1946.

Bruner, Jerome S. *The Process of Education.* 2d ed. Cambridge, Mass.: Harvard University Press, 1977.

CAS-Intensive Mathematics Project Curriculum [CAS-IM]. Module IV: Families of Functions, field tested. University Park, Penn.: CAS-IM, 2000.

Charles, Randall I., and Frank Lester. *Teaching Problem Solving: What, Why, and How.* Palo Alto, Calif.: Dale Seymour Publications, 1982.

Charles, Randall I., and Edward A. Silver, eds. *The Teaching and Assessing of Mathematical Problem Solving.* Research Agenda for Mathematics Education, vol. 3. Hillsdale, N.J.: Lawrence Erlbaum Associates, and Reston, Va.: National Council of Teachers of Mathematics, 1989.

Clement, Lisa L. "What Do Students Really Know about Functions?" *Mathematics Teacher* 94 (December 2001): 745–48.

Cobb, Paul. "Individual and Collective Mathematical Development: The Case of Statistical Data Analysis." *Mathematical Thinking and Learning* 1 (1999): 5–43.

Cobb, Paul, and Heinrich Bauersfeld. *The Emergence of Mathematical Meaning.* Hillsdale, N.J.: Lawrence Erlbaum Associates, 1995.

Copes, Larry. *Potent Problem.* Institute for Studies in Educational Mathematics, 2003. http://www.edmath.org/potent. World Wide Web.

Coxford, Arthur F., James T. Fey, Christian R. Hirsch, Harold L. Schoen, Gail Burrill, Eric W. Hart, and Ann E. Watkins. *Contemporary Mathematics in Context: Course 1, Part B.* Chicago: Everyday Learning Corporation, 1999a.

———. *Contemporary Mathematics in Context: Course 3, Part A.* Chicago: Everyday Learning Corporation, 1999b.

Cuoco, Al. "Action to Process: Using Functions to Solve Algebra Word Problems." *Intelligent Tutoring Media* 4, no. 3/4 (1993): 117–27.

Cuoco, Al, E. Paul Goldenberg, and J. Mark. "Habits of Mind: An Organizing Principle for Mathematics Curriculum." *Journal of Mathematical Behavior* 15 (1996): 375–402.

Davidovich, Boris M. P. E. Pushkar, and Uri V. Chekanov. *Mathematical Analysis in Mathematical Classes of School 57.* Moscow: MCNMO, Chero, 1998.

Davidson, Neil, and Toni Worsham, eds. *Enhancing Thinking through Cooperative Learning.* New York: Teachers College Press, 1992.

Davis, Brent. "Listening for Differences: An Evolving Conception of Mathematics Teaching." *Journal for Research in Mathematics Education* 28 (May 1997): 355–76.

Davis, Robert. B. "Understanding 'Understanding.'" *Journal of Mathematical Behavior* 11 (1992): 225–41.

Delpit, Lisa. "The Silenced Dialogue: Power and Pedagogy in Educating Other People's Children." *Harvard Educational Review* 58 (August 1988): 280–98.

Dewey, John. *How We Think: A Restatement of the Relation of Reflective Thinking to the Educative Process.* Boston: D.C. Heath & Co., 1933.

Driscoll, Mark. *Fostering Algebraic Thinking: A Guide for Teachers Grades 6–10.* Portsmouth, N.H.: Heinemann, 1999.

Driscoll, Mark, Sydney Foster, and John Moyer. "Linked Learning in Mathematics Project." *Mathematics Teacher* 92 (January 1999): 72–73.

Driscoll, Mark, John Moyer, and Judith Zawojewski. "Helping Teachers Implement Algebra for All in Milwaukee Public Schools." *Mathematics Education Leadership* 2 (spring 1998) 3–12.

Driscoll, Mark, Judith Zawojewski, Andrea Humez, Johannah Nikula, Lynn Goldsmith, and James Hammerman. *The Fostering Algebraic Thinking Toolkit: A Guide for Staff Development.* Portsmouth, N.H.: Heinemann, 2001.

Economopoulos, Karen, and Susan Jo Russell. "Coins, Coupons, and Combinations: The Number System." A grade-2 unit in Investigations in Number, Data, and Space. Cambridge, Mass.: Dale Seymour Publications, 1998.

Education Development Center. "What Is Mathematical Investigation?" A professional development module in Connecting with Mathematics, Grades 6–12. Newton, Mass.: Education Development Center, 2002.

English, Lyn D. "Engaging Students in Problem Posing in an Inquiry-Oriented Mathematics Classroom." In *Teaching Mathematics through Problem Solving: Prekindergarten through Grade 6*, edited by Frank K. Lester, Jr., and Randall I. Charles, pp. 187–198. Reston, Va.: NCTM, 2003.

Feinberg-McBrian, Carol. "The Case of Trapezoidal Numbers." *Mathematics Teacher* 89 (January 1996): 16–21.

Fendel, Dan, Diane Resek, Lynne Alper, and Sherry Fraser. *Interactive Mathematics Program.* Emeryville, Calif.: Key Curriculum Press, 1997.

Fey, James T. "Mathematics Teaching Today: Perspectives from Three National Surveys." *Mathematics Teacher* 72 (October 1979): 490–504.

Fey, James, William Fitzgerald, Susan Friel, Glenda Lappan, and Betty Phillips. *Getting to Know CMP: An Introduction to the Connected Mathematics Project.* Washington, D.C.: National Science Foundation, 1996.

Finzer, William, Timothy Erickson, and Jill Binker. Fathom Dynamic Statistics, Ver. 1.1. Emeryville, Calif.: Key Curriculum Press, 2001. Software.

Fomin, Dmitry, Sergey Genkin, and Ilia Itenberg. *Mathematical Circles (Russian Experience).* Providence, R.I.: American Mathematical Society, 1996.

Fuson, Karen C., William M. Carroll, and Jane V. Drueck. "Achievement Results for Second and Third Graders Using the Standards-Based Curriculum 'Everyday Mathematics.'" *Journal for Research in Mathematics Education* 31 (May 2000): 277–95.

Fuson, Karen. C., Yolanda De La Cruz, Steven. T. Smith, Ana Maria Lo Cicero, Kristin Hudson, Ron Pilar, and Rebecca Steeby. "Blending the Best of the Twentieth Century to Achieve a Mathematics Equity Pedagogy in the Twenty-first Century." In *Learning Mathematics for a New Century,* 2000 Yearbook of the National Council of Teachers of Mathematics (NCTM), edited by Maurice. J. Burke and Frances R. Curcio, pp. 197–212. Reston, Va.: NCTM, 2000.

Glaser, Robert. *Toward New Models of Assessment.* Pittsburgh, Penn.: LRDC, 1990.

Glass, Brad. "Students' Reification of Geometric Transformations in the Presence of Multiple Dynamically-Linked Representations." Ph.D. diss., University of Iowa, 2001.

Goldenberg, E. Paul. "Getting Euler's Line to Relax," *International Journal of Computers for Mathematical Learning* 6, no. 2 (2001): 215–28.

Goldenberg, Paul. "'Habits of Mind' as an Organizer for the Curriculum." *Journal of Education* 178, no. 1 (1996): 13–34.

Good, Thomas L., and Jere E. Brophy. *Looking in Classrooms,* 7th ed. New York: Addison-Wesley Publishing Co., 1996.

Greeno, James. "Situative Research Relevant to Standards for School Mathematics." In *A Research Companion to"Principles and Standards for School Mathematics,"* edited by Jeremy Kilpatrick, Deborah Schifter, and W. Gary Martin, pp. 304–32. Reston, Va.: National Council of Teachers of Mathematics, 2003.

Hancock, Chris, James J. Kaput, and Lynn T. Goldsmith. Authentic Inquiry with Data: Critical Barriers to Classroom Implementation. *Educational Psychologist* 27 (1992): 337–64.

Henningsen, Marjorie, and Mary Kay Stein. "Mathematical Tasks and Student Cognition: Classroom-Based Factors That Support and Inhibit High-Level Mathematical Thinking and Reasoning." *Journal for Research in Mathematics Education* 28 (November 1997): 524–49.

Hiebert, James, and Thomas P. Carpenter. "Learning and Teaching with Understanding." In *Handbook of Research on Mathematics Teaching and Learning,* edited by Douglas A. Grouws, pp. 65–97. New York: Macmillan, 1992.

Hiebert, James, Thomas P. Carpenter, Elizabeth Fennema, Karen Fuson, Piet Human, Hanlie Murray, Alwyn Olivier, and Diana Wearne. "Problem Solving as a Basis for Reform in Curriculum and Instruction: The Case of Mathematics." *Educational Researcher* 25 (May 1996): 12–21.

Hiebert, James, Thomas P. Carpenter, Elizabeth Fennema, Karen Fuson, Diana Wearne, Hanlie Murray, Alwyn Olivier, and Piet Human. *Making Sense: Teaching and Learning Mathematics with Understanding.* Portsmouth, N.H.: Heinemann, 1997.

Hiebert, James, and James W. Stigler. "A Proposal for Improving Classroom Teaching: Lessons from the TIMSS Video Study." *Elementary School Journal* 101 (September 2000): 3–20.

Hiebert, James, and Diana Wearne. "Interactional Tasks, Classroom Discourse, and Students' Learning in Second-Grade Arithmetic." *American Educational Research Journal* 30, no. 2 (1993): 393–425.

Hong, Lily Toy. *Two of Everything.* Morton Grove, Ill.: Albert Whitman & Co., 1993.

Huntley, Mary Ann, Chris L. Rasmussen, Roberto S. Villarubi, Jaruwan
    Sangtong, and James T. Fey. "Effects of Standards-Based Mathematics
    Education: A Study of the Core-Plus Mathematics Project Algebra and
    Functions Strand. *Journal for Research in Mathematics Education* 31
    (May 2000): 328–61.

Jackiw, Nicholas. The Geometer's Sketchpad, Ver. 3.06. Emeryville, Calif.:
    Key Curriculum Press, 1997.

Kahan, Jeremy A. "Ten Lessons from the Proof of Fermat's Last Theorem."
    Mathematics Teacher 92 (September 1999): 530–31.

Kilpatrick, Jeremy. "A Retrospective Account of the Past Twenty-five Years of
    Research on Teaching Mathematical Problem Solving." In *Teaching and
    Learning Mathematical Problem Solving: Multiple Research Perspectives,*
    edited by Edward A. Silver, pp. 1–15. Hillsdale, N.J.: Lawrence Erlbaum
    Associates, 1985.

Kleiner, Israel. "Evolution of the Function Concept: A Brief Survey."
    College Mathematics Journal 20 (September 1989): 282–300.

Kline, Morris. *Mathematical Thought from Ancient to Modern Times.* New
    York: Oxford University Press, 1972.

Konold, Clifford, and Traci L. Higgins. "Working with Data." In *Developing
    Mathematical Ideas: Collecting, Representing, and Analyzing Data,*
    edited by Susan J. Russell, Deborah Schifter, and Virginia Bastable,
    pp. 165–201. Parsippany, N.J.: Dale Seymour Publications, 2002.

Laborde, Jean-Marie, and Franck Bellemain. Cabri Geometry II. Dallas,
    Tex.: Texas Instruments, 1994. Software.

Ladson-Billings, Gloria. "Making Mathematics Meaningful in Multicultural
    Contexts." In *New Directions for Equity in Mathematics Education,* edit-
    ed by Walter G. Secada, Elizabeth Fennema, and Lisa Byrd Adajian,
    pp. 9–56. New York: Cambridge University Press, 1995.

Lampert, Magdalene. *Teaching Problems and the Problems of Teaching.*
    New Haven, Conn.: Yale University Press, 2001.

Lampert, Magdalene, Peggy Rittenhouse, and Carol Crumbaugh. "Agreeing
    to Disagree: Developing Sociable Mathematical Discourse." In
    *Handbook of Education and Human Development: New Models of
    Learning, Teaching, and Schooling,* edited by David R. Olson and Nancy
    Torrance, pp. 731–64. Cambridge, Mass.: Blackwell Publishers, 1996.

Lane, Suzanne, and Edward A. Silver. "Fairness and Equity in Measuring
    Student Learning Using a Mathematics Performance Assessment:
    Results from the QUASAR Project." In *Measuring Up: Challenges
    Minorities Face in Educational Assessment,* edited by Arie L. Nettles and
    Michael T. Nettles, pp. 97–120. Boston: Kluwer, 1999.

Lappan, Glenda, James T. Fey, William M. Fitzgerald, Susan N. Friel, and
    Elizabeth Difanis Phillips. *How Likely Is It?* Glenview, Ill.: Prentice
    Hall, 2002a.

————. *Thinking with Mathematical Models.* Glenview, Ill.: Prentice Hall, 2002b.

————. *Moving Straight Ahead.* Glenview, Ill.: Prentice Hall, 2002c.

Lester, Frank K. "Research on Mathematical Problem Solving." In *Research in Mathematics Education,* edited by Richard J. Shumway, pp. 286–323. Reston, Va.: National Council of Teachers of Mathematics, 1980.

————. "Musings about Mathematical Problem-Solving Research: 1970–1994." *Journal for Research in Mathematics Education* 25 (December 1994): 660–75.

Lubienski, Sarah Theule. "Perspectives on Problem-Centered Mathematics Teaching." *Mathematics Teaching in the Middle School* 5 (December 1999): 250–55.

————. "A Clash of Class Cultures? Students' Experiences in a Discussion-Intensive Seventh-Grade Mathematics Classroom." *Elementary School Journal* 100 (March 2000a): 377–403.

————. "Problem Solving as a Means Toward 'Mathematics for All': An Exploratory Look through a Class Lens." *Journal for Research in Mathematics Education* 31 (July 2000b): 454–82.

————. "Are We Achieving Mathematical Power for All? A Decade of National Data on Instruction and Achievement." Paper presented at the annual meeting of the American Educational Research Association, New Orleans, April 2002. (Available at http://www.public.iastate.edu/~stl/)

McClain, Kay, Paul Cobb, and Koeno P. E. Gravemeijer. "Supporting Students' Ways of Reasoning about Data." In *Learning Mathematics for a New Century,* 2000 Yearbook of the National Council of Teachers of Mathematics (NCTM), edited by Maurice J. Burke and Frances R. Curcio, pp. 174–87. Reston, Va.: NCTM, 2000.

Mason, John. *Thinking Mathematically.* New York: Prentice Hall/Pearson, 1985.

Mason, John, Leone Burton, and Kaye Stacey. *Thinking Mathematically.* Reading, Mass.: Addison-Wesley Publishing Co., 1982.

Mathematical Sciences Education Board (MSEB). *Everybody Counts: A Report to the Nation on the Future of Mathematics Education.* Washington, D.C.: MSEB, 1989.

Means, Barbara, and Michael S. Knapp. "Cognitive Approaches to Teaching Advanced Skills to Educationally Disadvantaged Students." *Phi Delta Kappan* 73, no. 4 (December 1991): 282–89.

Milne, William J. *A Mental Arithmetic.* New York: American Book, 1897.

Moore, David S. "Uncertainty." In *On the Shoulders of Giants,* edited by Lynn Arthur Steen, pp. 95–137. Washington, D.C.: National Academy Press, 1990.

National Center for Research in Mathematical Sciences Education and Freudenthal Institute. "Comparing Quantities." Middle-grades unit in Mathematics in Context. Chicago, Ill.: Encyclopedia Britannica Educational Corporation, 1998.

National Council of Teachers of Mathematics (NCTM). *Curriculum and Evaluation Standards for School Mathematics*. Reston, Va.: NCTM, 1989.

———. *Professional Standards for Teaching Mathematics*. Reston, Va.: NCTM, 1991.

———. *Assessment Standards for School Mathematics*. Reston, Va.: NCTM, 1995.

———. *Principles and Standards for School Mathematics*. Reston, Va.: NCTM, 2000.

———. *The Roles of Representations in School Mathematics*. 2001 Yearbook of the NCTM, edited by Albert A. Cuoco and Frances R. Curcio. Reston, Va.: NCTM, 2001.

———. *Navigating through Data Analysis in Grades 6–8*. Reston, Va.: NCTM, 2003.

National Research Council. *Adding It Up: Helping Children Learn Mathematics*. Report of the Mathematics Learning Study Committee, edited by Jeremy Kilpatrick, Jane Swafford, and Bradford Findell. Washington, D.C.: National Academy Press, 2001.

Pólya, George. *How to Solve It*. Princeton, N.J.: Princeton University Press, 1945.

———. *Mathematical Discovery: On Understanding, Learning, and Teaching Problem Solving* (Combined ed.). New York: John Wiley & Sons, 1981.

Rasmussen, Chris. "New Directions in Differential Equations: A Framework for Interpreting Students' Understandings and Difficulties." *Journal of Mathematical Behavior* 20 (2001): 55–87.

Ray, Joseph. *Ray's Algebra: Part First. Rev. ed.* Cincinnati, Ohio: Van Antwerp, Bragg & Co., 1848.

———. *Practical Arithmetic*. Cincinnati, Ohio: Wilson, Hinkle & Co, 1857.

Resnick, Lauren B. "Treating Mathematics as an Ill-Structured Discipline." In *The Teaching and Assessing of Mathematical Problem Solving, Research Agenda for Mathematics Education, Vol. 3*, edited by Randall I. Charles and Edward A. Silver, pp. 32–60. Hillsdale, N.J.: Lawrence Erlbaum Associates, and Reston, Va.: National Council of Teachers of Mathematics, 1989.

Riordan, Julie E., and Penrod E. Noyce. "The Impact of Two Standards-Based Mathematics Curricula on Student Achievement in Massachusetts." *Journal for Research in Mathematics Education* 32 (2001): 368–98.

Rothstein, Richard, Martin Carnoy, and Luis Benveniste. *Can Public Schools Learn from Private Schools?* Washington, D.C.: Economic Policy Institute, 1999.

Schifter, Deborah, and Catherine T. Fosnot. *Reconstructing Mathematics Education: Stories of Teachers Meeting the Challenge of Reform.* New York: Teachers College Press, 1993.

Schoen, Harold, Kelly Finn, Sarah Griffin, and Cos Fi. "Teacher Variables That Relate to Student Achievement in a Standards-Oriented Curriculum." Paper presented at the annual meeting of the American Educational Research Association, Seattle, Wash., 2001.

Schoenfeld, Alan H. *Mathematical Problem Solving.* New York: Academic Press, 1985.

———. "Learning to Think Mathematically: Problem Solving, Metacognition, and Sense Making in Mathematics." In *Handbook of Research on Mathematics Teaching and Learning,* edited by Douglas A. Grouws, pp. 334–71. New York: Macmillan, 1992.

———. "Making Mathematics Work for All Children: Issues of Standards, Testing, and Equity." *Educational Researcher* 31, no. 1 (2002): 13–25.

Schroeder, Thomas L., and Frank K. Lester, Jr. "Developing Understanding in Mathematics via Problem Solving." In *New Directions for Elementary School Mathematics,* 1989 Yearbook of the National Council of Teachers of Mathematics (NCTM), edited by Paul R. Trafton, pp. 31–42. Reston, Va.: NCTM, 1989.

Sfard, Anna. "Balancing the Unbalanceable: The NCTM Standards in Light of Theories of Learning Mathematics." In *A Research Companion to "Principles and Standards for School Mathematics,"* edited by Jeremy Kilpatrick, Deborah Schifter, and W. Gary Martin, pp. 353–92. Reston, Va.: National Council of Teachers of Mathematics, 2003.

Sfard, Anna, and Liora Linchevski. "The Gains and the Pitfalls of Reification—the Case of Algebra." *Educational Studies in Mathematics* 26 (March 1994): 191–228.

Shen, Alexander H. *Mathematics from the Class of 2000 (Section B) of School 57.* http://www.mccme.ru/schools/shen/2000v/. World Wide Web.

Siefert, H. O. R. *Principles of Arithmetic: Embracing Common Fractions, Decimal Fractions, Percentage, Proportion, Involution, Evolution, and Mensuration: A Manual for Teachers and Normal Students.* Boston: D. C. Heath & Co., 1902.

Silver, Edward. *Assessment and Mathematics Education Reform in the United States.* Pittsburgh, Penn.: LRDC, 1992.

Silver, Edward A. "On Mathematical Problem Posing." *For the Learning of Mathematics* 14, no. 1 (1994): 19–28.

———. "The Nature and Use of Open-Ended Problems in Mathematics Education: Mathematical and Pedagogical Perspectives." *Zentralblatt für Didaktik der Mathematik* 95, no. 2 (1995): 67–72.

Silver, Edward A., ed. *Teaching and Learning Mathematical Problem Solving: Multiple Research Perspectives.* Hillsdale, N.J.: Lawrence Erlbaum Associates, 1985.

Silver, Edward A., and Jinfa Cai. "An Analysis of Arithmetic Problem Posing by Middle School Students." *Journal for Research in Mathematics Education* 27 (November 1996): 521–39.

Silver, Edward, and Patricia Kenney. *Sources of Assessment Information for Instructional Guidance in Mathematics.* Pittsburgh, Penn.: LRDC, 1995.

Silver, Edward A., and Patricia A. Kenny, eds. *Results from the Seventh Mathematics Assessment of the National Assessment of Educational Progress.* Reston, Va.: National Council of Teachers of Mathematics, 2000.

Silver, Edward A., Jeremy Kilpatrick, and Beth Schlesinger. *Thinking through Mathematics: Fostering Inquiry and Communication in the Mathematics Classroom.* New York: The College Board, 1989

Silver, Edward A., and Suzanne Lane. "Can Instructional Reform in Urban Middle Schools Help Students Narrow the Mathematics Performance Gap? Some Evidence from the QUASAR Project." *Research in Middle Level Education* 18 (1995): 49–70.

Silver, Edward A., Margaret Schwan Smith and Barbara Scott Nelson. "The QUASAR Project: Equity Concerns Meet Mathematics Education Reform in the Middle School." In *New Directions for Equity in Mathematics Education,* edited by Walter. G. Secada, Elizabeth Fennema, and Lisa Byrd Adajian, pp. 9–56. New York: Cambridge University Press, 1995.

Silver, Edward A., and Mary Kay Stein. "The QUASAR Project: The 'Revolution of the Possible' in Mathematics Instructional Reform in Urban Middle Schools." *Urban Education* 30 (January 1996): 476–521.

Simon, Martin A. "Reconstructing Mathematics Pedagogy from a Constructivist Perspective." *Journal for Research in Mathematics Education* 26 (March 1995): 114–45.

Smith, Margaret. "A Comparison of the Types of Mathematical Tasks and How They Were Completed during Eighth-Grade Mathematics Instruction in Germany, Japan, and the United States." Ph.D. diss., University of Delaware, 2000.

Stanic, George M.A., and Jeremy Kilpatrick. "Historical Perspectives on Problem Solving in the Mathematics Curriculum." In *The Teaching and Assessing of Mathematical Problem Solving.* Research Agenda for Mathematics Education, vol. 3, edited by Randall I. Charles and Edward A. Silver, pp. 1–22. Hillsdale, N.J.: Lawrence Erlbaum Associates, and Reston, Va.: NCTM, 1989.

Stein, Mary Kay, Barbara W. Grover, and Marjorie A. Henningsen. "Building Student Capacity for Mathematical Thinking and Reasoning:

An Analysis of Mathematical Tasks Used in Reform Classrooms." *American Educational Research Journal* 33, no. 2 (1996): 455–88.

Stein, Mary Kay, and Suzanne Lane. "Instructional Tasks and the Development of Student Capacity to Think and Reason: An Analysis of the Relationship between Teaching and Learning in a Reform Mathematics Project." *Educational Research and Evaluation* 2, no. 1 (1996): 50–80.

Stein, Mary Kay, Suzanne Lane, and Edward A. Silver. "Classroom in Which Students Successfully Acquire Mathematical Proficiency: What Are the Critical Features of Teachers' Instructional Practice?" Paper presented at the annual meeting of the American Educational Research Association, New York, 1996.

Stein, Mary Kay, Margaret Schwan Smith, Marjorie A. Henningsen, and Edward A. Silver. *Implementing Standards-Based Mathematics Instruction: A Casebook for Professional Development.* New York: Teachers College Press, 2000.

Stigler, James W., and James Hiebert. "Understanding and Improving Classroom Mathematics Instruction: An Overview of the TIMSS Video Study." *Phi Delta Kappan* 79 (1997): 14–21.

———. *The Teaching Gap: Best Ideas from the World's Teachers for Improving Education in the Classroom.* Washington, D.C.: Free Press, 1999.

Stodolosky, Susan S. *The Subject Matters: Classroom Activity in Math and Social Studies.* Chicago: University of Chicago Press, 1988.

Suydam, Marilyn N. "Untangling Clues from Research on Problem Solving." In *Problem Solving in School Mathematics,* 1980 Yearbook of the National Council of Teachers of Mathematics (NCTM), edited by Stephen Krulik and Robert E. Reys, pp. 34–50. Reston, Va.: NCTM, 1980.

Thompson, Denisse R., and Sharon L. Senk. "The Effects of Curriculum on Achievement in Second-Year Algebra: The Example of the University of Chicago School Mathematics Project." *Journal for Research in Mathematics Education* 32 (2001): 58–84.

Thorndike, Edward L. *The Psychology of Arithmetic.* New York: Macmillan, 1922.

Treffers, Adrian. *Three Dimensions: A Model of Goal and Theory Description in Mathematics Instruction—the Wiskobas Project.* Dordrecht, Netherlands: D. Reidel, 1987.

Upton, C. B. *New School Algebra.* Boston: Athenaeum, 1900.

———. *Social Utility Arithmetics—First Book.* New York: American Book, 1939.

Velleman, Daniel J., and Gregory S. Call. "Permutations and Combination Locks." *Mathematics Magazine* 68 (October 1995): 243–53.

Wearne, Diana, and Vicki L. Kouba. "Rational Numbers." In *Results from the Seventh Mathematics Assessment of the National Assessment of Educational Progress*, edited by Edward A. Silver and Patricia A. Kenney, pp. 163–91. Reston, Va.: National Council of Teachers of Mathematics, 2000.

Wentworth, G. A. *Plane and Solid Geometry*. Boston: Ginn & Co., 1899.

Wilson, James, Maria Fernandez, and Nelda Hadaway "Mathematical Problem Solving." In *Research Ideas for the Classroom: High School Mathematics*, edited by Patricia S. Wilson, pp. 57–78. Reston, Va.: National Council of Teachers of Mathematics, 1993.

Wirtz, Robert. *Banking on Problem Solving in Elementary School Mathematics*. Washington, D.C.: Curriculum Development Associates, 1976.

Yackel, Erna, and Paul Cobb. "Sociomathematical Norms, Argumentation, and Autonomy in Mathematics." *Journal for Research in Mathematics Education* 27 (1996): 458–77.

Yackel, Erna, and Chris Rasmussen. "Beliefs and Norms in the Mathematics Classroom." In *Beliefs: A Hidden Variable in Mathematics Education?*, edited by Günter Törner, Erkki Pehkonen, and Gilah Leder, pp. 313–30. Dordrecht, Netherlands: Kluwer, 2002.

Ziebarth, Steven. "An Evaluation of the Modeling Innovation in Mathematics Education Project (MIME)." NSF Summative Evaluation Report Document. Western Michigan University, Kalamazoo, Mich., 1998. Photocopied.

———. "PRIME-TEAM: The University of Iowa Local Systemic Change Project Final Evaluation Report." NSF LSC Summative Evaluation Report Document, University of Iowa, Iowa City, Iowa, 1999. Photocopied.

Teaching Mathematics through Problem Solving

Grades 6 –12

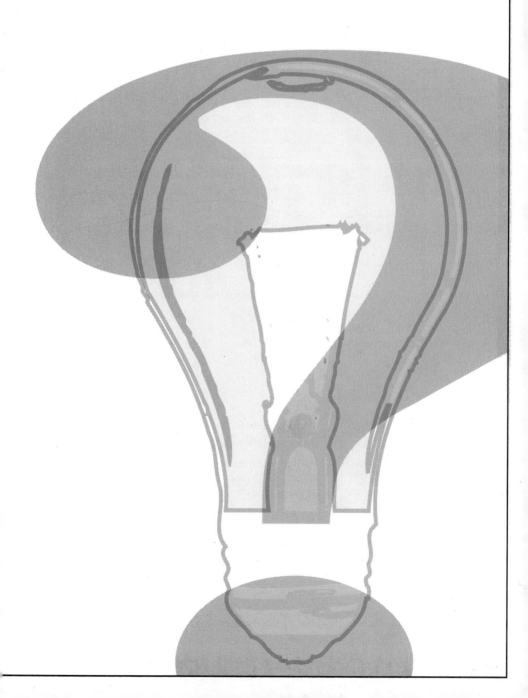